"An essential resource for early years professionals, transforming trauma-informed theory into practical magic."

Lisa Cherry, International Trainer, Consultant and author on trauma-informed practice

"The uniqueness of this book is how accessible it is, explaining and unpicking a complex and heavy subject. He leaves the reader feeling empowered to make a difference."

Sonia Mainstone-Cotton, Nurture Consultant and author

"This complex subject is clearly explained, with detailed and practical examples as well as simple play activities. An essential read to understand a range of behaviour through a trauma-informed lens."

Rachel Thynne, SEMH Outreach Lead Teacher and author of *Behaviour Barriers and Beyond* and *Understanding Anxiety at School*

TRAUMA-INFORMED PRACTICE IN EARLY EDUCATION

Many young children arrive in our settings carrying past trauma. And all children will face challenges in their future lives. Trauma-informed practice helps us support them all by offering safe and responsive relationships and environments.

This book provides a clear, research-based framework for understanding what trauma feels like, how it affects behaviour and learning, and what this looks like in daily practice. It shows how early years educators can support recovery and resilience through everyday care, co-regulation, and practical strategies, and how joyful settings can be created even in the face of stressful or systemic challenges. With chapters on staff wellbeing and secondary trauma, this is a hopeful, hands-on guide.

Trauma-informed practice is not an extra - it's high-quality early education adapted for everyone in the setting. This book shows how to do it well, for every child and adult. It is essential reading for all current and future early years educators, and those who train and support them.

James McTaggart is an educational psychologist with nearly 20 years' specialist experience in early childhood and psychological trauma. A popular trainer and speaker, he has worked with many children, practitioners, and families facing challenges and as a survivor of childhood trauma himself is passionate about applying this learning to help change lives.

TRAUMA-INFORMED PRACTICE IN EARLY EDUCATION

Making a Lifetime's Difference

James McTaggart

LONDON AND NEW YORK

Cover image: Getty Images

First published 2026
by Routledge
4 Park Square, Milton Park, Abingdon, Oxon OX14 4RN

and by Routledge
605 Third Avenue, New York, NY 10158

Routledge is an imprint of the Taylor & Francis Group, an informa business

British Library Cataloguing-in-Publication Data
A catalogue record for this book is available from the British Library

ISBN: 9781032915456 (hbk)
ISBN: 9781032915432 (pbk)
ISBN: 9781003563808 (ebk)

DOI: 10.4324/9781003563808

Typeset in Interstate
by Apex CoVantage, LLC

CONTENTS

SAFETY NOTICE - READ THIS FIRST!

This book is about childhood adversity and trauma. It is not an easy subject to write about, or to read about. I will do my best to make it as comfortable as I can, but there will be some examples of trauma and the effects on children. I've presented this material many times in training events and conferences and it is usually fine, but sometimes people find it upsetting or it reminds them of experiences they have had themselves.

Please make it a priority to notice if you find any of this content difficult. Do what you need to do - take a break for minutes or days, allow for recovery time, and seek out support if you wish. Most people do well if they attend to the basics of getting some exercise, outdoor air, nutritious food, sleep, time with family and friends, doing things we enjoy. Or they use the natural emotions this content might prompt to renew a determination to help children manage and recovery from the difficult experiences that should not be in their young lives.

If things in this book make you angry, that is as it should be. Throw the book if you want, or shout at the screen. There are things that shouldn't happen to children. If it makes you feel helpless, that is ok too. I have wept writing it, so if you do too as you read it, that is not a surprise. There is too much suffering in these young lives and we know that because we see it every day. And - I will show - we as early educators can make a lifetime's difference for every child just by doing what we do well. I hope you can stay with me as we see how trauma-informed practice can be effective, enjoyable and the best response we can make to the way the world is.

Introduction

Ten Reasons to Be Trauma-Informed

- Reason #1 - Trauma is common

Up to 20% of preschoolers meet criteria for post-traumatic stress disorder - and more are affected by trauma without meeting those criteria (Woolgar et al., 2022). That's 1 in every 5 of the children we work with. It's often disguised though, presenting in behaviour or reduced learning that puzzles us. In Chapters 3, 4, and 5 we'll see how trauma-informed thinking can help us recognise what we are seeing. In Chapters 7, 15, 16, and 18 we make the links to safeguarding.

- Reason #2 - There will be troubles ahead

Jason is a happy 4-year-old. He's never experienced anything overstressful. But he will one day. Life will bring its ups and downs from unexpectedly high bills to bereavements. As we will see in Chapters 11–13, trauma-informed practice is an effective way to "future proof" children, so they have a deep well of resilience to draw on when life gets tough.

- Reason #3 - Trauma has long and deep impacts

We often see the immediate effects of trauma in young children, but they can last for a lifetime. Even a relatively simple single incident can stay with someone for decades, while developmental trauma can change the whole course of development, impacting on learning and wellbeing now, and on health and even life expectancy into adulthood. We'll see how and why in Chapters 2 and 3.

- Reason #4 - Early education can make a huge difference

But this is a hopeful book, even if we will spend most of the time talking about difficult experiences. Early educators can make a lifetime's difference in two ways. Firstly, recent research shows that it is not the amount of trauma that has the most influence, but the quality of relationships around the child (Bellis et al., 2017; Hambrick et al., 2019). Simply learning and growing in a safe, stimulating and kind environment is protective. These both have measurable consequences decades later. And we can do them - Chapters 8–13 provide detail on how.

DOI: 10.4324/9781003563808-1

- Reason #5 - It helps everyone learn!

Who doesn't learn best when they feel safe, they have strong positive relationships, others understand their emotions and provide just enough but not too much challenge? What effective early education doesn't involve being aware of children's development, noticing and promoting their strengths, and adapting to and working with them on the gaps? This is the essence of trauma-informed practice too - so the more trauma-informed a setting is, the better everyone will learn (and see Reason #2 for why everyone needs this). Throughout the book you'll have moments when you say "but I do that!" Trauma-informed early education is high-quality education and vice versa.

- Reason #6 - Trauma-informed approaches solve a lot of our hassles

Working with young children is an endless series of "events", from sudden disputes over whose turn it is to inconsolable sadness at drop-off to baffling refusals to do something they happily engaged in yesterday. It's fun, but hard work. Trauma-informed thinking helps unlock the reasons for these hassles, and find new ways to prevent and solve them - or, even better, make them moments of learning.

- Reason #7 - We can make a huge difference to families

If children have experienced trauma, so often have their families. And just having a traumatised child can be difficult and upsetting for parents. Early educators are not family therapists, but there is so much we can do in supporting understanding and signposting to help. More than that, much trauma goes along with systemic issues, such as families that are marginalised or stigmatised. Our settings can be safe places where they feel wanted, valued, respected, and included. Chapter 16 looks at our role in supporting families - again we are more powerful than we might realise.

- Reason #8 - Settings (yes, us) can unintentionally traumatise children

This is a hard thought, but a necessary one. We work hard to provide spaces and experiences that are nurturing, fun, and interesting for children. And we do our best to offer kind and sensitive relationships and responses to difficulties. But one of the effects of trauma is that people find it hard afterwards to feel safe even in safe places. Children who have experienced relational trauma can have difficulty recognising positive relationships and drawing on them. And sometimes, even with the best will in the world, settings can be stressful places for children - even small transitions can be hard. In Chapter 15 we'll look at how we can reduce this.

- Reason #9 - It's good for us too!

We are people too! So we might have our own past or present experiences that are difficult or traumatic. And the job is hard work and the stresses can spill over into the rest of our lives. A trauma-informed setting tends to be better for staff wellbeing, with the adults feeling better supported themselves, as well as happier and more effective as educators (Douglass et al., 2021; Simons et al., 2022). Chapters 17 and 18 cover staff wellbeing, including the risks of secondary stress if we work with a lot of trauma and how that can be prevented and managed.

- Reason #10 - It's becoming policy and good practice

For all these reasons, and more, trauma-informed practice is becoming recommended or even mandated by national and local policy-makers. It is increasingly becoming the standard for good practice, built into quality frameworks. In the USA, the Every Student Succeeds Act explicitly calls for trauma-informed practice in education, while both UNESCO and UNICEF promote it. But it is not just down to educators - we are enabled and limited by the systems around us. Chapter 15 considers what we can do to be trauma-informed when the policy or resource environment makes it harder.

How This Book Can Help

- Explaining related concepts

Childhood trauma and adversity is complex, affecting sometimes the whole of child development. "Trauma" itself can often mean many different things that need different understandings and responses from educators. It might refer to a single incident that happened recently, things in the past we will never know about, or the more pervasive effects of neglect or abuse. In Chapters 1-5 we will unpack these concepts showing the differences and what they mean for practice, and how they relate to other concepts, such as attachment, nurture, and toxic stress. In Chapter 14 we set all this in the context of more systemic factors such as poverty or racism.

- Presenting up-to-date research

This is a complex field, and one which has changed a lot in the last few years. We are starting to understand better how children adapt to trauma, and how this can bring strengths to work with as well as issues to support. I've offered one example already - how the emphasis is gradually shifting in research and practice from "what's happened to you" to the quality of relationship around a child. Another is an increased understanding that every trauma is different, and so is every child and family, so measures such as "ACE scores" need careful interpretation. We'll cover recent research on the effects of different kinds of adversity for education and more widely.

- Jargon-free content

A lot of the evidence for what works and why in trauma-informed practice is highly technical - decades-long studies tracking outcomes, neuroscientific studies on complex brain regions. This book is written so far as possible in non-technical language, using everyday examples. We do cover the different roles of the amygdala and the orbito-frontal cortex and we do consider epigenetics, but in intuitive ways you can relate immediately to practice. There is a glossary for the more specialist terms.

- Relating to everyday educational practice

There is nothing more practical than a good theory, and this book aims to provide rigorous, up-to-date, and clear treatment of current knowledge about trauma in young children - precisely because understanding this makes the practice implications clearer and easier to do. Seeing, for example, how a refusal to do anything other than play with wheeled toys might be a fear-driven avoidance, or alternatively the working out of difficult memories of a car accident, can help us work out the difference and what to do to help. Also, this book is for educators. We are not therapists, which means it needs a different angle. In fact, as we will see, there are many things we can do to help children as educators that therapists can't - but we will consider in Chapter 8 exactly what our role and limits are, as well as the immense potential of our work to make a difference.

- Including the contexts in which we work

If you put together all the hours I have spent doing training with practitioners on trauma-informed practice, it would go on for weeks (!). But one question always comes up. "I see the point of all this, but how do we do it if . . .". And then practitioners rightly raise the different wider system barriers to putting trauma-informed thinking into practice, whether this be resource limits, pressure to raise attainment, lack of time, or just that there is so much to deal with. This book is about best practice, yes, but it is not an imaginary ideal. In Chapter 14 and throughout we will have an eye on how to be trauma-informed in a context which isn't, because that's how most of us work. And we think too about what we need. Chapter 15 includes material on what we should expect in our working environment in order to do this difficult, vital, wonderful work.

Onward

I hope I've convinced you to stay with me and read on. As you do, please remember the Safety Notice and take breaks when you need to.

Section 1 looks at how we can recognise and understand trauma in young children. Then in Section 2 we add detail on how as educators we can respond and help. Section 3 sets this in the wider world context of how we can work in communities and with families, and how to build effective partnerships with the services around us. We begin with a surprising encounter in a coffee shop . . .

Section 1

Understanding Trauma

1
How Our Brains Manage Stressful Events

This chapter will provide:

- Understanding of how the brain assesses situations, particularly stressful ones
- Knowledge about key brain systems that are involved
- What fight, flight, freeze, and flop behaviours are and why people do them

By the end of this chapter and the next two we will have seen how and why traumatic experiences can have long-lasting effects for young children. We'll have the concepts and tools to make sense of some of what we see in our settings and work out how we can help children recover, as well as learn and develop as well as they can. Along the way we will also have some ways in to understanding other adults, and ourselves, and why we react to things the way we do sometimes.

We will get there in three stages. Firstly, we need to understand how the brain works minute to minute to figure out what is going on and what we need to do about it. Most of the time we only notice all of this when it goes wrong. Billions of brain cells work together to get us through the day and every so often we catch them at it when they make a mistake - we drop the cup, or say the thing we instantly regret, or munch the extra biscuit despite best intentions.

Once we've got a sense of how the brain smoothly navigates the complexities of human life, we can then in the next chapter see how it copes with highly stressful experiences. We are really good at this - there are emotional and action responses built into us that get us through threatening or frightening experiences. We also have responses built in that try to safeguard us against future repetitions of those experiences. We'll see how well these work, but also how that can result in longer term problems.

Then, thirdly and finally, we can apply this to the young developing brain. We will see how traumatic experiences and their effects over time can be different for children than for adults. There are sometimes different and disguised signs that children have become traumatised. I'll describe those and what they might look like in your setting. And we'll also consider some of the myths around childhood trauma and how it can be invisible to the adults for many different reasons.

DOI: 10.4324/9781003563808-3

Before we go any further, please revisit the Safety Notice at the start of the book. In this chapter I am deliberately going to use light-hearted examples that I am sure will not have happened to any reader. That's not to minimise trauma and its impact, but to make sure it is a smooth and easy experience for you, so far as I can. But do remember that even talking about trauma can be uncomfortable, so do what you need to do for your own wellbeing.

Our Amazing Brains

Well, that sounded a bit heavy, so let's go out for a cup of coffee. Do this literally if you want to, but what I mean is let's imagine going to a coffee shop. I'm going to take you through a story that actually did happen to me, and try to show you what went on in my brain to cope – and this will give us what we need for understanding how the brain assesses situations and creates behaviour to deal with them.

> Well, it was exhausting typing that introduction so I decide to go to the nearest coffee franchise outlet and order myself a triple shot mocha with extra whipped cream. It is a towering mugful of things my doctor tells me I shouldn't have. I pick it up from the counter and step backwards, taking a first delicious, rich, creamy sip – ah, that's better. At that moment, someone bumps into me from behind quite gently, but enough to push my nose into the cream, tip the mug so that hot coffee spills over my new shirt and splashes my shoes.

Hopefully you can picture the scene, so I have a question for you. What might I do in that moment? I don't mean "what should I do?" but instead, what are the range of actions available to me as a reasonably functional adult human being? Maybe look away and make a short list.

I do this activity quite often with groups and it amuses me sometimes how long it takes before someone comes up with things like:

- Shove back
- Turn round and empty my coffee over their head
- Step on their toes

Instead, people come up with more appropriate actions such as:

- Turn round and give them a "look"
- Say, "look what you've made me do"
- Ask them to pay for a replacement coffee and/or shirt

Also, being British and quite shy, it's possible that I might:

- Apologise to them for being in their way
- Ask them if they are ok
- Do nothing and hope it all goes away

Actually, I could go on for pages and pages listing possible responses, from breaking into song as though this is a scene in a Broadway musical to sitting on the ground and crying for my lost beverage. Adult humans know how to do an almost unending list of things. And this is the main question here – how, out of that huge list, does the brain so quickly choose what to do and then put it into action often quicker than we can think about it?

One answer is that it might depend on how I feel. Faster than thought, I have an immediate emotional reaction to the event and produce an action that fits the emotion. It would be odd if I shoved back if I wasn't really that bothered about it, or if I asked them to buy another coffee if I was alarmed and scared. So there is a match here:

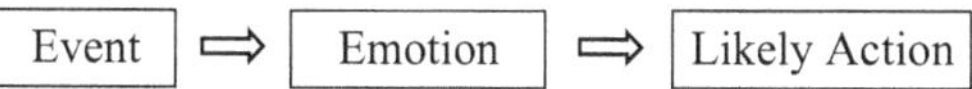

And this is how it works in fact. Deep in the middle of our brains is a set of stress systems whose job is to make a rapid appraisal of the significance of what's going on using two basic questions:

1) How big a deal is this?
2) What kind of a deal is this?

If the appraisal is that this is a BIG deal and a scary one, I might react in one way (shove?) to defend myself. If the appraisal is that this is actually not that big a deal, and perhaps an awkward or embarrassing one, I might react another way (smile and say "oh!"). One more thing about this system is that adults can come up with a very wide range of answers to each question. In response to my coffee calamity, I might be calm, edgy, irritated, annoyed, cross, angry, furious, incandescent – a whole continuum like notes in a scale or temperatures on a thermostat. And I've sufficient life experience to know that this could be an experience that is the biggest I've yet encountered or, given the kind of day I tend to have, actually quite routine. These two points will both be relevant when we think about children later. But for now we've got a major part of our amazing brain mapped already:

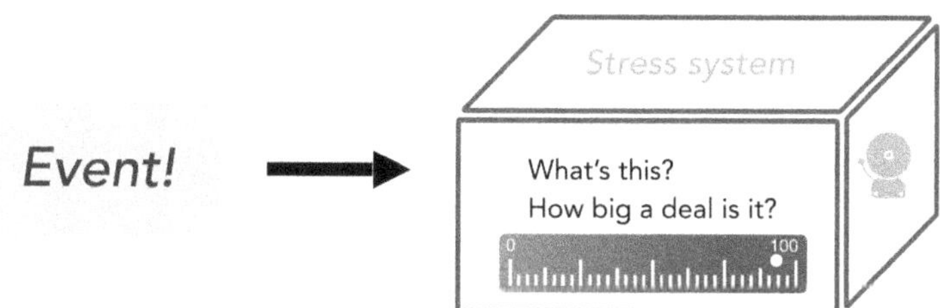

Figure 1.1 How our stress system responds to an event

There is one more element to add, and then we will have the whole map. We'll have a simple way to understand pretty much anything people do in response to events.

So, back to that moment in the coffee shop where I feel the push from behind, get a nose-full of whipped cream, a coffee-striped shirt and a hot splash. Supposing I am actually surprised and furious – how come I don't do any of the first three things on my list? How come, assuming I don't (and I'm not going to tell you what I actually did), I don't give them a shove back? Here are a few possibilities:

- I notice they are bigger than me and think better of the idea
- It occurs to me that people are watching and I don't want to look bad
- Perhaps there is a law enforcement officer nearby who will occupy the rest of my day with questions
- It's wrong to shove people deliberately in coffee shops
- It turns out to be only a kid who'd overbalanced
- I just don't, and calm myself down

We can see here the brain has a second stage of deciding what to do. The stress system has had a first go, and has said "this is a big deal, and an annoying deal, so let's shove back to defend ourselves!" But other brain systems now take a look and come to a different view. And look at the amazing resources they have available to do that:

Reason not to shove	*Knowledge and skills involved*
They are bigger than me	Comparison Fine judgement Processing and comparing consequences Future thinking
People are watching	Sense of self Social norms Understanding of other's minds
Law enforcement nearby	Social rules Structure of society Modelling possible futures Judging different outcomes
Wrong to shove	Sense of right and wrong Applied morality
Only a kid	Understanding others Cause and effect thinking Empathy and sympathy
I just don't	Self-soothing Stopping impulsive actions (inhibition)

That's quite a lot of skills and knowledge all getting deployed quite quickly and effectively. It involves multiple brain systems, some of which I will describe at the end of the chapter. For now, we can call them all "regulating systems" for short. Looking down that list on the right-hand column you can see how much we depend on, and how much has to come together, for us to make reasonably correct behavioural decisions in real-time complex situations.

Now we can see the whole model for behaviour. An event happens, and the stress system makes a quick judgement about whether this is a big deal, and what kind of a deal. It can make quite fine judgements about this and create finely nuanced emotional reactions (which I've represented as a 0–100 scale). This judgement gets passed to the regulating systems, which then have another look and bring to bear knowledge and skills including stopping immediate impulses, reasoning about consequences and morality, taking into account who and what is there, and so on. This then results in an overall judgement that gets passed to the action systems - the areas of the brain that move us around. These then create the action out of a huge repertoire of things we know how to do.

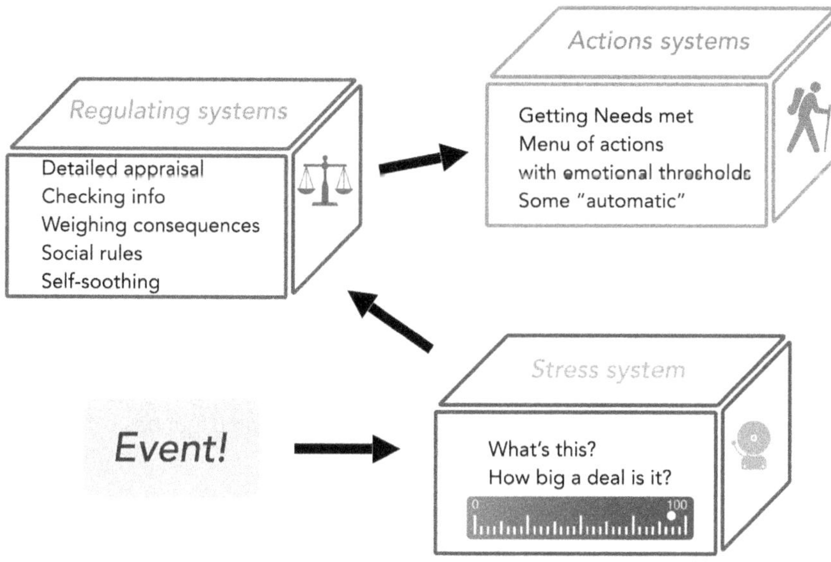

Figure 1.2 How the brain decides what to do

The whole process takes about 0.5 seconds. You might have experienced this in action if you've ever been tapped on the shoulder unexpectedly from behind, or a family member has jumped from behind a door and gone "boo", or there is a sudden crash in your home. Most people hunch or flinch and go "aah!" or something like that. Then we realise what it is (a friend, our child playing a joke, the dog knocking over the table), un-flinch and go "ooh!". "Aah" is the stress system, and "ooh" is the regulating systems ("it's only the dog") - roughly 0.5 seconds between those for most people.

Reflective Activity

Think of a time when you nearly acted on impulse but didn't - perhaps when you decided not to have another biscuit, or stopped yourself sending an email. What stopped you? Can you map this onto any of the regulating systems in the picture?

All hopefully quite interesting, but so what? We now have a model for understanding what happens during potentially traumatic events, how we can prevent traumatisation, what we might see people doing even years after trauma, and how we can help. To get there, I need to take you in slow motion through a difficult experience. As promised, I will keep this as light as I can, using a silly example that cannot have happened to you. I'm also going to describe it as though it is happening to me, so it is my experience we are talking about. But, and I can't overemphasise this, remember the Safety Notice and do what you need to do if this next section is uncomfortable.

An Overwhelming Event

We are going to take that brain model we have just developed and see how it copes with an overwhelming event. Imagine the same story as we started with. So I'm off to the local coffee shop, have ordered my lovely and forbidden drink, and am sinking myself into it when suddenly . . .

> I feel a push from behind, as suddenly the Loch Ness Monster shoves its head through the shop window, past the queuing customers and takes a huge bite (chomp!) out of the counter. Nessie then ranges her head from side to side looking what to munch next.

We looked before at what was the whole range of possible responses, and that range is still available. But a different question this time - what sorts of things might it make sense to do in that moment? In other words, if you were watching from a safe distance, what might you expect to see me doing?

If we made a list, it would probably be variations on the following four basic themes. I might:

- Throw my coffee at the Monster
- Run away
- Root to the spot in terror
- Faint and fall to the ground

None of these might work that well if Nessie is hungry and enjoys feasting on coffee-covered psychologists - but all of them would make sense as a way to respond. Let's give them their formal names:

- Throw my coffee at the Monster - FIGHT
- Run away - FLIGHT
- Root to the spot in terror - FREEZE
- Faint and fall to the ground - FLOP

These are the "four Fs", the basic responses that are built into human beings (in fact every complex animal so far as we can tell) and deployed when we meet an overwhelming threat.

It is important to notice what is not there, as this tells us what the brain cares about in times of high stress, and what it is prepared to let go. I might think what I'd like to do is film the whole thing live on my phone and make my social media fortune. Perhaps those who often encounter Loch Ness Monsters in coffee shops would be able to do this. But I'm very unlikely to. Nor am I going to start a seminar discussion about why Nessie has appeared in this shop - does she like coffee? - or the biology that might have preserved a dinosaur over so long. And there are other things I don't care about either. I'm not bothered if anyone laughs at me if I run away screaming, or if they criticise me for throwing my coffee at a rare and possibly endangered species.

So we can look inside my head and see what is going on with the brain systems. My stress system is on high alert, and is using a direct line to the action systems to get fight, flight, freeze, or flop going as quickly as possible. The regulating systems are struggling to catch up, but their main assessment is also that it's not safe; I have to defend myself or escape.

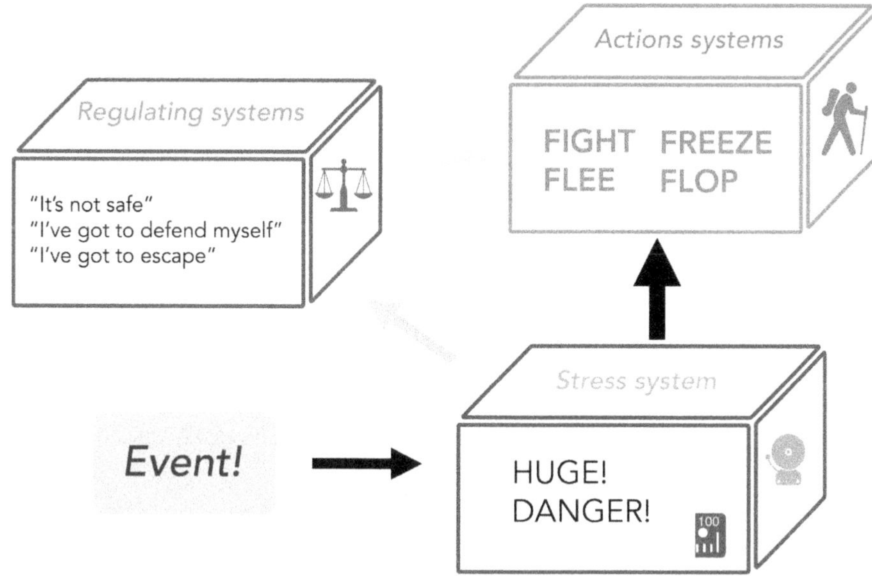

Figure 1.3 The brain under very high stress

My brain cares about one thing, and one thing only - getting me safe. Once safe, we can worry about other things. And this is what the four Fs are for - quick, built-in, action responses that aim to make us safe under overwhelming stress.

We've got enough now to take a brief look ahead to how trauma-informed thinking can give us a simple way to understand complex or baffling behaviour, and come up with ideas as to how to help. The four Fs are all about getting us safe at all costs. So we can turn this around and wonder if, when we see behaviour that has elements of fight, flight, freeze, or flop (or any combination of those) it is all about trying to get safe. In which case, what the person needs from us is to find ways to help them feel safer in that situation. For example:

> Aaron is usually quite happy playing with his friends and exploring the setting. But when the "tidy up" music starts he often refuses to clear up, and matters quickly escalate into pushing and biting the adults who try to get him to.

Fight, flight, freeze, or flop? There are elements of fight here, for sure. But perhaps you also spotted a bit of freeze in the refusal to clear up? He will do anything but that. There is more to it of course and we will come back to Aaron who'll be helping us in later chapters, but we have a quick and easy assessment - we are seeing FFFF-like behaviour, so perhaps there is something about the music, or tidying up, or transitions in general that makes Aaron feel unsafe. His young biology then produces FFFF actions in response. We also therefore have some quick and easy ideas for what to do next time. What might make the situation feel safer? Over time we might try different things to see what works, but these might include giving advance warning, turning the music down, making sure someone is there to comfort Aaron just before, asking him to help an adult tidy, and so on. You've probably already had better ideas than those, which is the point of thinking this way.

Reflective Activity

Make a short list of some of the behaviours you encounter working with children that cause problems for you or for them. For each one, can you notice any elements of fight, flight, freeze, or flop in them?

Back to me and the Loch Ness Monster as there are a few more things to notice. We've learned so far that under high stress the brain starts to prioritise getting safe through deploying FFFF reactions. This means other systems have to be turned down so as to focus on the essentials. Looking back at the figure above of the regulating system and its tasks, we can see just how much my brain is putting aside to allow this focus:

- Comparisons
- Fine judgements
- Processing and comparing consequences
- Future thinking
- Sense of self
- Social norms
- Understanding of other's minds
- Social rules
- Structure of society
- Modelling possible futures
- Judging different outcomes
- Sense of right and wrong
- Applied morality
- Understanding others
- Cause and effect thinking
- Empathy and sympathy
- Self-soothing
- Stopping impulsive actions (inhibition)

That's quite a lot of what helps us function in adaptive and appropriate ways in daily life. But it can all go, temporarily. If you had an actual brain scanner with you in that moment, you would see different areas of my brain powering down and becoming less available - precisely the ones that do these things - and the ones needed to produce FFFF actions powering up.

Looking ahead again, you might be able to think of times when people seem not to have those regulating systems available. Perhaps they struggle to reckon with consequences of actions, or are clear what they should do but find themselves doing something else instead.

We might have worked for hours with a child to teach them to ask for help rather than throwing the pencil at us, but in the heat of the moment all that hard-earned knowledge seems to have disappeared. And, from the point of view of the child, it has - it's not available! This is a frequent problem for people who have traumatic memories when these are triggered in ordinary situations. Aaron above seemed to lose all his skills at the sound of the tidy-up music.

It's not that they are bad people, but that they may temporarily not have available the brain systems that enable them to produce expected behaviours. Instead, their stress system is pushing towards versions of fight, flight, freeze, or flop. But one of the common effects of difficult experiences is that people often do think it is their fault, or that they are bad people. This is especially so for children, for reasons we will explore in later chapters. A large part of helping consists of showing them that they are not bad through the ways we relate to them, and the opportunities we provide to create a new sense of self.

There is much more on this in chapters to come. What we have seen in this chapter is how the brain works in ordinary times, and then under extreme stress. In the next chapter we look at what makes a stressful event traumatic, how memories of trauma can be very different to ordinary memories, and the problems these can then cause day to day. In Chapter 3 we will focus all of that onto young children and their experiences so as to understand what we see and what we can do.

In More Depth and Detail

This chapter has covered a lot of mainstream neuroscience understanding of how our brains deal with stressors without going into too many technical terms and detail. This section aims to fill in some of that background and point towards further reading if you are interested in this. The brain and its wonderful abilities are so complex that any short description is going to be as inaccurate as it is correct, and the following is no exception. In this section I'll identify the main brain systems, give a more formal account of how they work together, and conclude by relating to some common metaphors (lizard brain, emotional hijack) and some pointers for how to tell if an account is oversimplified.

Key Brain Systems

The "stress systems" are a wide range of different brain areas mostly found towards the deep middle of the brain. They include the amygdala and the hippocampus. If you want to see where these are in the brain, then typing "limbic system" into any search engine will provide plenty of images. What I have called "regulating systems" is many distinct brain areas and functions, including the prefrontal cortex and the orbitofrontal cortex.

We are used to thinking of ourselves as a single thing, and of ourselves as being in charge of that thing and making all the decisions. That is what it feels like, but the reality is different. Intuitively we know this, as when we say "I'm in two minds about . . ." or "I don't know what made me do it . . .". Evidence from brain scans and other experiments confirm this impression, and show that the brain consists of many different parts, all of which have different tasks, and all of which have to work together in order to get anything done. For example, it's been known for over 150 years that some areas of the brain specialise in language and others in processing vision - these all need to work together in sync for us to be able to say, "look at that over there!"

Brain anatomy can be as complicated as you want it to be. There are roughly 100 billion neurons and over a trillion glial cells (Herculano-Houzel, 2009). The neurons have upward of 100 trillion connections between each other. Or we can zoom out, and see that all these can be mapped into different areas within the brain. For example, we can see that the outside surface of the brain forms a thin sheet, called the cortex, wrapped around other parts. The cortex itself has folds that separate it into four areas called lobes, named after their location under the skull - frontal, parietal, occipital, and temporal. The whole brain also has a left and right half, which are richly interconnected, but also do slightly different things. So the left half controls the right side of the body (and sees the right side of the visual field from either eye) and vice versa.

It quickly becomes complicated, but for understanding trauma, we only need to include the front part of the cortex (the "frontal lobe") and some structures deep inside called the limbic system. The story about the Loch Ness Monster earlier follows what we know about how a response to a threat builds in stages, from initial judgement down in the limbic system to reappraisal once that and the cortex have had a second look (for a staged model, see Smith & Lane, 2015; and for scanning evidence, see Morawetz et al., 2020).

The first step, an immediate judgement of what's going on and how much it matters, happens in the limbic system - brain regions such as the amygdala, but also the insula and others (Fusar-Poli et al., 2009). These then work together with areas towards the front of the brain, including the prefrontal cortex, to produce an overall emotional state. Then the last stage is one of adjustment, which is done mainly by more regions at the front of the brain. For example, the dorsolateral prefrontal cortex makes adjustments to the "what's going on and does it matter" judgements, and then different systems in the ventromedial prefrontal cortex help to tune the levels of arousal accordingly (Nejati et al., 2021).

As we will see in just a moment, the limbic system often gets a bad press, being described as a primitive "lizard" brain, or else an irrational monster just waiting to take us over. In fact, it is far from mindless. The amygdala, for example, is often described as the brain's fear centre, but it does much more than just react. One part of it (the basolateral amygdala) looks at what comes in through the senses and decides how important it is, while another (the centromedial) helps create the emotional response, coordinating other systems and keeping it under control. Both are richly connected to other brain areas, such as the orbito-frontal cortex - and it is this connection that may be responsible for when we "just don't" overreact (Gao et al., 2021).

Traditionally, this was seen as a top-down process (Buhle et al., 2014) where "higher" parts of the brain regulated the less rational emotional parts. But more recent evidence suggests it is more collaborative, where cortical regions work together with limbic systems and each listens to the other (Pessoa, 2017). And, just as sometimes the best thing to do is to think carefully, and other times we just need to do something, the balance between these systems seems to change according to circumstances (Underwood et al., 2021). What this means in practice is that we can quickly produce reactions tuned to the level of threat and the time available for thinking about it.

An example of this flexibility is shown in the different ways the brain processes unpleasant events. Regulating happy or pleasant experiences (how pleased should I be about this birthday present, for example) use mostly general resources. But negative or frightening happenings get additional input from other areas (Golkar et al., 2012; Silvers et al., 2015). This makes sense, as the risks of my getting too happy, or not happy enough, about my new socks are not as high as the risks of making a mistake about the Loch Ness Monster.

Not all of this is conscious. In fact, much of it happens faster than we can be aware of in real time. But these "automatic" processes are still us - we are not being taken over in any way. That's because they involve a whole library the brain has built up of our past actions and habits, our overall goals and desires, what we have learned about acceptable behaviour in different contexts, and some deep memories of how stressful experiences went in early childhood (Xie et al., 2019).

What's Missing from This Account?

This account reflects faithfully the state of current knowledge as to how the brain handles stressful experiences, but it does simplify. I've also missed out some other important systems that put the stress response and actions into practice. So if you were reading wondering when I was going to mention cortisol (a stress hormone) or the hypothalamic-pituitary-adrenal axis or the vagal nerve, we will see these when we look in more detail at traumatic memories in Chapter 2. When we cover what's different in trauma for young children, I will relate all that as well to the developing brain and the ways this means children experience events differently, have different vulnerabilities to being traumatised by them, and express that differently to adults or older children.

Before we get there, there are some metaphors in common use for the way the brain works and handles stress that you may be familiar with, and I want to relate them to what we have seen so far.

Some Common Metaphors

If nothing else, the previous sections will have shown how complex the brain is, and how we are still only at the beginnings of understanding it. As with all complex things, it can be useful to use metaphors to help grasp what we need. Urban traffic systems, for example, can be compared to plumbing! We talk about traffic *flow* and *bottlenecks*. But taking a metaphor too far just confuses - nobody talks about *drinking* cars.

With the brain there are two common metaphors in particular that can be useful but also can get in the way of understanding about trauma and how people experience it. The first of these is the "triune brain", the idea that our brains consist of a base reptile brain, with a mammal brain and then a sophisticated human brain wrapped around it in the course of evolution (MacLean, 1990). The reptile does emotions and impulses, restrained and guided by the wiser and rational human brain. You can see how this reflects the brain anatomy we've already mentioned - the limbic being reptile and the cortex human. And it is helpful for seeing the broad different functions of brain areas. But it does not fit the facts of brain evolution (Cesario et al., 2020), and hopefully you can see from this chapter that the limbic system can itself be quite rational, making complex judgements about what is going on and why it matters, and also the potential costs and benefits of a course of action (Dixon & Dweck, 2022). Also some of the automatic processes are indeed found in the limbic system, but others are in the cortex (Phillips et al., 2008; Xie et al., 2019). This is important because when the brain decides on fight, flight, freeze, or flop, it is about a considered appraisal of the situation rather than throwing reason to the winds.

There is a similar problem with another common metaphor - that of emotional hijack, sometimes also called amygdala hijack (LeDoux, 1996). This is the idea that under stress the limbic system takes over, overwhelming or ignoring the rational parts of the brain that might know better. Although, as we will see in Chapter 2, parts of the limbic system do have direct connections to motor areas and thus an influence on what we do (LeDoux & Pine, 2016), what we have also seen is that the full response comes from all the relevant brain areas working together. Which system has most influence over what we do is determined depending on the situation - so if the limbic system is leading, that is what the whole brain has decided is best.

One reason to spend time on these metaphors and their drawbacks is that we will need it when understanding the experiences of people with traumatic memories and how we can help them. It is, for example, very common for them to feel shame about the events, or about their reactions to them. The neuroscience tells us something different - their brains have prioritised their survival, and nobody can be blamed for that.

In the next chapters we will look at how this exquisite and wonderful system deals with potentially traumatic experiences, how and why some people are traumatised by these, before we see what is different about this for young children and how we can recognise this and help them in educational settings.

Chapter summary:

- Our responses to stressful situations are produced by many brain systems working together
- As stress increases, fight, flight, freeze, and flop responses become more likely
- We can understand these as attempts to become safe at all costs
- Other things, such as reasoning about consequences and social norms, become less important

Practice points:

- Recognise the elements of fight, flight, freeze, or flop in difficult behaviour
- Respond in ways that reduce, rather than increase, stress
- Be aware of our own stress reactions and fight, flight, freeze, or flop-like reactions

2
Living with Traumatic Memories

This chapter will provide:

- Understanding of how and why traumatic memories form
- An account of what it is like living with traumatic memories
- Information on triggers, intrusions, avoidances, and dissociation

In the last chapter we looked at how our brains manage difficult and stressful situations. Different areas worked together to create responses that fitted the situation, whether this was an accidental nudge in a coffee shop or the sudden appearance of a hungry Loch Ness Monster. As stress and threat levels increased, I became more likely to do a version of fight, flight, freeze, or flop. These are the responses built into me to help me survive when under threat. Finally, we also saw that threat is in the eye of the person experiencing it - it is my brain's assessment of the situation that influences what I do and how I feel, not the objective situation itself.

So we also have all the ingredients for understanding how traumatic memories can develop after a difficult experience, why this happens, why they can stay fresh for decades, and what it is like living with these memories. I will describe this first with an adult example before we look at young children in the next chapter. This is partly because adult trauma is simpler, but also to ground later chapters on practitioner wellbeing (18 and 19), and working with families and systems in Chapters 15 and 16.

We are going to be discussing what trauma and traumatic memories are and what they feel like, so please do bear in mind throughout the Safety Notice and your own needs. I'm going to use a light-hearted example again to make it as comfortable as I can.

Traumatic Memories

Let's imagine the unfortunate incident with the Loch Ness Monster is now a few days in the past. Nothing terrible has happened since then, so in order to once more put off writing this chapter, I head back to the coffee shop with my sights set on a caramel latte and a muffin. It doesn't take too long to get to the front of the queue, when suddenly . . . .

DOI: 10.4324/9781003563808-4

I feel a push from behind

What kind of reactions might be understandable here? This is the place and situation where only a few days ago that gentle nudge turned out to be a large monster chomping things up before my eyes. Just at this moment, remember, I don't know exactly what is happening. Look at it from my brain's point of view. It could be (perhaps most likely is) someone just accidentally jostling me in the busy queue. In which case, all that we saw in the first half of Chapter 1 might apply - anything from a grumpy rebuke to a polite smile would fit. On the other hand, last time it was a scary and dangerous monster that I only just escaped, so in that case it would make sense to flee, or hide, or defend myself. For the brain, this is a simple choice. The chomping monster is the biggest risk so that's what I act on. However, my brain is, as we saw, a complex system where different regions work together to get a full picture. It might not be the monster again, but just the person behind me. Putting that together means that I might not do full fight, flight, freeze, or flop, but something "fighty", "flighty", "freezy", or "floppy". So I might snap or shout at them (fighty), flinch or suddenly decide I don't want a coffee and leave (flighty), appear momentarily overwhelmed and unable to respond (freezy), or just fall apart (floppy).

Suppose you are a bystander, just watching this. There is a lot that *you* know that I don't. You can see that what is actually happening is that the person behind me was bumped by the person behind them when they were moving to let the door open. So it's mildly annoying, or even amusing depending on mood, but hardly threatening enough to warrant fight, flight, freeze, or flop. And it is very puzzling when I snap or shout at them all, or leave the coffee shop in tears.

But also - there is a lot that *I* see that *you* don't. My brain has a very clear memory of what happened before, when the nudge on the back was the prelude to a Loch Ness Monster attack. And this is the essence of trauma-informed practice. It is realising, and putting into practice the realisation, that people presenting us with unexpected or inconvenient behaviours are not experiencing the situation the same way that we are. And secondly, that people who have experienced trauma can, as we will see in more detail, often experience ordinary situations as unsafe. The rest of the book simply adds some depth and detail to the following three principles matched to practices and applied to young children:

	Principle	*Practice*
1	People who have traumatic memories can experience situations very differently from how they look	We need to let go of what we think is happening and look through their eyes
2	In particular, they might easily feel very unsafe even in safe places	Almost every way of helping is about supporting people to feel safe
3	They will have feelings and impulses to act according to their experience of the situation, not the situation itself	Unless we address the need for safety, we can't make progress with managing feelings or behaviours

These are all easy to say but can be difficult to remember and to do. Most situations are quite fast moving, and we have our own built-in fight/flight/freeze/flop responses, not to mention layers of assumptions. Thinking in a trauma-informed way is a learned, or learnable, skill. It is not that different to something we might do routinely in the ups and downs of friendship or working together. To show this, and the difference it can make even in ordinary life and work, I am offering a short Reflective Activity to try.

Reflective Activity

Think back to a minor disagreement with a friend or a colleague - about something like what to do next, or where to put a table, or what to have for lunch.

Look at your different opinions - how many ways can you find that you and they saw the same situation differently?

How did their view make sense to them in a way it didn't make sense to you? What was more important to them and less to you?

Let's get back to that moment when I am nudged from behind, and my brain starts to assume this is the Loch Ness Monster all over again. If you could read minds and look inside my head, what might you see? Feelings of panic, certainly, perhaps also fleeting fear and terror. You might see some thoughts like "Oh no, it's happening again" "I've got to escape" "It's not safe". And you'd see the action areas starting to get together the necessary ingredients of fight, flight, freeze, or flop, priming the muscles and starting to move them. The picture would be something like this:

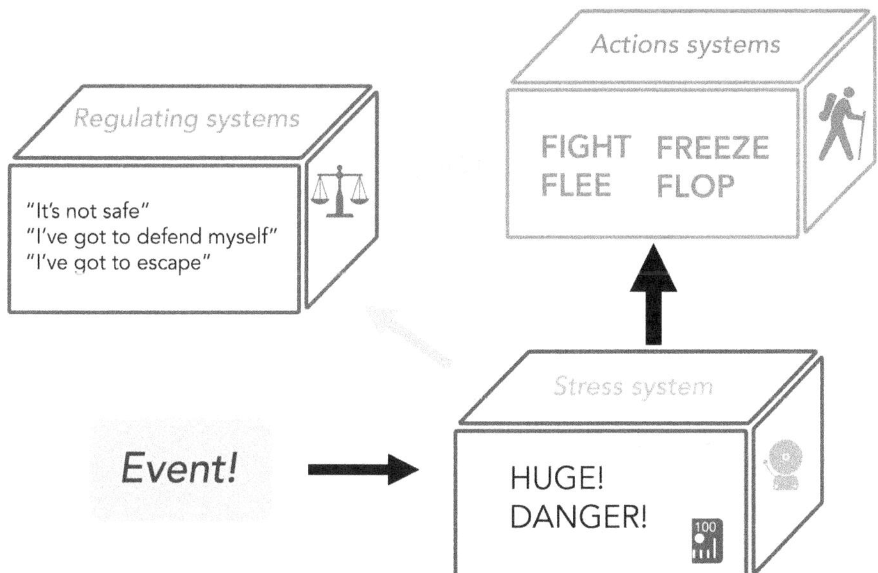

Figure 2.1 The brain under very high stress

You might think you've seen this before, and of course you have. It is the brain scan picture from when the Monster actually appeared in Chapter 1. It is the same, because the brain has made the safety-first, faster-than-thought, decision that it is all happening again, and has started to produce the same responses. And hopefully you can see how, from my point of view, this makes sense. This is the place where only a week ago I was under serious threat and had to fight, flee, freeze, or flop. Something has happened which is almost the same as what started all of that off last time. So a similar response might be needed, and the risk of assuming otherwise is too high.

And this is what a traumatic memory is, essentially a copy of the brain and body state that I had at the time of the overwhelming event (Buchanan, 2007; Kearney & Lanius, 2022). They form during these very threatening times so that the brain has them quickly to hand in case the event happens again in the future (Bryant, 2019). As such, traumatic memories are quite different to ordinary memories for experiences, and there is evidence that they are stored differently in the brain (Patel et al., 2012; Shalev et al., 2024; Thome et al., 2020). A typical ordinary memory is usually quite sketchy. If I think now about what we had for supper last night, I can remember that it was fish, and not much else. By contrast, a traumatic memory does not fade over time, but can be as fresh and vivid as the original event even years or decades afterwards (Brewin, 2015). Ordinary memories feel like the past. If I think of supper last night, it does not feel like it is happening now, as if I can taste the fish even as I type. Traumatic memories, when they come forward, feel like the present, not the past. They feel like they are happening right now (Hackmann et al., 2004; van der Kolk et al., 1997). And lastly, ordinary memories are under our control. I deliberately thought about that meal, and now I can just as easily stop thinking about it. When traumatic memories are "triggered", they unpack whether we wish them to or not (Berntsen, 2001). And they can be very difficult to get out of our minds again.

When Do Traumatic Memories Form?

Not everyone forms a traumatic memory after a difficult experience. Whether they do depends on two different sets of factors - things about the experience, and things about the person. We will briefly look at each in turn before we come back to how and why living with traumatic memories can be difficult. It is important to emphasise that it is never, ever someone's fault if they are traumatised by an experience. I say this because it is very common that people blame themselves. People think they have been weak, should have handled it differently, shouldn't feel like this, should have got over it by now, or that it only happened because of something they did or didn't do (Brown et al., 2019). This is even more strong when the traumatic event is something secret and highly personal, such as sexual abuse or domestic violence. There is also a phenomenon known as survivor guilt, where people feel they should have protected someone else, or that they did not deserve to survive, and don't deserve to recover (Kip et al., 2022). All of this is usual after trauma, but none of it is true - or if elements are true, they are still not as true as people think and feel. Often they have been heroic in their coping and care for others.

Factors About the Experience

It is not the event itself that is traumatic as much as how the person experiences it. I can't give you a list of things and say "these are traumas", and I advise you not to believe anyone who does. Two different people can go through the same event, and experience it very differently - one might be overwhelmed with terror and another might not.

Having said this, there are some characteristics of how people experience an event that make it more likely to be traumatic. The elements are all there in my Loch Ness Monster experience. It was sudden and unexpected, potentially very threatening, and there was not much I could do to make it stop. And, although there were lots of people around, none of them was of potential help in the fast-moving moment. These make up a triad, shown in the figure below, but which can be summarised simply as "something awful is happening, and I have no control over it".

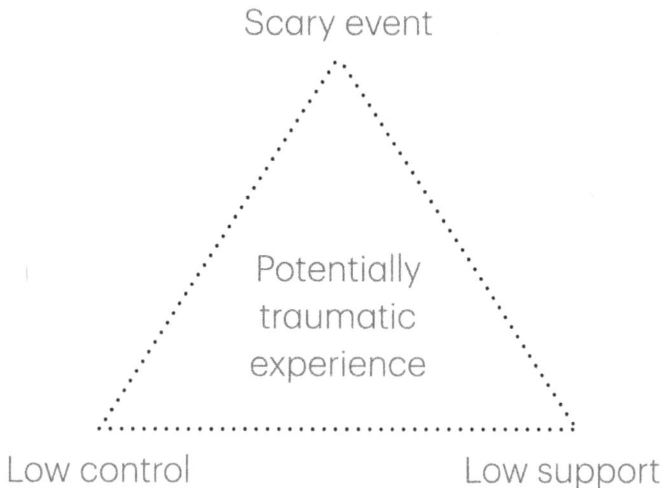

Figure 2.2 The trauma triad

As we will see, and will make much use of in the second section of the book, this triad also shows how we can help *prevent* experiences from being traumatic. Suppose, for example, I have to go to the dentist, and I find this a scary experience. There are some things we could do about that, such as providing more information about what will happen, and not happen. But skilled dentists also work hard to provide us with support and encouragement, explaining what they are doing. And they increase our sense of control by asking permission to do the next step, whether we feel we need more pain reduction, and so on.

Factors About the Individual

Trauma-informed thinking involves realising that different people can experience the same situation in very different ways, and the same goes for potentially traumatic events. One person might develop traumatic memories after an experience while for another it is a good story to tell and nothing more. Perhaps you'd have got the phone out and sped to social media fame with your picture of the Loch Ness Monster eating a banana muffin.

There are some factors about individuals that might make them more likely to be traumatised. We can immediately rule some candidates out, though. It is not, ever, about being weak. Traumatic experiences are traumatic experiences and even the apparently "strongest" person (whatever that might mean) can be traumatised. Indeed, part of the shock of trauma is that our coping capacities are overwhelmed, and this can be particularly difficult for people who are generally used to coping.

The trauma triad shows us some of these individual characteristics. The more traumatic experiences someone has had, then the more likely they are to experience any situation as unsafe (Breslau et al., 1999). They may also, if they have experienced many difficult and uncontrollable events have a lower sense of control over what happens to them generally. Perhaps most important is their history of positive relationships. Having nurturing and caring relationships with others (be this friends, family, parents, etc.) can be protective (Gunnar, 2017).

Small things can make all the difference between a nasty experience and a traumatising one. Here's a couple of parallel stories showing how this can play out for children and how we can respond. See if you can spot the differences where Di is offered more control and support:

> Fi was in a minor road accident with her mother driving to the shops one day. While her mother sorted out the insurance with the other driver, she sat quietly in the car. The journey proceeded and she seemed fine. But over the next few weeks she started sleeping poorly, and being aggressive towards her mother.
>
> Di was in a minor road accident with her mother driving to the shops one day. "Oops, that was a bump!" said her mother. "Are you ok? I've just got to talk to the other lady about getting our cars fixed. Do you want to come out with me, or stay in the car with Juggles [the plush rabbit]?" When they got to the shops, Di ran about a bit in the car park shouting "bang". She was a bit weepy at home for the next few days but quickly got distracted by plans for a trip to the zoo next weekend.

Chapter 6 is about how we can support recovery and help prevent the process of traumatisation after a difficult event. The whole of Chapter 4 is devoted to how we can offer care and compassion after a potentially traumatic event. The first step, as we see with Fi and Di, is realising that an experience may be one where the three points of the triad are all in operation, and adjusting what we do to compensate.

Living with Traumatic Memories

We have seen that traumatic memories differ from ordinary memories. They consist of strong feelings, and urges to fight, flight, freeze, or flop, along with sketchy thoughts such as "It's not safe" or "I must defend myself". Once established, they stay fresh and vivid, not fading over time like ordinary memories. And when triggered, they feel like *now*, as though the original event is happening all over again.

Living with traumatic memories can therefore present two sets of problems. Firstly, they can be triggered, flooding us with those strong feelings and urges to act. This is called an *intrusion*. It can be just an inconvenience, such as feeling unease at a supermarket checkout. Or it can be a major issue, as our fight response leads to a difficult argument over nothing with a friend. Life can become very bumpy and difficult. Intrusions can be unpleasant and frightening, which leads to the second set of problems. People will, without having to think about it, develop *avoidances*, so that they do not encounter triggers so often. We will look at each of these in the next two sections.

Triggers and Intrusions

A trigger can be almost anything that serves as a reminder of the original traumatic event (Bryant, 2019; Ehlers et al., 2004). It might be something obviously connected. So if I watch a blockbuster monster movie, that could be a trigger for my Monster memory. But there are many other possible reminders. What is or is not a trigger can be quite individual and unpredictable. To show some possibilities, I've grouped some potential triggers for me in the table below.

Type of trigger	*Example for the Loch Ness Monster memory*
Sensory	Drinking a hot liquid
Thematic	A coffee break at work
Explicit reminders	"Tell me about that time you met the monster"
Internal	Being thirsty
Emotional	Suspense in the last five minutes of a close football match
Associative	Seeing reptiles at the zoo

When a traumatic memory is triggered, often the only thing the person is aware of is that they have strong feelings of terror, rage, or numbness, along with an urge to do something along the lines of fight, flight, freeze, or flop. They might also be aware of thoughts such as "it's not safe", "I've got to defend myself", or "I've got to get away", and might start to behave accordingly. All that the people around them are aware of is the behaviour that they see, just like in the example of the accidental bump in the café above.

Meanwhile, the brain has two contradictory pictures of reality to deal with. I'll use one of the examples from the table to illustrate what this can be like to experience.

> Wandering the corridors of my office to avoid writing a report, I bump into a colleague I have not seen for a few days - shall we take a break, he asks? Great idea, and we head for the staff room, chatting happily about a recent absurd meeting we were both at. We enter the staff room and I start to feel tetchy. My colleague jokingly asks me if I am ever planning on getting that report done. "Yes", I snap, "I think I'll go and do it now".

Of course you can see the trigger here and you can recognise the fight-like response. I want to try to demonstrate what experiences of "the past in the present" are like. Here are the two contradictory pictures of reality:

The picture of the present	*The picture of the memory*
We are having a laugh while we wait to make a coffee	Something terrible is happening and I am in great danger
My colleague and friend is teasing me	I am under attack
I have lots of options to respond	Fight!

This is where the insistence in Chapter 1 that we are not just hijacked by our emotions is so important. I know, and part of my brain knows, that it is just friendly banter, and I am preparing to give as good as I get! But the trigger has activated a traumatic memory, so I feel, and part of my brain is convinced, I am under huge threat. These parts are all well connected and can dialogue, so what comes out is not actual "fight", but instead a grumpiness that is acceptable even if it is out of proportion.

So not too bad an outcome, except that the experience is horrible. The colleague, who I trust and admire, is there in front of me with my brain labelling them as a clear and present danger to me. This happens because brains do not like having two contradictory pictures of reality – they work hard to create a single coherent sense of what is happening. As a result, even though I know they are not a threat, I feel they are a threat. Even though I know how to behave at work, I find myself snapping about nothing. Even though my colleague thought he knew me, he is starting to change that view and how he reacts to me in future.

Avoidances

Intrusions are unpleasant or disruptive and can impact on how others relate to us. People with traumatic memories may therefore often do their best not to encounter triggers. This is not often a conscious thought-out process but the result of internal messaging in the stress systems of the brain. In simple trauma, when someone has "only" one or two traumatic memories that are quite contained, this may not result in much difficulty. I could stop going to that particular coffee shop, for instance, and it would not matter as there are plenty of others. Nor would it majorly impact my life, work, or relationships if I decided to only drink tea from now on. But even in simple trauma, there can be triggers (and efforts to avoid them) that do cause more changes to how one lives. Suppose, for example, I find it difficult to even go past that coffee shop. In this case the whole street might be tricky to go down, and I will end up doing lengthy detours or having to come up with unconvincing reasons why I can't meet a friend at the bar next to the coffee shop. Remember that this may not be something I am consciously aware of – all I know is I don't want to meet there. And that might affect the relationship – "But we always go there on my birthday" "No let's go somewhere else" "Why?" "I don't know, stop asking me!" With complex trauma, life can start to feel full of jaggy bits as there are often lots of triggers, and one traumatic intrusion can set off another.

These patterns of behaviour are called avoidances and they can have three different kinds of impacts on people's lives. Firstly, life starts to get smaller. Not going to a particular coffee shop is not a big deal. But being unable to be in the same room as the smell of coffee, or having a strong desire to flee if I hear the clink of a cup, or a radio – these can severely reduce my options for what to do and where to go. Secondly, as hinted above, the options for who to do it with start to reduce as I might need to avoid people and encounters that involve triggers. As well, not everyone is going to be willing to go along with some of my apparently strange and unreasonable requirements for avoiding places or activities. Thirdly, look at some of the things I am starting to avoid, or at the least endure rather than enjoy (in the case of the workplace coffee-meeting). These are likely to be factors in my life that give it meaning, enjoyment, or even in the case of the workplace, a means to live. So my sources of resilience and recovery are becoming fewer. No longer the relaxing Friday drink in the bar that helps me unwind from the working week. Still taking the Saturday walk in the park with the dog, but steering away from the coffee stall – and anxious all the time in case the dog runs in that direction. And all of this without necessarily knowing why.

Dissociation

Dissociation is not easy to describe in words and different people experience it in different ways. It functions as a way of defending against difficult feelings and one way to think of it is that the emotional systems shut down – at least at a conscious level. What this can feel like is being very cold (literally sometimes), numb, or else cut off from what is going on, or even fragmented (Lanius et al., 2010). I have heard various descriptions including:

> It's like I'm stuck in a cage of ice unable to reach through it to people
> Every so often this glass wall comes down
> I don't feel any pleasure in the things I used to enjoy
> I know I am here, but it feels like I am not
> I'm somehow sort of a little to the left of my body

To the people around them, someone dissociating might come across as uninvolved, unemotional, lacking empathy, or just somehow "not connected".

There is nothing unhealthy about dissociation in itself. We all use it from time to time as a way of dealing with unpleasant experiences (Frewen et al., 2017). I spend most of a visit to the dentist pretending to myself that it is not happening, and I am not really there. Nor, I guess, am I the only person who sometimes "zones out" of a less than interesting meeting. Other frequent examples include the way we can read a book or watch TV and not really take it in – we are "elsewhere". And most people are a bit dissociated when they have a fever.

Like all coping mechanisms, it has the purpose and benefit of getting us through something. But habitual dissociation comes at a high cost. Here, for example, is the mother of a 6-week-old baby:

> I do all the things she needs to care for her, but it's like I am just going through the motions. I don't feel any joy in it, and I don't feel any love for her. Does that make me a bad mother? Am I a bad person?

You can't have got this far in the book without being able to answer that question for her: of course not! This mother may well have the problem of too much feeling, not too little. Without going into likely traumatic history, there is something about caring for her baby that contains triggers, and her emotional system goes "offline" to deal with it. She's a great mother, because despite not having the feelings to drive her care, she still does all the baby needs – and the baby will know this at some level too.

Dissociation becomes a problem because it can drain the colours out of life, the taste out of food, the love out of friendships and the meaning from whatever we used to value doing. It is also a problem because this cuts us off to an extent from the very things that might help us cope when we have traumatic experiences. As my friend might put it:

> Look, James wants to do something different and go somewhere else and that's fine, we try it. But when he turns up, it is like he's elsewhere. It's just not so much fun meeting anymore, and I have better ways to unwind if he's not wanting to bother

The tragedy is that I would be wanting to bother, would be desperate to be with my friend, and "with" him when I am there. Life slowly, or quickly, gets smaller and the sources of resilience more sparse.

Types of Trauma

One of my grumps with some writing about trauma is that it can lump a lot of different things together by talking about "trauma" without being clear about the different types. By types here, I do not mean different kinds of experience (bungee jumping, shark-wrestling, watching football, etc.) but different ways traumatic memories are laid down. These have important differences for how people manage, and how we can help them.

Simple trauma usually refers to a single incident, with few complicating factors. A bump in the car, a near-miss accident, one instance of bullying at work, things like that. It is not really a great name since, as we have seen, even a single and simple trauma can make life more complicated for the person with a traumatic memory. But one way to look at this is that they are quite likely to cope day to day. So after my Monster encounter, I am mostly fine – you'd never know. I play the piano, practise psychology as well as I ever did, eat my greens and so on. But there are some specific triggers that can cause difficulties and although these can generally be avoided it can make some aspects of life harder for me or for those around me.

Complex trauma by contrast tends to be a cascade of many events, or a single experience that goes on and on, or stops and is repeated. Potential examples include ongoing workplace bullying, domestic violence, or just a lot of difficult things happening all at once. It can also be a single incident where there are complicating factors. For example, a traumatic bereavement such as by accident, suicide, homicide, or difficult illness can result in complex traumatic responses. Or there might be other complications such as when the incident results in linked disasters and losses. So a small house fire that is rapidly put out might not be traumatic, or complex, in itself – but it could be if one of the things lost is the only photo album with pictures of loved ones.

Complex trauma is well named because it can make life complicated, and make day-to-day coping a constant struggle with intrusions. As well, people might develop wide ranges of avoidances of triggers, or things that might be triggers. They might be more constantly on the alert, or dissociated, and therefore on the edge of fight, flight, freeze, and flop reactions. Remember they might not know why, or make the connections to their past experience. So one of the most powerful reinforcers of longer term complex issues is how people come to think of themselves and how others start to think of them too. Here's a possible workplace description from a colleague:

> James used to be a helpful, humorous and pleasant colleague in the office, always with a cheery word or an idea to solve problems. But in the last few months he has become a grumpy so-and-so, tending to be sarcastic or dismissive. He focuses on risks and problems, and co-workers dread him coming to meetings.

So how will I start to feel about myself then? My sense of self is influenced by what I experience in myself, what I see myself doing, and how others react to me. So I might come to see myself as a tetchy, difficult person with poor self-control and a bad attitude to other people. And then of course I become more likely to interpret what happens to me and what I do according to that script, and more likely to act it out.

Concluding Thoughts

This chapter has some heavy material. It describes how and why people can form traumatic memories after a difficult experience. We also saw how this can have a big impact on life and their wellbeing. One of the first steps in trauma therapy and recovery, however, is to become aware of what is happening. It can help if a person can see that the behaviours or distressing feelings they struggle with are due not to their weakness or badness but to something that happened in the past. And that the intrusions and avoidances are neither random nor fully chosen, but rather the brain working "too hard" to try to keep them safe. Knowing these things, we can start to take more control, explain ourselves to others to gain their support, and gradually find experiences less overwhelming.

We will use the main points of this chapter in the second part of the book to show how we can help prevent traumatisation after a known recent event, how we can understand children's baffling or difficult behaviour in trauma-informed ways, and how we can use this to help them recover and flourish. As a last step of preparation, the next two chapters will apply what we have learned to young children. First we look at simple trauma in Chapter 3, and then in Chapter 4 we take it a stage deeper to consider more far-reaching developmental trauma.

Chapter summary:

- Traumatic memories form under conditions of overwhelming stress, low control and low perceived support
- They consist of strong feelings, body sensations, impulses to fight, flight, freeze, or flop, and only very simple thoughts
- When triggered by reminders, it feels like the original event is happening again
- People develop coping mechanisms such as avoidances and dissociation

Practice points:

- Realise traumatised people are not bad or weak, but coping with very difficult memories
- Understand a wide range of difficult behaviour as either intrusion or avoidance
- Use the trauma triad to help anyone feel safer in any situation

3
Trauma and Young Children

This chapter will provide:

- Application of the content of the previous chapter to young children
- A developmental account of trauma in young children and how it can present
- An introduction of key ideas of co-regulation and positive relationships

The first two chapters have described how the brain deals with day-to-day stressors and shown how different areas work together to create a level of response that deals as effectively as possible with the situation. We then looked at how the same systems deal with highly stressful events, where an overriding need to become safe creates fight, flight, freeze, and flop responses, along with feelings of terror. At the same time, thinking and reasoning functions, along with anything else that might slow us down, are reduced temporarily. Then we saw how sometimes these reactions can become part of a traumatic memory, a process designed to keep us safe in case the difficult experience happens again. These memories can be triggered by non-threatening events that are in some way like the original trauma, again because the brain takes a safety-first approach that if a really bad thing might be happening, it is best to assume that it is until proved otherwise.

Living with traumatic memories gives people two sets of difficulties. They can intrude suddenly and unexpectedly into our everyday lives when we meet a trigger. In addition, they can keep us on a state of higher alert than we might have been, as the brain is constantly scanning the world around us for signs that the trauma might be repeating. And, secondly, because the intrusions are unpleasant and upsetting in themselves, people may end up avoiding situations so as not to experience them. This can extend to times, places, and people that would otherwise provide pleasure and resources for coping and recovery. Or, it can make it harder to do the things that we have to do, whether this be going into shops, looking after children, going to work or taking a break.

With this background in place, we can understand how young children experience difficult events and under what conditions they might develop traumatic memories. We can see how

DOI: 10.4324/9781003563808-5

those memories might be different to those of adults, and how they might present as intrusions and avoidances.

Can Children Be Traumatised?

It can be a common assumption that children do not experience trauma. It is an assumption we might encounter in colleagues or families. There can be different reasons for it – children are "too young to understand" or else childhood is an innocent time that is its own protection. Or, how can we have traumatic memories from times before we have any memories at all? And sometimes children seem "fine at the time", and we only see the effects in more challenging environments as they get older.

In fact, post-traumatic stress is common in early childhood, with children under 6 up to twice as likely as older children to develop this after a difficult experience (Dunn et al., 2017). One reason for this is they are quite likely to have potentially traumatic experiences both for the reasons given above and because young childhood is a challenging time (Briggs-Gowan et al., 2010; Jimenez et al., 2016). Exact figures are difficult to provide as there are debates as to how to measure trauma in children, but roughly a quarter of children might develop traumatic memories in some form after a difficult experience (Woolgar et al., 2022). None of this is really surprising, since our basic threat detection and response systems are ready from birth (Sokolowski & Corbin, 2012) as are the relevant memory systems (Rovee-Collier & Cuevas, 2008). As a result there is evidence that infants even younger than one and certainly older show signs of post-traumatic distress and behaviours when they encounter triggers (Bogat et al., 2006; Bornstein et al., 2004; Gaensbauer, 2002).

A particular consideration for young children is that trauma for a loved one can be traumatic to them too. The reason for this is that, as we have seen, the children rely on the adults to provide safety and to help them manage threats. So one of the most important predictors for whether a young child will be traumatised is whether their caregiver is too – leading to the idea that we should describe early trauma as actually relational rather than just individual in nature (Scheeringa & Zeanah, 2001).

Having established that young children can experience trauma and develop long-lasting traumatic memories, we can go on to how these might be different from those of adults, and how what we see in our settings might be different too.

The Developing Brain

What's the difference between me and a baby? Or a toddler? "Not much, sometimes, James", my nearest and dearest might say. There's a serious point in that which we will come back to. But for now, let's put both me and a 6-month-old through a minor stressor and watch what happens inside our heads. The event will be the same – feeling hungry – but the *experience* will be very different, and show the differences in brain development and what these mean for traumatic memories.

In Chapter 1, I introduced a model for how the brain handles stressors and creates responses matched to the challenges of life. The systems involved include:

Stress systems	Rapid assessment What kind of event? How big a deal is it?
Regulation systems	Detailed assessment Soothing or ramping up stress system Knowledge of norms, consequential reasoning, etc.
Action systems	Producing actions to meet the need Fight, flight, flee, flop responses ready for high threat
Interconnections	Information sharing Creating a common response Coordinating that response

So let's take me (middle aged adult) and also me (aged 6 months) to compare and contrast how these systems respond to a feeling that I am hungry. I've set this out as a summary below:

	Hungry!	
	Adult	*Baby*
Stress systems	Hungry, again? Feels not great, but No big deal	Hungry! Huge! Survival at risk!
Regulation systems	Yes - had a good breakfast so won't starve It's lunch in an hour - manage till then? Or pop into a shop and get a snack? By the way, it's wrong to grab other people's snacks in the park, and they might object	Hungry!
Action systems	Here's 100 things I know of what to do about this . . . Do nothing then? Ok, turn down that snatch response	Cry? Scream? Give up?
Interconnections	Carried the information flow back and forth Allowed for confirmation and negotiation	Capacity exceeded Stress → action emergency link activated

For an adult, being hungry is a routine event. I've been hungry tens of thousands of times before and lived through it each time. It's not a perfect experience, but it is nothing compared to some of the other things I've coped with. It's also not a big deal because I know that I have a huge range of possible solutions available from making a snack to just ignoring it until the next meal that I know is coming soon enough. The baby at 6 months has none of this. At that age, I don't have tens of thousands of memories of being hungry and then being fine, and there is very little I can do about it. So the threat level is higher in itself (it really is a survival issue for a baby) and because I haven't had a lot of life experience yet, so don't have any comparisons.

As we experience more of the world and other people, our stress systems gradually become able to make finer judgements. You may remember from Chapter 1 that the adult stress system can manage quite fine differences, almost as if there is a scale from 0 to 100 for how strongly we should feel about something. So I can make assessments ranging from "ok" to "hmm" to "peckish" to "hungry" to "ravenous" to "starving". For a 6-month-old the scale is basically ok/not-ok. But that understates it - it is more like having only 0 for safe and 100 for threat, and none of the numbers in between - rather as though your home thermostat only has freeze and baking hot as the available temperatures. More on exactly how this develops in a moment, after we've looked at the rest of the brain.

Babies therefore probably have a stronger stress reaction to most things than adults. But also, we can see that many of the adult regulating systems are simply not there. There is no knowledge of cultural rules, such as it is polite to wait, or how to ask for food. Nor can a baby so easily soothe themselves and just manage. And even if they could, they are not as good at selecting and controlling actions, so even if the baby did not intend to cry or scream, they might end up doing that anyway.

But even if the baby was, unusually, good at selecting actions, the available menu is still very small. The differences between my actions systems now and what they were when I was 6 months old are fairly simple. Firstly, I know many more things to do, and therefore have a wide range of potential solutions for my brain to choose from. This not only calms the stress system in the first place, but also means that I gradually accumulate more and more memories of solving problems. So then, when I meet a new problem my brain can more quickly discard responses that don't work or make it worse and already can have the ones that do at the top of the list of suggestions.

But there is a difference between selecting an appropriate action and managing to do it. I can move myself to a shop, say what I need, manage a transaction, and so on. All of that requires both physical capability and developmental capability. Six-month-old me has neither of these. I couldn't move by myself, and I wouldn't have the words to express what I needed. So all I have is to cry, scream, or do nothing.

Then, putting it all together into a successful solution requires coordination. There is a sequence involved that has to be done in the right order and with the right timings. Apart from making demands on attention systems that have not yet developed, putting complex action sequences together can be difficult for young children. It is also error prone, sometimes resulting in all the right actions but in the wrong order, or else just apparent disorganisation. To give one example, a child may know not to touch the TV screen, but the impulse to do so is faster, quicker, and easier than any alternative yet - and so they touch the screen faster than they can stop themselves. Or a toddler, faced with the perfectly manageable challenge of being asked to put their coat on, produces the form of chaos otherwise known as a tantrum.

Lastly, as we saw in Chapter 1, the brain's responses to stressors require fast and clear connections between the different brain areas so they can create finely adjusted actions. The young brain has less efficient connections, so again actions may not be well adjusted to the situation. Instead, the brain draws either on built-in reactions (such as versions of fight, flight, freeze, or flop) or ones that are well learned already even if they don't fit.

Reflective Activity

Think about the children you work with. How do you think their brains differ from yours in how they experience stressors (big, small, etc.) and what they can do to regulate the feelings by themselves? Does this explain what you see sometimes in what they do or how they react?

All of these differences will help us to see how children experience potentially traumatic events, why they might experience different things to adults as traumatic, and what traumatic memories look like in young children. There is one more difference to consider before that.

Sensitive and Reflective Care

The example above showed how an infant's response to a stressor is limited because it is based on brain systems that are yet to develop to adult capacity. This is what we would see if we could look inside my 6-month-old brain:

	Baby
Stress systems	Hungry! Huge! Survival at risk!
Regulation systems	Hungry!
Action systems	Cry? Scream? Give up?
Interconnections	Capacity exceeded Stress → action emergency link activated

Even a simple, ordinary, experience of being mildly hungry can rapidly become felt as an escalating, life-threatening crisis. Does this mean young children are very vulnerable, and need to be shielded from all stress in case their development is damaged? There are two reasons why not that we explore in this section.

The first reason is that babies and young children don't have to solve any of these crises on their own. They have us to solve it for them, or to help them solve it for themselves if they can. What I want to highlight here is what goes on in our brains as we do this, so here is a column with a sketch of a caregiver's brain as they attend to the baby's needs:

	Caregiver brain
Stress systems	Baby needs something!
Regulation systems	No big deal, I can work it out Been a while since feed Yes, this feels manageable
Action systems	Let's offer a feed and see if that solves it
Interconnections	All working together Response confirmed

Babies are very good at creating alarm calls that go right through the adult head! We are set up to respond to the tone and pitch of an infant's cry and our stress systems initially respond strongly to it. So the first response to a baby cry is often a rapid peak of high stress. But for most people, and in most situations, this has gradually become a routine event and we have many memories of solving whatever it was (more or less). So the regulating systems can quickly damp it all down - it's urgent and important, yes, but not a big, life-threatening deal. And the adult action systems know lots of things to try, including offering a feed, jiggling about, or starting the soothing noise of the washing machine. So we can move quickly to a solution and, if that does not work, we have lots of others to try.

There's nothing more important than making sure baby is fed. But! There is something hiding in this ordinary sequence that happens billions of times each day around the world that is, I would argue, *as important*. This is hard to explain, because our culture and everyday experiences make us think of human beings as isolated individuals. I am me, and you are you. What goes on in your head goes on in your head, and it is separate to what goes on in mine. But this isn't quite true, as I can easily show. You've just read this paragraph. It was in my head, and now it is in yours - so something in me has changed something in you. There is lots of research showing that when people interact, their brain activity gets into sync. Again this is obvious in a way. If we are both looking at a dog and talking about the dog, our "talking about dogs" brain areas are going to be activated. But it goes several levels more profound than that.

Although the neuroscience is complicated, the essential point is simple. The baby doesn't have a nuanced adult stress system, effective regulating functions, and a long list of actions. But we do. And when we interact sensitively with young children we are effectively lending them our capabilities. The toddler can't get the top off the jar (fortunately). But her parent can, so delicious food can be provided. The 4-year-old can't quite manage the stress of being dropped off at their early education setting. They are torn between delight at all the things to do, and anxiety at their parent leaving them. And they can't yet understand their experience. But we do understand, and we can respond accordingly, offering ways to say goodbye and manage the feelings.

This kind of sensitive care does much more than help a child cope in the moment. It is also what, with many repeated and reliable experiences, builds the stress, regulation, and action systems. The more times that 4-year-old is helped to cope with the separation, the more their stress system will start to recalibrate the drop-off as a minor issue. And their regulating systems will pick up the pattern of stress-comfort-ok as a more general rule for facing difficulties. And then, being calmer and more in control, they can learn and experiment with different actions that might solve them.

Reflective Activity

Think about a time when you helped a child to manage some small thing they were finding difficult - anything from waiting for a turn, to climbing another rung, or coping with there being no more fruit. What did you "lend" them from your ability to manage stress, or take effective actions?

The whole process from baby to adult takes years, with many ups and downs along the way. We will see in detail how it all happens in Chapters 8–13, along with how we can restore these processes for children who have had more traumatic developmental pathways. In the rest of this chapter we will apply what we have seen so far to understanding how young children might experience trauma differently to adults and how the resulting traumatic memories might be different. In the following chapter we will take this a stage deeper to consider developmental trauma, which is when the overall process of brain development adapts to cope with frequent and severe early adversities.

Young Children and Traumatic Experiences

In Chapter 2 I showed why we can't make a list of "traumatic experiences" since trauma is about the person's experience of the event rather than the event itself. There were three features of an experience that made it more likely to be traumatic, which can be summarised in the trauma triangle.

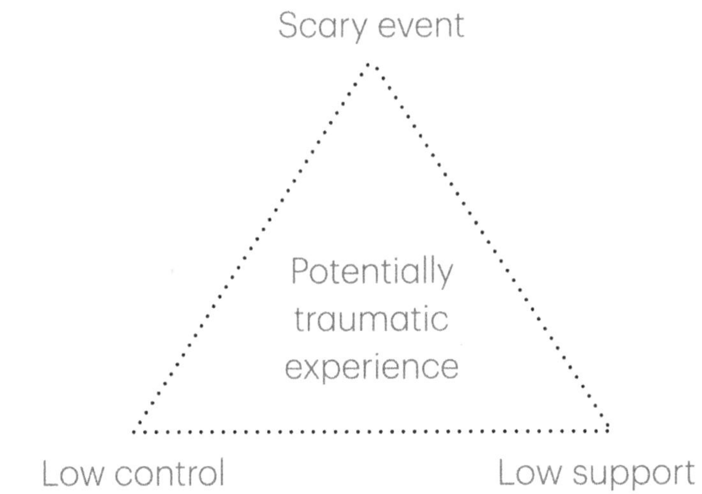

Figure 3.1 The trauma triad

We can see from this how young children might be more likely to find experiences traumatic that the adults may see as routine, or even may not notice at all. Their stress systems have stronger reactions, especially to unfamiliar events. Regulating systems are less developed and they have fewer actions available that they are good at doing. Those together mean that they have much less sense of control over what is happening (and they are right about this). Finally, young children, as we have seen, are much more dependent on adult support to manage even ordinary stressors. In practice this means that when an experience is highly stressful, even a well-meaning and effective adult who is there to help them may feel less available. But the other side of this is that if adult support to cope can get through and be effective, then it can counter that part of the triangle. What might have been traumatic turns out not to be because the adult has effectively "buffered" (Humphreys et al., 2022).

Here are two simple and hopefully non-traumatic examples that show the difference this support can make (I'm making it something annoying rather than "very bad" just to keep things comfortable).

> Miles carefully carries his ice cream cone towards the bench. He stumbles on a step and the lovely ice cream falls splat onto the ground.

> Miles carefully carries his ice cream cone towards the bench. He stumbles on a step and the lovely ice cream falls splat onto the ground. His dad sees, comes over, crouches down with a gentle touch and comforts him, suggesting they go and try the swings to forget about it.

The same "event" can be a different experience with different outcomes. Dropping your ice cream can be an earth-shattering disaster for a young child, but in the second instance it becomes transformed into an experience of being supported and of coping. The meaning of dropping an ice cream has changed, or begun to.

What this means in practice is that it is even harder to predict what might turn out to be traumatic for a young child. They can be unaffected by what seem like huge things, but carry traumatic memories from quite small ones. A lot depends on the meaning they make out of it (Tronick & Hunter, 2024). They might be surrounded by supportive adults but also be for whatever reason unable to feel this, or use it. For example:

> Patsy was with her family at a shopping mall. She was skipping ahead of them and got into the lift just as the door closed. The next thing she knew the door had opened two floors above and what seemed like an army of strange adults crowded around asking questions.

It was hardly life threatening, but it felt like it. The adults were being helpful, but what Patsy saw was an army firing questions at her. Something bad was happening, she couldn't stop it, and she wasn't getting any accessible help. Contrast:

> Padma was with her family at a shopping mall. She was skipping ahead of them and got into the lift just as the door closed. The next thing she knew the door had opened two floors above – what an adventure. And all these people taking an interest in her!

The key question is therefore not "was that experience traumatic?" but "were they traumatised by it?" More on this when we look at myths about children and trauma at the end of the chapter. Before that, we can see how traumatic memories might develop differently for young children and the consequences for how life feels to them, and what we might see in our settings.

Young Children's Traumatic Memories

We have seen that traumatic memories are different to the "story-like" memories we have for ordinary experiences. Traumatic memories are unprocessed, vivid bundles of strong feelings, FFFF responses, and fragmentary thoughts such as "I've got to get out". A useful metaphor is to think of them as a frozen snapshot of the brain state at the time of the event, that the brain can unpack whenever it judges the trauma is likely to be happening all over again.

We have seen the differences between the adult's brain and the young child brain, so we can expect that the traumatic memory might look rather different too. When I met the Monster in Chapter 2, my memory was a snapshot of an adult brain since I was an adult at the time. Suppose instead I had met the monster aged 2. The snapshot would have been of my 2-year-old brain, so when it is triggered that is what will come forward. We sometimes refer to this phenomenon as an "emotional stuck point". The effect is that if this memory is triggered what I have immediately available are the coping resources of a 2-year-old. Children might appear to lose skills or regress temporarily (Moner et al., 2022). For example, a teenager may present as though they are a toddler – just a toddler with a bigger and stronger body and a much wider vocabulary!

In practice this means that the two problems of intrusions and avoidances can present differently for young children who have developed traumatic memories. Remember from Chapter 2 that intrusions happen when the memory is triggered and starts to affect how we experience the present, while avoidances often arise as ways to prevent this happening. We will look at each in turn.

Intrusions

The first sign of the intrusion of a traumatic memory for a young child will be in what they do. Often, as with adults, this does not fit the actual situation but the triggered memory. So we will see versions of fight, flight, freeze, and flop. But what happens might be different to adults because of the differences in brain development. Because the stress system has a smaller range of responses, for example, children may show "all or nothing" emotions:

> Angie was described to me as a "Jekyll and Hyde" girl. One minute she would be happily playing and laughing, following instructions and so on. The next, she would be "a nightmare", screaming and kicking and then going into floods of tears and refusing to be comforted.

Secondly, because the regulation systems are less developed, the fight, flight, freeze, and flop responses may not get toned down in the way they are with adults. Remember that when my memory was triggered in the staffroom in Chapter 3 I was just grumpy rather than fighting? That's because my regulation systems were able to process the situation and judge it to be safe and could plan and evaluate actions and consequences. The result was a compromise between the regulating systems saying "it's ok" and the stress system saying "it's not safe". Young children do not have this available, so we are likely to see stronger action responses – even actual fight, flight, freeze, or flop – as with Angie just now.

A third difference is part of the same issue. The different brain systems, as well as being less mature, are not so well connected. So even if Angie's regulating systems realise that whatever is happening it is not the traumatic memory over again, and even if we have taught Angie some alternative solutions such as telling an adult what the matter is, the regulating systems can't tell the stress system. And by the time they get through to the actions systems it is too late, the fight response is already in progress.

A fourth difference is a difficult emotion that can affect children more powerfully than adults. This is shame. In Chapter 2 we saw how much of the reasoning functions of the brain turn down during an overwhelming experience, so that a resulting traumatic memory contains only sketchy thoughts such as "I'm not safe" or "I've got to get out". For reasons we do not fully understand, young children tend to acquire highly negative thoughts about themselves, such as:

> "I am bad"
> "I should be punished"
> "Bad things that happen are my fault"

They might not be aware of these, and probably would not express them exactly like that, but we can see their influence in what they do. Subjectively, these will feel like shame. Not only is the child experiencing the distress of high emotion and urges to fight, flee, freeze, or flop, but a powerful voice is telling them that what this means is that they are bad and should be punished. This can then feed an escalating cycle of stronger feelings and therefore stronger actions to deal with them. We will see in Chapters 8-10 how important it is for adults to counter shame, and how effective some quite simple ways to do this are. One headline is to avoid getting pulled into the worldview that the child is bad and must be punished. Another is to make sure that any sense of rupture or disruption to a relationship is swiftly followed by a repair of the relationship - a repair in which the adult has to take the lead and the main responsibility. This has implications not just for what individual staff members do but for the ethos, processes, and policies of the whole setting. We look at these issues in Chapter 15.

Apart from the usually quite visible fight, flight, freeze, and flop responses, there are some other signs of intruding traumatic memories for young children that we might see, or that they might describe themselves (Chu et al., 2025; Hensley & Varela, 2008; Lieberman & Van Horn, 2009; Moner et al., 2022). These include:

- Changes in eating or sleeping
- Nightmares and terrors
- Being generally fussy (as a younger child)
- Other apparent regressions, sometimes just in the moment or more generally
- Aggression towards themselves - hitting, banging head, pulling hair, holding breath
- Taking undue risks or trying to put themselves in danger
- Aggression towards key caregivers (who should have kept them safe); this can transfer to other caregivers too
- Being highly aware of potential threats, constant vigilance
- Easily startled
- Frequent crying
- Fears of separation, even small ones such as toilet visits
- Tummy pains or headaches, or other odd pains

Traumatic Play

A particular form of intrusion for young children can sometimes be seen in their play (Moner et al., 2022) where they can seem to be re-enacting the traumatic experience (e.g., Cohen et al., 2010). This might be directly, for example in repetitive collisions of toy cars. Or it can be more indirectly, for example in frequently bumping into other people or things, perhaps also shouting "bang". Witnessing this can be distressing for families and for practitioners alike, and it can be hard to know if the play is healthy and helpful, or else is doing further harm.

For some children the play may be a compelled acting out of an intolerable memory, while for others it may be a way of examining a memory and making sense of it or coming to terms with the feelings (Chazan & Cohen, 2010). We might be able to tell the difference from how it feels to us. Does it feel dry, repetitive, and without relief? Or does it seem to bring some comfort? And does it have some of the features of regular play, including that a child might let us become involved in it and even steer towards a positive resolution? It is always a good idea to seek some specialist advice if you notice elements of traumatic re-enactment in a child's play.

Avoidances

> Wilma had been playing happily with Rafi, who was showing her what he had learned about counting buttons. He was making a mistake in counting the same buttons twice, so she gently took his hand to go "one, two, three . . .". Rafi shook her off and wandered away. For the next few days, he refused to work with her, which was inconvenient as she was meant to be doing an observation for his profile.

Here is the past sending its reach into the present and painting every day, trusted, beloved people or situations with the emotional stain from a memory. Rafi at one level knows that Wilma is Wilma, the kind and interesting person who plays and learns with him, and who helps him solve the daily problems of being a young child. But superimposed on this clear image of Wilma is another one, and Rafi's behaviour is telling us that this second image is frightening. He develops an avoidance as a result.

Young children's avoidances can be quite disguised. We might notice a lack of compliance, refusals to do certain things or only to do them in certain ways. Alternatively, children may persist in an activity so as to avoid what is coming next, or else to avoid difficult emotions connected to change and uncertainty. They may temporarily lose competencies, such as the ability to climb the frame or wash their own hands, as a way of avoiding feelings of responsibility and control. Finally, young children can dissociate, just as adults can. This might take the form of cognitive dissociation and look like inattention, poor listening, or carelessness. Or more emotional forms such as seeming to lack empathy or feelings, and behavioural errors that relate to these.

Looking Ahead

The second part of the book contains ways to respond to both triggers and avoidances and how early educators can help children to manage traumatic memories and to an extent resolve them, or some of the effects.

It is also important to recognise that this work, while essential for the children, can have an impact on the adults. Being a witness to a trigger moment, especially if we have in some way brought it about, can be shocking, frightening, and frustrating. These emotions easily change into others such as anger, blame, or helplessness – whether about ourselves or about the other person. If we react according to those feelings, then things may well not get better.

Once the adult in a situation becomes frightening, the child has lost their main source of safety and solutions, so things are only likely to escalate. We will look at this in slow motion and some detail in Chapter 10. But we must also consider the practitioners and our wellbeing so that we can stay in there for Rafi and for others without a high cost to ourselves. That is the subject for Chapters 16–17, and you may want to turn to this now if any of this material has been difficult to read or think about.

In the following chapter we take all this a stage deeper. We have so far considered the impact of simple trauma on children. But when traumatic experiences occur early enough and often enough, this can affect how the brain develops in order to cope with and adapt to them. The next chapter is therefore about this, developmental, trauma.

Chapter summary:

- Young children can be traumatised by a wider range of experiences than adults
- Traumatic memories surface in developmentally influenced ways, including through play
- Sensitive and reflective care is the essential foundation both to prevent traumatisation and to support day-to-day coping

Practice points:

- Consider how ordinary experiences in the setting might have aspects of high stress, low control, and low support for some children
- Be aware of, and consider, the possibility of traumatic origins for a wide range of common problems in education settings
- Prioritise providing safe and positive relationships in ways that suit each child

4
Developmental Trauma

This chapter will provide:

- A detailed account of developmental trauma and its differences from simple trauma
- A model for understanding developmental trauma that enables positive action
- Clarity between different concepts such as toxic stress and adverse childhood experiences

In the first four chapters we have been considering what is usually called "simple trauma". We've seen enough to understand that trauma of any kind is far from "simple", but the term refers to experiences that have generally happened only once or twice, quickly over, and with not many other complicating factors. Trauma becomes more complex when it is repeated or inescapable, carries on for a long time, or stops and starts, or when there are complicating factors. These can include when the trauma is caused by someone significant to us, especially if they are in a position of care – a parent or a partner, for example. If someone experiences lots of simple traumas, especially in a short space of time, this can become complex trauma also.

This chapter is about a third type of trauma that is specific to children, particularly young children, but that can have effects over the whole lifetime (and into the next generation, as we will see). When traumatic experiences are deep enough, and happen early enough in life, and go on for long enough, then the way the brain is developing changes in order to cope with them. There are different names for this from different research traditions, so you may have heard it referred to as developmental trauma (the term I use in this book), toxic stress, or adverse childhood experiences. I'll show how these terms relate and differ along the way.

Here is some of the most potentially difficult content in the book. As usual, I will include some lighter examples and metaphors to make it as comfortable as possible, but we will be discussing some of the worst experiences for young children, so please do remember to pace yourself as needed. If any of what follows is upsetting, then that is because it is. No child should go through what is discussed here. We should, as caring adults, feel upset and even angry about it. It's a healthy response, as long as we also remember that we are very powerful to prevent it, and to help children who have experienced it. If this chapter gives an

DOI: 10.4324/9781003563808-6

understanding of the impact of developmental trauma my hope is that it also energises us to respond in our role as educators - and the second half of the book is packed with ideas for that.

How Child Development Works

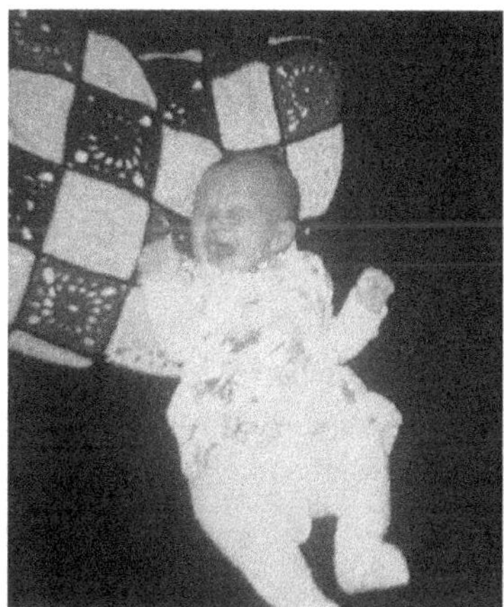

Figure 4.1 Spot the difference

Here are a couple of pleasant pictures to start us off. On the left is me - aged a few months! On the right are some lambs, born in the field next to my house. We could now play the world's worst game of "spot the difference". It's not very difficult - woolly, not woolly; four legs, two legs; edible . . . . I want to draw attention though to one very important difference. Look how advanced these lambs are, at roughly the same age, compared to me. They are not quite independent yet, but they are basically little sheep almost ready to take on the world. It will take baby James many years to get to the same level.

This is where human beings are strange animals. We have these long childhoods. And look how we change, from infant to toddler to young child to tween to teen to young adult. The whole program takes about 25 years in terms of complete brain development. All this time, the developing youngster is expensive in time, resources, and dangerously helpless unless able to rely on elders. Why are we not born ready, or at least with the ability to get ready faster, like those lambs?

There are a number of reasons, but the key one for us is this: being born incomplete allows the child to develop to match their environment. Rather than a one-sheep-fits-all approach, humans can develop quite differently depending on what kind of world they are born into. This is why people can live almost anywhere on the planet, but also have survived through very different and sometimes difficult epochs - times of famine, predators, cold, heat, as well as times of plenty. To flourish in an easy world needs a different brain and body from flourishing in a difficult and dangerous one. We'll look at exactly what this means next, and then relate it to childhood trauma, as this will give us a very powerful way to understand children and how to help them. But for now, we can sum up all the complexities of child development (everything you might have read in textbooks about Piaget, Vygotsky, and all the others) as being about two basic questions:

1. What kind of world is this?
2. What kind of brain and body do I need to develop to do well in it?

Different answers to these questions have different consequences for how the brain and body develop. We often see these consequences in our settings. And in our settings, we are very effective in changing those answers, as we shall see.

A Difficult and Dangerous World

Instead of listing all the ways in which childhood can be difficult and dangerous, I want to use one more imaginary story. Just suppose that when you opened this book for the first time a Golden Ticket dropped out (or if you are reading on a screen, a Golden QR code flashes up). Yes, that's right! Somehow I persuaded the publisher that everyone who reads this book should be rewarded with a free holiday. It is no more than we all deserve and need after the last three chapters.

Here's the deal. You'll be picked up by taxi from your door, taken to the airport, flown to the destination, and dropped off in a pleasant looking forest clearing, with a bag full of comfortable clothes and supplies for three days. A signpost points down a path to your luxury beach hut accommodation. As you pass, you notice that the sign is a little battered, with some strange scratches, and then on the beach you see the footprints. Yes, there is a catch. The only place available for the publisher at short notice and within budget is an island known as Jurassic Park, roamed by a variety of annoyed and hungry dinosaurs. Enjoy your holiday!

Over time, the publisher assesses the feedback and online reviews for this experience and notices two things. Firstly, people didn't always enjoy it that much, but secondly, there aren't that many reviews. Closer investigation reveals that not everyone got home - some people, for some reason, didn't survive their holiday. Follow up focus groups with survivors revealed that they had a few things in common (apart from a strange lack of gratitude for their free break).

Here's a question for you to pause and consider. What do you think made the difference for each person as to whether they survived their holiday? What skills did they have, or other characteristics?

Some of these are fairly obvious, and some less so. Being good at running away from hungry dinosaurs would be one thing. And you can't run for ever, so being quiet and still and finding hiding places would be good too. And if the dinosaur finds you, then being able to have a good go with a stick or some rocks also helps. We've seen these before - they are our old friends fight, flight, freeze, and flop. But these are not just fleeting reactions to a single experience or a trigger. They need to be a general lifestyle, as it is dinosaurs, dinosaurs everywhere. So we need a body that is always ready for action, which means having energy and water available to supply the muscles. And it is one thing after another, so we need to be constantly alert for danger, homing in on tiny cues such as a snapping twig or a shaking branch. It's a sad fact too that we might get bruised or scratched or bitten, so we need our body to be ready to repair wounds and to fight back against any infections that might get into cuts. Lastly, although we'd like to think that if we met other unfortunates we would all band together and help each other, those who nobly sacrifice themselves so their companion can escape won't be one of those survivors we are talking to.

We can sum this up in a list of things we would need to be able to do, and the kind of brain and body that could make these possible. For example, to spot the danger, we need a brain that is alert for it. Here's some of the ideas in a table. As you look at them, maybe reflect on whether you see any signs of these with children you work with - we are very close to a full understanding of developmental trauma.

I need to be able to . . .	*So I need a brain and body that is good at . . .*
Run or fight	Ramping up my muscles quickly Providing lots of energy at short notice
Spot dangers	Always being on the watch Assuming the unknown is a threat
React fast	Switching attention quickly Fast, impulsive responses Acting first, thinking later Relying on myself
Recover from injury	Fending off infections Healing any wounds

We'll look at what this means for child development in conditions of adversity, but there are two more key things to learn from this horrible holiday experience. Firstly, and perhaps obviously, those of us who do survive to return home might not be feeling fully relaxed. Whether your usual idea of an ideal holiday is doing nothing on a beach for a week, or speed cycling in the Appalachians, one usually comes back more refreshed - even if that feeling doesn't always last so long. But after this one, we are exhausted, strung out, likely to be snappy with colleagues and family, with wobbly feeling legs and high fatigue. Living, even for a while, in a difficult and dangerous environment is taxing and tiring on body and mind. More on this in a moment.

The second thing is less obvious but just as important. Imagine on day 6 of your "holiday" with the dinosaurs that a helicopter lands and a representative of the publisher gets out. They tell you there has been a terrible mistake (you don't say), and you were meant to be dropped off at the neighbouring Paradise Island, so they transfer you straight away. There are lovely pools, with open bars, friendly people chatting, all kinds of interesting things to do, and long sumpluous buffet meals. Very nice - but what might you be doing? You've just spent six days being hunted by dinosaurs, so you might well jump at any unexpected sound. You've been on the run, so you may grab food from the buffet and run off with it. You've been reacting rather than thinking, so you may suddenly hide under a lounger if a champagne cork pops, or be irritable if someone says "hello". It'll naturally take a while for your brain and body to adjust to this new place, and meanwhile you will come across to the others as quite strange. They may even think there is something wrong with you.

But there isn't. And, as we will see, in the same way there is not much "wrong" with the traumatised children we work with. It's time to make the connections with real children's worlds.

Real Childhoods

The truth is that many children grow up not among dinosaurs, but in equally scary places, where scary things happen and among scary people. We know the different ways in which this can be so. Perhaps the neighbourhood is a violent one, with shouts in the streets as the little one tries to sleep. Perhaps there are daily unbearable worries of how to provide food, shelter, or care. Perhaps the family is often in danger, or faces repeated disasters – repossessions, evictions, house fires, sickness, incarcerations, separations. Perhaps, as well, the people who the developing infant and toddler might have expected to provide safety, nurture, care, and fun are themselves the source of violence, neglect, or abuse. Don't be misled by accounts that talk about "stone age brains" and evading predators – from prehistory to the present, the main danger to humans has been other humans (Perry, 2009). And this remains so in the cities, towns, and villages all around us.

We can consider this in the light of our understanding of child development and its two key questions:

1. What kind of world is this?
2. What kind of brain and body do I need to develop to do well in it?

The first question is clear. For whatever reason, this seems to be a difficult and dangerous world. So what kind of brain and body do I need to do well in it – even to survive into adulthood? We know this already, as we had a rehearsal in Jurassic Park:

I need a brain and body that is good at . . .

- Ramping up my muscles quickly
- Providing lots of energy at short notice
- Always being on the watch
- Assuming the unknown is a threat
- Switching attention quickly
- Fast, impulsive responses
- Acting first, thinking later
- Relying on myself
- Fending off infections
- Healing any wounds

Most early educators have met young brains and bodies like these. Here's one, who I knew a few years ago – see if you can spot some of the aspects in the table above:

> Marta is a lovely 4-year-old girl, who enjoys playing with water and mud. But she is best left by herself. When other children try and join in, she gets agitated and can end up throwing things around or even biting the other children. She tends to "disappear" from time to time, taking herself off to a corner of the setting and sitting there, refusing to come out and not accepting adult comfort or hugs. Her language is delayed, and mostly consists of single words. She's not interested in any of the mark-making resources. But she does love being read to in an adult's lap, even if she sometimes chews the pages or tears them. But what worries the staff most is that she is always on the alert. The

> smallest change or surprise can set her off into a tantrum, or to start attacking adults or objects. And they are concerned about whether she will be ready for school as she rarely settles to anything for more than a few minutes.

There are lots of ways we could describe this in terms of things wrong with Marta, and we might even give them some names of disorders. We might see some issues around attachment, in her insecure or even disorganised way of relating to the adults in the setting. There is language delay and also perhaps some issues of cognitive development too. Her behaviour is difficult to say the least - are there some early signs here of conduct disorder? Or perhaps, given her short attention span we should be thinking of ADHD. And we should consider autism too, given her difficulty in handling social situations with peers or adults. Lastly, there seem to be some sensory issues in her preoccupation with water and mud.

I'm not saying any of that is wrong, or we shouldn't think in this way. In some educational systems, indeed, it is the only way to access additional help for her. But I am suggesting that a trauma-informed approach offers a simple and intuitive way to understand that unlocks some ways to help Marta quite quickly. I have some additional information for you:

> Marta now lives with foster carers, having experienced high levels of neglect and inconsistent care in her first year of life. Nobody is quite sure what else happened, but it is likely there was also violence in the home between the adults.

What we can now see is that Marta has been living in a real-world and prolonged version of your imaginary nightmare holiday. Instead of dinosaurs, she has had scary people and scary happenings. And here is the key difference. Her young brain has been working on the two big questions of child development:

1. *What kind of world is this?* — A difficult and dangerous one
2. *What kind of brain and body do I need?* — The one we see in our setting

So what we saw in the setting, and what troubled us, was the result of Marta's wonderful brain doing its very best to adapt to the world that it thought she was growing up in so as to ensure her survival in that world. When she came into a quite different kind of world - our lovely calm, nurturing, kind, and interesting setting, she didn't match it. Marta had been developing to match a difficult and dangerous world, not a safe and interesting one, and so she sticks out in our setting, she looks disordered. That's not a surprise, because so did we when we were transplanted from Jurassic Park to Paradise Island. It would have taken us a few days to adapt; it'll take Marta, with suitable help, perhaps years to.

Adaptation and Its Costs

This is all about adaptation, growing and developing so as to do as well as possible in the world that presents itself. We've looked at adaptation to a difficult and dangerous world, so what about a safe and reliable one? If, for example, there isn't a terrible threat round every corner, it doesn't make sense to be in a state of high alert all the time. For one thing, this is very costly in energy and more, as we will see below. For the other, we might miss opportunities - if we run in terror from every bee or butterfly, we lose out on learning and wonder. Alternatively, if the world is fairly stable, and does not contain lots of surprises (nasty or nice) then it pays to develop concentration and focus on what is in front of us rather than attention that flits from one thing to the next. If people in the world turn out to be reliable, then a balance of seeking help from them when we can't manage something ourselves is the best way to be.

I need to emphasise how deep these developmental choices go. It's not like going on holiday to France and picking up a few words of French here and there. To take one example, when we are born, we are small and helpless and lots of different things happen to us. To cope with this, our sensory system is initially set up for defence. As we encounter an ordered world where needs are met, this defensive system changes so that it can tell the difference between good and bad stimuli (Bundy & Lane, 2020). And if we encounter a different kind of world, our sensory system remains in "threat mode", with consequences for how we experience almost anything thereafter.

So we can't expect Marta to go "oh, turns out things are fine, I'll be different". This developmental process happens at the level of networks in the brain. And because each development is built on the last, these alternatives gradually become more fixed. Children will literally develop different bodies and different brains to adapt to the world their brain thinks they are growing up in. These choices involve trade-offs (Szepsenwol, 2022). We can't develop two brains at the same time in one head. So increasing vigilance for danger by building an attention system that keeps scanning from one thing to another means not building one that prioritises focusing stably on one thing for long periods. Putting more resources into developing fast actions means fewer available for developing language.

Having seen the consequences for Marta, and the staff in her setting, we can fill in some detail in terms of developmental milestones and learning, relating this to the concepts that are used in curriculums and developmental frameworks around the world. These include:

- Language and communication
- Cognitive development
- Executive function (attention, memory, controlled action)
- Stress regulation
- Social and self (views of self, social rules, help seeking, etc.)

Let's imagine two basically similar children, Diego and Daniel, growing up in very different circumstances, and see what developmental pathways are needed in those different worlds.

	Diego	*Daniel*
What kind of world?	Difficult & dangerous	Mostly safe & stable
Language & communication	Act rather than talk Reduced language	Express needs & negotiate More language
Cognitive development	Rapid assessments Concepts for action Coping with randomness In the moment	Deepened thinking Complex concepts Cause & effect Reasoning about future
Executive function	Scanning environment Changing focus often Low impulse control	Controlled focus and attention Higher impulse control
Stress regulation	Vigilant, reactive	Calm, self-soothing

(Continued)

(Continued)

	Diego	*Daniel*
Social and self	Negative expectations Self-reliance Reduced help seeking	Positive expectations Confidence Help seeking

The most important point here is that neither of these pathways is "better" in itself. Neither is the right one. If we transplanted Daniel from his safe and stable childhood into Diego's difficult and dangerous one, he might not do that well. He is not adapted to that kind of world. But Diego does brilliantly in it, as he is developing to match it. However, if we transplanted Diego to Daniel's world, he would struggle too - just as Marta did, and just as you did when moved from Jurassic Park to Paradise Island.

But the two pathways do have very different consequences in our 21st century world. We've seen the immediate implications for Marta as she struggles to adjust to an alien environment. We can play out how her life might develop. Because she is reluctant to seek help and comfort, she may end up experiencing less help and comfort - which pushes her further into developing for a world in which there is no help and comfort. Fizzing from one thing to another, she may not engage enough with anything to catch an interest, deepen an exploration, and so develop those focusing skills. With reduced language, she might have fewer conversations, and so her development of communication will remain slow and fall further behind relative to others. And with her difficult behaviours, she is already being labelled a problem by others, and it won't be long before she starts to see herself that way.

There are further costs, though. The processes described in this chapter do their job well in adapting us to the world we seem to be growing up into. Their aim is to get us to adulthood, and over thousands of years they have done this for humans in good times and bad. On the difficult and dangerous pathway, however, there are limits. Let's look once more at the brain and body that is needed (Baumeister et al., 2016; Del Giudice et al., 2011; Matson et al., 2024; O'Mahony et al., 2017; Seal & Turner, 2021; Tronick & Hunter, 2024):

I need a brain and body that is good at . . .

- Ramping up my muscles quickly
- Providing lots of energy at short notice
- Always being on the watch
- Assuming the unknown is a threat
- Switching attention quickly
- Fast, impulsive responses
- Acting first, thinking later
- Relying on myself
- Fending off infections
- Healing any wounds

As you look at that table, you might well be thinking that this looks like a lot of hard work. A body always near the edge of action - rather like an athlete before a competition. A mind based on vigilance and switching, a life designed around self-reliance - it seems very tiring! And it is. This kind of brain and body is expensive to run and, without being overtechnical about it, might well wear out more quickly.

Adverse Childhood Experiences

This is what the adverse childhood experience (ACE) studies find. These are a family of research projects that have roughly the same design. They measure two things – how much adversity and trauma someone experienced in childhood, and their state of health in adulthood. It won't be a surprise by now that usually a connection is found between these. If you compare a group of people who experienced lots of adversity and trauma with a group who didn't, then the first group are more likely to have certain diseases or even to have a shorter lifespan.

Before we look at why, there is an important clarification that too often gets missed out or misunderstood. The ACE findings are not about individuals. I experienced lots of trauma in my childhood, including early on. But this does not mean that I have a higher risk. The relationship only holds for groups or populations (Baldwin et al., 2021; for other cautions about ACE scores in screening see Finkelhor, 2018). So if you had a lot of trauma, that does not – repeat, does not – mean you are going to get sick. Or if you have some health problems, that does not mean they were caused by earlier experiences. The risk is only seen when we look at large numbers. An example might help. I live in Scotland, where everyone likes to joke that we eat a diet consisting of deep-fried pizza and chocolate. So we could do some research to show that on average French people eat more vegetables than Scots. This is true. But it does not mean that if we pick a Scottish person at random (me, say) and a French person (Henri) that I eat fewer veg than Henri does. Actually I eat lots and Henri loathes them. In the same way, there is a higher risk of disease in groups of people who have experienced lots of childhood trauma, but that does not mean any individual (me, for example) has a higher risk.

Sometimes, as well, people misunderstand the "10 ACEs" as a list of the main or most important traumas of early childhood. In fact the ACE measure is simply a list of common events that may or may not be sources of adversity. It was compiled to use in research to estimate exposure to adversity. For example, it does not include important factors such as unpredictability (Koss et al., 2025) or neighbourhood quality (Marini et al., 2020). As we saw in Chapters 2 and 3, whether a given happening is actually traumatic depends on many factors, including the individual's experience of it and the support available. There can be discussions of limited value about whether something is an ACE. What matters is not whether it is on a list but whether it has an impact for the child and their family. We need more nuanced approaches to capture this, including the impact of poverty and other circumstances. For example, exposure to abuse has different consequences for brain development compared to experiencing neglect (Keding et al., 2021).

I spent some time on these points so as to make it safer to interpret the ACE findings here. This is because they are actually quite remarkable. For a whole range of adult diseases, the risk of getting them is related to experiences in early childhood. People sometimes get stuck on this, though, and do not go on to the main implication (or the most useful one) which is that for a wide range of adult diseases the risk of getting them *can be substantially reduced in early childhood*.

Developmental Trauma in Early Education

Before we see how, and what a key role early educators can have in this, it is worth reflecting on this for a moment. What we do for and with (and to) young children can have effects reaching into their adult lives, affecting their health, welfare, prosperity. We know this for all children, but it is especially the case for those who have had a difficult start in life - in fact the influence we have can be out of all proportion to what we seem to be doing. Let's show this with some mud!

> Jessica goes outside with her group after a few days of rain. One corner of the yard which used to be a nice square of grass has become a swamp. Jessica hangs back and watches as another child recklessly jumps into the middle of the muddy puddle and creates a wild spray of yucky, cold water. Some gets on her face, and some on her coat. She shrieks and runs back inside.

So far not that different from a normal day in early education! But let's look closer, with the help of Jessica's keyworker.

> Jess is a sweet girl, but she's had a dreadful life. She is only 4 and in her third foster placement already. When she was 2, she was removed from her home, where there was a lot of domestic violence from her father, who frequently found fault with her mum and used that to control them both.

With the knowledge from this chapter, we can see what might be going on in Jessica's head. What kind of world is this? A dangerous one! So any new, or unexpected, happening is likely to be a threat. It was bad enough encountering this change to the yard - the lovely soothing soft grass has become this strange place overnight. And then a horrible splat of cold water, caused by the rapid movement of a male body. And also, what kinds of things lead to danger? Well, getting into a mess for one, and look what has happened to her coat.

As Jessica's educators, we have a couple of choices at this point. Both are fine and ok as responses, but one of them might just be part of transforming her life and even those of her children and grandchildren (if she has them). The first choice would be to do our best to accommodate her needs. So let's reduce challenge, find quiet corners for learning within what she can cope with, and accept the limits. As I say, there is nothing wrong with this - it is the right thing to do. And it can be the basis for doing some more as well, which is our second choice. In order to cope and flourish in the 21st-century world she is headed for, Jessica needs to shift developmental course. But can she, and can we help her to do so?

Changing the World

One of the advantages, apart from it best fitting the evidence, of understanding developmental trauma as a process of adaptation is that it allows us to see not just that it is possible to change the course of development, but also how to do it. There are strong grounds for hope. Take as an example prenatal stress. There is a lot of evidence now that when pregnant mothers experience very high levels of stress, this can have developmental consequences for the baby long after birth. To be clear, this does not mean the usual ups and downs of life and pregnancy, but major life-threatening levels of stress. Effects include higher stress reactivity (Tung et al., 2024) and slower language development (Laplante et al., 2004). Again, although it is natural to focus on these effects as poorer outcomes, which in our complex societies they are, something astonishing has been going on. Babies in the womb are scanning their surroundings to find out what kind of world they are going to be born into (Lester et al., 2018). They use their mothers' bodies to do this, for example picking up the levels of stress hormones in the placenta (Charil et al., 2010). If their mother has high levels of stress hormones, this tells them that the world is a difficult and dangerous one, so they then start to develop a brain and body that will help them survive in such a world. The process is called fetal programming (Sandman et al., 2011).

All of this fits with wider research into how young children adapt their development in adverse circumstances. Because this is adaptation, there are also some positive aspects – children will enhance their development in some directions to become talented specialists in their particular environment (Ellis, 2018; Frankenhuis et al., 2020). For example, people who experienced childhoods with high amounts of uncertainty perform better on some tests of cognitive function than those who didn't (Mittal et al., 2015). What is "better" development and what is a milestone depend on context and what we value within it.

An adaptation, rather than deficit or damage, model opens up the question as to whether there can be re-programming. Is it possible to change the baby brain's assessment of this world as difficult and dangerous, and will they develop differently as a result? You can't have got this far in the book without knowing that I would not have raised this issue at all unless the answer is "yes". How can this be done? Again the answer is surprisingly simple, and the example of prenatal stress illustrates it well. Bergman and colleagues (2010) measured mother's levels of stress during pregnancy and found that higher stress levels were associated with slower cognitive development in the infants. We can see how this makes sense – development is a matter of prioritising, and a difficult world rewards action (reaction) rather than thinking. But that is not the whole story. Bergman's sample could be divided in two. Some of the babies after they were born developed secure attachments with their mothers. And these showed *no effects* of the prenatal stress.

It is worth pondering on this briefly. Prenatal stress goes deep into our biology. It changes the very course of brain and body development, with health and other implications that reach far into adulthood. But positive relationships with at least one caregiver in early childhood can prevent or reduce this deep biological process (Nolvi et al., 2023). All we have to do is notice when babies have needs, respond to this, chat, and play with them – and a whole course of life can change. Nor is this only the case for very small infants. There is now plenty of evidence that the best predictor of outcomes is not so much the amount of adversity that happens to us but the quality of the relationships we experience in childhood (for example, Bellis et al., 2017; Hambrick et al., 2019; Puig et al., 2013).

What is going on? How can positive relationships, which remember is as simple as smiling and helping, be so powerful? The adaptation model shows us how. Let's imagine that baby brain in the womb picking up on high levels of stress from mum. Looks like this might be a difficult and dangerous world, better be born ready for it! So I need to get moving, but not so much the thinking and language, and I need to have an alert alarm system. But now I am born, this is really strange. People are looking after me, comforting me, and we are doing fun and interesting things. So looks like I got it wrong, this is a safe and interesting world – so I need lots of thinking and language, and I can turn down that alarm system too. In terms of flow, this is what has happened:

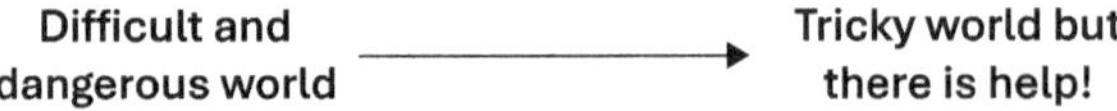

Meanwhile Jessica is waiting for our response to the mud incident, and this interlude has helped to see how high we can pitch our ambitions. But we do need to be careful about the goal here. Jessica's development is currently organised around assessments that this is a difficult and dangerous world. What do we want this assessment to be - a safe and interesting world, as in the examples above? Perhaps, but we have to consider two things. Firstly, Jessica is in a safe and interesting place with us. We are early educators, this is what we do for children! But her whole life is not like this. There are still bumps and difficulties at home. And the second thing is a main message of this book. No matter what has happened in each child's past, even if they have had a life of smooth safety and delightful stimulation so far, we can be sure that their future will contain troubles and even traumas. If we provide children just with safety, it is harder for them to get ready for this. So what we want for Jessica is the same shift. We'll meet her again in Chapter 10 and I'll show what we provided for her then, once we have a more in-depth understanding of how we can decide what to do.

Changing the Information

We have said a lot about gaining information about the world, and developing accordingly, but not much yet about *how* children's developing brains gather that information. Children's brains use their immediate experiences to tell them about the wider world (Ellis et al., 2022). Am I regularly fed? Then this is a world with plenty to eat so I don't need that expensive metabolism. Am I often hurt? Then this is a violent world and I need fighting muscles and quick reactions. Am I comforted when upset? Then this is a world where people help, so I should major on developing attachments rather than self-reliance. And are there safe and interesting things to do? If so, I should develop thinking and exploration.

That list gives us the basic four channels through which children pick up what kind of world they should be adapting to:

- Physical care
- Sensitive and reflective relationships
- Manageable and resolved stress
- Developmentally appropriate stimulation

We will look at these in much more detail in Section 2 and how we can change the messages the developing brain is receiving about the world. Meanwhile, if you look at this list and think, "but that's just what we do every day", you are right. In a high-quality early education setting, we care for children's physical needs, we comfort them when upset, we provide interesting and manageable stressors, not overwhelming ones, and we plan appealing things to do that stimulate further development.

Pause for Thought

There is a lot of material in this chapter about the long-term consequences of young children's experiences. These happen at the most basic of brain levels (Perry, 2009) and can affect almost everything that comes after. It can be overwhelming, which is why it is important to re-iterate that what all this research really tells us is how influential we can be on how things turn out. We are working with children at just the time that their brains are learning about the world and adapting to it. As we will see in Section 2, simply by providing experiences of physical care, sensitive and reflective relationships, manageable and resolved stress, and interesting things to do along with people to do them with, we are giving fundamental messages to that process.

Before we move on to that, though, we will take a pause for an interlude reflecting on our role in all this. Firstly, in the next chapter, how does reflecting in a trauma-informed way help us make sense of what we see day to day? And then, so what - we are educators, what exactly can we do? The answer will be that we cannot do everything, not by a long shot. But what we can do will make a lifetime's difference.

Chapter summary:

- Early experiences can have a profound effect on the course of brain development
- Children who experience adversity have made adaptations in order to do as well as they can
- By providing physical care, positive relationships, moderate and resolved stress and developmentally appropriate stimulation, we can change the course of brain development in the long term

Practice points:

- Consider how children present in terms of "what kind of world would this fit?"
- Plan responses by considering, "what kind of world do we want to show this is?"
- Be optimistic and realistic about how quickly the course of development can change

5
Recognising Trauma's Impact in Our Settings

This chapter will provide:

- Some examples of common behaviours or situations we might see
- Trauma-informed reflection on these in the light of previous chapters
- Signposts to the following chapters that cover what we can do

The previous chapters have shown how our brains deal with stressors and how this can lead to developing traumatic memories that can stay fresh for years. We saw the specifics of this for young children and how early trauma can impact the course of brain development. In this chapter we will use this to reflect on some examples that we might see in early education settings. The second section of the book contains extensive ideas for how we might respond, so I will only provide some indications here for the first two examples as an illustration. The main emphasis for this chapter is just to reflect on what we see and what it might mean. All of these are real people, suitably changed for anonymity. Hopefully even if you do not encounter exactly similar things, there will be enough to shed light on what you do see.

Leanne - A Reluctant Writer

What We See

Leanne is coming up to 5 years old. She is an active girl, who loves being out and about. She plays happily with other children and is keen to take on responsibilities, such as helping to set the table, though not so much for clearing up. Her parents are highly involved in her development and education, coming into the setting early some days at pick-up time to chat with staff. But Leanne poses a puzzle to them and to the staff. She will not pick up a pencil or crayon. Wherever mark-making tools are put out, she is suddenly elsewhere. If asked, she will sit at a table, but pushes the things about and tears the paper - if pressed, she puts her head in her hands or else slips away.

DOI: 10.4324/9781003563808-7

What Might We Wonder About?

It can be puzzling why a child like Leanne with all these skills and advantages just won't take the next step with literacy. Are these early signs of dyslexia, dysgraphia, dyspraxia? Could be, but trauma-informed thinking gives an additional perspective and ideas to try. If we stand back from wanting to know "why" this is happening, we can instead reflect on how Leanne might be experiencing it (key idea 1). What we might call refusal can be seen alternatively as avoidance. Slipping away is flight-like, and other behaviours such as hiding her head or not even picking up a crayon have elements of freeze. So Leanne may not be feeling unsafe, but is certainly uncomfortable (key idea 2). So it could be that either there is something about mark-making that she really does not like, or she is feeling forced, or she thinks she can't do it by herself.

How Then Might We Help?

We do not yet know which of these three is going on - could be one, all or none. But trying things out and further observation can shed more light on how Leanne experiences her world.

- Making it easier

So we might consider making the whole thing less "high stakes". Maybe the adult anxiety is communicating to Leanne and putting her off. Alternatively, as sometimes happens with able children, she may have some gaps and lags in development, such as fine motor control or hand strength, that make manipulating the crayon really difficult or unpleasant. Perhaps then she'll do this when she is good and ready. We can meanwhile provide lots of other stimulation for motor development and confidence.

- Increasing control

Everyone has got into a dynamic (or even an obligation) to "get her" to do it. Leanne may be picking up on this and feeling pushed and controlled. No small child likes this! But where there is reason for the reluctance, it pushes them towards flight or freezing. So we could back off, and instead have mark making available across the play settings that Leanne likes. Maybe she can choose the medium. If scrawling with mud on a wall (outdoors) suits her for now, that's fine.

- Increasing support

There is a delicate balance between providing support to do something and a child thereby feeling forced. What we can provide is some cheerful modelling of what to do in different play contexts (get your hands muddy!), and gentle and low key praise and encouragement when she tries something. And develop her confidence doing other creative things that make a mark - patterns with loose parts, potato painting, etc.

At this point I am half hoping you are wondering why Leanne is here as an example in a book about trauma. This is all about the literacy curriculum and there is no suggestion Leanne has experienced anything traumatic. I have two reasons. Firstly, to illustrate the process with an example that is not complicated by wondering about traumatic history. But mainly to show that trauma-informed thinking can help everyone develop and learn. It gave us a framework to think about Leanne's issue and a language to describe it in a practical way. So it is not just about identifying children who may be traumatised, but having a way of delivering education that is more effective for everyone.

Martina - Who Has Had a Recent Traumatic Experience

What We See

Martina loves coming to her setting where she very rarely gets on with what is offered as she is a real chatterbox. She tells anyone in range about what she had for breakfast and what the family dog got up to last night. If there is fun and laughter going on - especially if it involves making a mess - you can be sure that Martina is involved in it. But in the last few weeks, the staff have noticed a change in Martina. She has stopped chatting and become grumpy and fearful. If there are unexpected noises, she covers her ears and cries. And she has stopped making her usual beautiful drawings and now just scribbles circles over and over, with the crayon biting into the paper.

What Might We Wonder About?

Changes in behaviour and presentation like these can be unsettling. What was a happy child now seems unable to cope. A new member of staff who did not know Martina in the past might look at the sensory sensitivity and stereotyped behaviour and wonder if she has a social communication disorder. But we know two key things. Firstly, there is a clear "before and after". Martina's experience of our setting has changed. Secondly, Martina is showing us in lots of ways that she is not feeling safe, from grumpy reactions, heavy crayon pressure (fight), and covering her ears (flight, hiding), to the frozen patterns of action making her circles. So we might wonder what has happened in Martina's life to give her this fear and terror and how we can help her feel more comfortable with us.

How Then Might We Help?

The first thing we might want to do is talk to Martina's parents. But how we do this matters since they may well be worried themselves and anxious whether they might be blamed. They might react in different ways depending on how we approach the conversation. There are ideas about trauma-informed family engagement in Chapter 16. In particular, we want the conversation to be a psychologically safe and constructive experience for them. Sometimes, parents don't know what has happened. Lots that children do is not seen by adults, so we do not want to imply that they "ought" to know. So we can talk about how sometimes children are upset by things that seem small to us, but are big to them, or about what happens to loved ones rather than themselves.

What we want to do is put together a plan to support Martina. In Chapter 6 we will see how to do this more generally using the key elements of psychological first aid. While it helps to know what might have happened, there is a lot we can do even if we don't.

Contact and Engagement

We've already started this by engaging with her family, but what about Martina herself? In the past she has been quite independent, but she may welcome her key adults being a little closer to her for a while. We can make sure we spend time near her, playing quietly alongside her, or interactively if she wishes. We can follow the themes of her play, commenting, and see what develops.

Safety and Comfort

This may by itself help Martina to feel safer, but there is more we can do. Perhaps there are some activities that she enjoys and finds soothing? This can be individual. Some children love a quiet, cozy corner with soft toys – while others like to immerse themselves in rain, mud, and sticks. But we can increase these in her daily "diet", following what she seems to be drawn to. All the adults in the setting are kind and caring, but it is important that they do their best to reduce anything that they think might seem scary to a traumatised child, using gentle voices, slow approaches, and touching or not touching as Martina prefers.

Stabilisation

Martina's family might be glad to know that one of the best ways to help children recover is to "get back to normal" in terms of routines and family activities. If they always used to go to the park on Saturday afternoon, that's still a great thing to do. It is also helpful for them to know that the daily rhythms of our setting provide stability. So we need to make sure that they do!

Information Gathering

With careful observation, and often by chatting with Martina, we can work out some of the small events and transitions that seem to bother her. For example, the loud noises each Tuesday as the big bins are emptied outside is something we can anticipate and prepare for – either by distraction, by making a game of it, or making sure Martina is far away. She might even find it easier if she can go out and watch so she knows what is happening!

Practical Assistance

We all sometimes struggle a little with practical tasks when we are preoccupied, and a young brain working hard to process memories of a difficult event is no different. So we approach what might seem like "regressions" with the understanding that they are likely to be temporary capacity issues. And we can reassure families about this. Martina might easily be forgetting some well learned routines or self-care skills, and all we have to do is support as we would any child learning these until she can do them for herself again.

Connection with Social Supports

One of the main problems with talking, as we must, about the difficult and negative effects of trauma and how we counter these is that it can pull the focus away from what can help most, which is joy! And in particular, shared joy. So we can make sure Martina still gets to experience having fun, both by herself and with others. This may mean providing more support for social interactions to help her manage them, or making more time for quiet one-to-one play with a trusted adult. This again is an excellent theme to share with the family, who may be concerned to protect Martina and not risk encountering triggers. Some careful observation, and consulting her, can show what she might manage and enjoy (feeding the ducks, yes; swimming in a busy pool, not yet).

Information on Coping

Martina's parents may well be wondering what has happened to their girl. In struggling to understand, they may be drifting towards new ideas about her, such that she is now badly behaved and needs more control and punishment. This may well make things worse, as well as setting a tone for their future relationship that won't help when further difficulties come. In Chapter 16 we will see how early educators can work respectfully with families to help them see what is behind children's behaviours and how they can respond in partnership with us.

Bruno - Safely Adopted by Great Parents but Having Trouble Building Relationships

What We See

Nobody is quite sure what happened to Bruno in his first year of life. He was in foster care for a while before being adopted into a loving family at the age of three. His adoptive parents are devoted to him and look after him very well. In the setting he is keen on anything that involves running around, carrying, or throwing things. He has to be watched around food, as he tends to grab anything within reach and run off with it. The main issue of concern, however, is that Bruno has trouble settling with anyone but his parents. If left by himself, he gets into bother with other children. If a staff member is with him, then he does his best to get away, or else seems to deliberately provoke a confrontation through actions or words. If told "no" for something, he becomes helplessly upset - one staff member commented, "he just wants to be babied all the time".

What We Might Wonder About

Bruno seems to be seeking a lot of movement, so perhaps this is a developmental need. We don't know exactly what experiences he has missed out on in the past, but he certainly seems to be catching up on them. He also seems to be operating on assumptions that needs are not always met, so grab things (especially food) when you see them. As well, his models for relationships seem based on conflict, and he even brings this about so that the world makes more sense to him. But at the same time he yearns for care and nurture and is devastated if he thinks it is in jeopardy. Finally, much of his development seems "pegged" at infant/toddler level. In fact, if we think of him as a much younger child in an older body, a lot of what we see seems to fit.

Nina - Becomes Distressed at Tidy-Up Time

What We See

Although she had some initial difficulties settling in, Nina now happily separates from her mother at drop-off and engages with everything the setting has to offer. She has formed some great friendships and has a close relationship with her main keyworker. Unexpected changes can throw her, but the main difficulty she has is when the "tidy up" music starts towards the end of the session. She becomes inconsolable, crying and stamping her foot, or else sometimes starts throwing things off shelves that the other children have just tidied away! Once her mother comes to pick her up, all is then sunshine and smiles again.

What We Might Wonder About

What we might be seeing is an almost chaotic blending of fight, flight, and freeze responses, suggesting these are driven by overwhelming internal stress. It looks like Nina might have two sets of triggers, both to do with uncertainty. Firstly, any transition, especially if unexpected, can be difficult. And secondly the transition from one set of caregivers to another seems tricky. The tidy-up music serves as a signal that this change is coming. It is like she is fine with both, but the change is the issue - as if she has to swim from one island to another across a sea that might contain sharks. We might help Nina with these triggers using some of the ideas for co-regulation in Chapters 8-10, and further develop her abilities to manage them for herself using suggestions in Chapters 12 and 13.

Sofia - Comes from a Stigmatised Migrant Family

What We See

Sofia came into the setting a few weeks ago having been settled in the area with her parents by the refugee agency. She flits about the setting, not really engaging for any length of time with staff or children. She is reluctant to make eye contact, and often responds to adult initiatives by skipping away, or hiding her head. It is hard to work out how much she understands, and she does a lot of very simple repetitive play. Her parents shy away from any discussion about her, although they are very grateful to staff and recently brought in a huge plate of traditional pastries. Staff are wanting to raise with them the possibility that Sofia might be on the autistic spectrum but are at a loss how to do this.

What We Might Wonder About

We don't know what experiences Sofia may have had along the way, but not all of them will have been easy. In particular, as soon as she got used to a new place, new people, and new things to do, the family will have been off again perhaps at too short notice to prepare her. She is still doing the same thing, flitting, and not sticking to things or people. But she is finding a stability of sorts, even if a very limited one, in her repetitive play. Sofia needs us to meet her where she is with gentle positive relationships, in particular to approach what we see in a mind-minded way (Chapter 8). There is also a possible element of cultural difference.

Perhaps in Sofia's context it is rude to look someone in the eye, and as we see with her parents, relationships might be more low-key generally. Chapter 15 gives some ideas for culturally responsive practice with children and their families.

Emily and Maya - Early Education Professionals

What We See

Emily is an early education setting manager. She seems to spend all her time in meetings and emails with officials and managers who want to know why so many of her children are not "ready for school" and why she keeps recruiting more staff beyond her budget. She rarely emerges from her office now except to deal with whatever is going wrong on the setting floor - often a dispute between staff about how to handle a child who is "kicking off". Staff struggle with getting some children to sit for story, contain conflicts that break out over resources, and are reluctant to try new ideas for child-led play. Emily's evenings are spent trying to contact families to talk about problems with their child's learning or behaviour, or filling referral forms for behaviour and mental health services that keep getting knocked back.

Maya became an early educator because of her own experiences of struggling in the education system. She has a strong vision of how children who have experienced difficult starts in life can be helped in the early years. Skilled in "tuning in" to children's emotions, she is often assigned to youngsters who present difficult behaviour, and works hard to create partnerships with their families. But lately, she feels she is "losing it". She gets through the day, but inside feels on the edge of saying something she shouldn't. At home she has become cranky with her own children. All she wants to do in the evening and at the weekend is flop down and rest. She has stopped going to her walking group and is thinking she can't go on with the job much longer.

What We Might Wonder About

Both Emily and Maya are working in a context with high levels of adversity and trauma and working hard each day to provide what the children and the staff need in response. In addition, they are working in an overall system that makes this more difficult, with high pressure to achieve targets that do not necessarily correspond that well with the needs of the children. This can both lead them to think they are doing a bad job, and have an increasing impact on their wellbeing and effectiveness. Over time, and despite their best efforts and intentions, the ethos of the whole setting may become more negative resulting in a self-reinforcing pattern of more issues with the children and less effective adult responses. In Chapter 18 we look at ways that practitioners can support their own wellbeing, but Chapter 17 places this in the context of the whole setting and the wider system. Finally, we also have to consider that staff may well have their own memories of trauma, so there are some ideas to provide support with this in Chapter 19.

Conclusion

This section of the book was all about trauma, what it is, and how it might relate to what we see in early education settings. The next section focuses on how we can respond and help.

We start with considering recent and known traumas - what we can do if we know a child and/or family have had a difficult experience. Then we look more generally at trauma-informed education and what it can do for children and for practitioners.

However, at this point, there might be an uncertainty, a question, and even a challenge. We are educators, not therapists. What exactly is our role, and how come it is so important? So we will start with an interlude considering this as a foundation and framework for what follows.

Chapter summary:

- Reflecting on what we see in a trauma-informed way can give us a simple understanding of children's and adults' experiences
- This can open up ways to respond that can help both in the moment and in the longer term
- We need to consider the adults in the setting as well as the children

Practice points:

- When encountering unexpected or difficult responses, consider whether these tell us about how the person is experiencing the situation
- And/or whether this is telling us something about their feelings of safety or ability to manage it
- Make sure that adult wellbeing is promoted in setting policy and practice

Section 2

Trauma and Adversity in Early Education

Interlude – The Role of the Educator

When I do training or consultation with early educators there are two common and reasonable sets of concerns that we talk through. The first is a sense of overwhelm. Trauma's impact can be huge – what can we really achieve in the time we are with the children? Secondly, people wonder how trauma-informed practice fits with their role. We are educators, which means our primary task is to deliver the curriculum and help children learn. Isn't the trauma side really more for specialists to deal with? Is there a risk we could do harm? And there are seven chapters coming on strategies – how can we do all of this in addition to everything else?

It can be uncomfortable and distressing to realise how many children are affected by trauma. There will be several at least within any nursery or kindergarten class or group. But the research also tells us that the most important factor in these young lives is not so much the trauma as the quality of relationships that they encounter. That, we can do. And we can do so in the knowledge that this will benefit every child in the setting, not to mention the adults. The research also shows us how trauma can impact on children's development and learning. Whether this be about language development, managing feelings, coping with social challenges, or even learning how to move in a coordinated way, all of that is part of the core business of early education for any child. Those who have experienced trauma just need it more, and more help to feel safe so that they can explore and grow.

We can prevent trauma interfering with learning. By helping children manage the triggers that bar them from useful experiences – whether playing with others, or splashing in a puddle, or picking up a pencil – we help them to access these with their brains fully engaged. By building their resilience from basic sensory processing upwards, we create with them the foundations for literacy, mathematics, and everything else.

Yes – we are educators, not therapists. What this means, though, is that there are many things we can do that a therapist cannot. A therapist can offer trauma-specific therapies that can help resolve traumatic memories. They can see a child or a family a few times, perhaps once a week for a couple of months. But we are with them sometimes every day for a year or more, providing an environment that feels safe and offers interesting ways to develop and learn. We have time to get to know them, to learn what parts of life feel difficult for them, and what helps them to feel safe. We have chances to help them manage challenges as they arise, and to show them the progress they are making. They learn with us new ways to be with people, developing trust, love, and joy in shared meaningful activity. We build relationships

DOI: 10.4324/9781003563808-9

with their families, providing yet another arena of safety - from support with daily hassles to influencing the home environment.

We might not be able to heal or resolve traumatic memories. But we can help children to grow the rest of their lives. Years and decades later, they may not remember us or what we did. But the effects will be with them, and making what could be all the difference.

Section 2 is all about how we can make that difference. Chapters 8-10 provide practical detail about how we can provide positive relationships and the differences these can make. Chapters 11-13 show how we can build on that foundation by offering experiences that match children's developmental needs. Then Section 3 sets this in wider context, looking first at the whole setting, and the world in which it is set. Finally in Chapters 17-19 we turn to our own needs, considering what promotes wellbeing for practitioners as well as reducing the impact of working with children who have experienced trauma.

Trauma's impact is, indeed, huge. But so are the effects of simple and reliable positive relationships, and offering interesting things to do that meet children where they are. It is the pathway we can help create - from childhood trauma to joy and flourishing. In walking it with them, we can find a joy of our own.

6
Recovery After a Known Event

This chapter will provide:

- A simple but comprehensive approach for recovery after a difficult event
- Detail on how early educators can support children and families
- Information about when to be concerned or seek further advice

As educators, we have a powerful role for children and families who have experienced trauma. What most people need after a difficult experience is not so much lying on a couch and talking about it as being helped to get back to a day-to-day sense of safety within a world that makes sense.

In this chapter, we will cover what can be done to support children and families in early educational settings after a known event. Without giving an exhaustive list, this might include anything from a minor bump in the car on the way in to a major community-wide event such as a natural disaster. Early educators are well positioned to help in many different ways. Firstly, and perhaps most simply, we cannot underestimate the value of just being there. Our settings can be islands of stability and welcome during difficult times. They can be not only a way for life to "go on" but a sign of what we all value for our children and in each other. Secondly, and still quite simply, for families who are under pressure either because they have a lot to organise or because they are under severe emotional strain, being able to provide some assistance through trusted care for children can make all the difference. It gives families a bit of extra resource in terms of space, time, and even respite that might make the difference from coping to flourishing.

But there is much more than this, none of which takes us out of the ordinary role of an early educator, even if we might be doing this with particular purpose and in extraordinary times. In the next sections we will cover what research tells us that people need in the days and weeks after difficult experiences, how this can help prevent re-traumatisation, as well as how to adapt it to provide some specifics for young children. As we go along, we will see that although this has the rather technical sounding title of "psychological first

DOI: 10.4324/9781003563808-10

aid" (Vernberg et al., 2008), it actually comes down to common sense human kindness and avoiding a few "don'ts". It also maps almost exactly onto what we know is high-quality early education - just by doing what we do in a trauma-informed way we can help children and families recover as well as they can from whatever they have experienced (Gilbert et al., 2021).

There is a natural tendency to think of these kinds of events as rare. And fortunately, for most families and communities, they are. However for many, disasters and adversities can come thick and fast. Also, what is a 1 in a 1000 chance of event for any family is a 1 in 10 chance for a setting with 100 families. So we need to be prepared for this, have a plan for how we might provide support, and have this aligned to local guidance and practice for critical incidents (Chang et al., 2018; Machado & Anderson, 2022).

What Do People Need?

It can be scary and disturbing to think about, but what people need from us is actually quite simple and do-able. To show this, I will first cover what people need after a potentially traumatic experience in an intuitive way, before bringing out some practice detail for children, families, and practitioners. I need to take you back once more to that coffee shop and the unexpected visit from the Loch Ness Monster in Chapter 2. Imagine, if you will, that you were there and witnessed the whole thing from watching me queue, to seeing the Monster push me out the way, rampage around a bit and then leave. There I am, in a bit of a state after this experience. Suppose you decide to see if you can help me - what might occur to you to try?

We can rule out some things straight away. I don't need a lecture on the different theories of whether the Loch Ness Monster exists, or what species it might be. Nor am I possibly in much state to sit on a bean bag and tell you how I feel about it all, and how this relates to an early experience with a free toy from a cereal packet. Maybe look away from the page for a few minutes and make a short list - what might help me, that you can do in the next few minutes?

The first thing you might do is come over, maybe touch my sleeve, or crouch down to me if I'm on the floor. You might start talking gently, asking if I am ok. Another natural thing would be to say that it is alright, the monster has gone. Perhaps offer me some water from the counter, or even a muffin or apple. As I start to recover, you'll probably keep gently talking, and maybe help me to a chair and then start to talk about what happened - "wow, that was scary!" If I seem to be ok, you might then ask me if I need anything, where I live, do I know how to get home. And then help me do what I need, perhaps call a cab for me, or walk me to the bus stop. You might ask if there is anyone at home who can check on me, and if you know them actually send them a message to let them know what's happened. And you might give me some useful advice, such as making sure I get some rest, that I might consider not going in to work, get some food, as well as go to the doctor if I am not feeling well later or can't sleep.

You might have thought of slightly different things than these. We all have different personalities and histories and therefore different styles of coping. But everything that we might try would very likely come under one of the following headings.

Contact and engagement	Coming over, talking gently
Safety and comfort	Asking if I am ok, checking it is safe
Stabilisation	Offering some water, sitting with me
Information gathering	Asking what I need
Practical assistance	Helping to get home
Connection with social supports	Seeing who can check on me later
Information on coping	Advice to get some rest or help
Linkage with collaborative services	Connections to doctor, work

These are the headings for the guide to psychological first aid provided by the National Child Traumatic Stress Network (2006). There are different ways to categorise what we might offer (Wang et al., 2024), but they tend to come down to the same activities. I am using this one as it is (at time of writing) available for download from their website for readers who wish to know more. It has the same aims as other versions to promote people's sense of safety, ability to be calm and to take what action they need, as well as feeling connected to others and hopeful for the future (Hobfoll et al., 2007).

Psychological First Aid

This section will cover each core aspect of psychological first aid for young children and their families with some applications within an early education setting. There are three key points to make at the start. The first is that young children, as we will see in Chapter 5, rely greatly on the coping and resources of others. Adults do too, of course, but as well as the obvious aspects of care and safety, children need those around them to help them manage feelings, work out what is happening - *and* what it means. An adult who is struggling with their own experience and recovery is less likely to be able to provide the calm and assured care that a child needs in order to know they are safe now. What this means is that an essential part of supporting children to recover is also (and even first) supporting their important adults. These include family and caregivers, and also sometimes ourselves. While there is a natural tendency to "think of the children first", we can only help them into a lifeboat if we are out of the water ourselves. An important way early educators can help is therefore often to remind parents, carers, and colleagues to consider their own needs and take steps for themselves (Terranova et al., 2015).

The second key point is that, as we saw in Chapters 2 and 3, whether an experience is traumatic has as much to do with people's experience of it as with the event themselves. So while we might easily see natural or public disasters as traumas, or big events such as a house fire or witnessing violence, we have to remember that for young children it can also be apparently small things that are big for them. It could be a pet's unexpected demise, a caregiver's illness, or even a sudden loud noise. How can we know? Two principles can help us. Firstly, we need to abandon our adult assumptions about what feels safe. There is more on this in Chapter 3. Secondly, young children will soon tell us through what they do whether they are disturbed or troubled by an experience. We can look out for these signs and respond accordingly.

> Mateo is a cheerful and adventurous young boy usually, but his parents noticed a change in his behaviour at home. He had become reluctant to go to sleep, at first stretching out bedtime as long as possible with pleas for another story, more cuddles. Then he began insisting on his stuffed animals being in a line on the shelf and would endlessly get out of bed to re-arrange them. The last straw was when he wanted everything in the house to be unplugged. At his early years setting by contrast, he was as relaxed and happy as ever, if a bit tired. After a chat with Mateo's keyworker, his parents realised that something must have happened to upset him, and he was in a spiral of trying to deal with it that was just making him more anxious. Careful thought reminded them he had accidentally seen a fire safety advert on TV one evening – he'd seemed fine at the time, but it had all started then.

> Ava loves coming to her setting, to the extent that she ignores the carefully planned drop-off process and just gets stuck into her play. She has made some great friends and there is almost nothing, apart from stopping to wash her hands before snack, that she is unwilling to try. However, staff noticed that she has been arriving later than usual, and is reluctant to let go of her father who drops her off. In the setting, she explores less than she used to, and is more easily upset. She has also started some new behaviours, throwing items against the wall and running into other children. Her father, and her keyworker, wondered if she had been upset by a recent public disaster where a ship had crashed into a road bridge.

We have to resist the adult assessment ("for goodness sake, it was just a 90 second advert on TV"). For Mateo this was a big thing, and his parents' quickly realising this with the help of his keyworker stopped it being a big thing for them and for the whole family.

The third key point is that although some difficult experiences are relatively simple or only involve the child or family, many are more complex and public events. A large-scale industrial accident, a pandemic, or a natural disaster are just a few of the big and complex experiences that can affect a whole community. In this case early educators are working within a wider network of professionals and voluntary supporters and need to be aware of what this is and what is going on. For example, there may be plenty of practical assistance going around but little chance for parents or carers just to sit and chat if they wish. Or you might notice that a child is becoming always late for their session, and open up a conversation that reveals how parents are stretched, and you can connect them with a source of support. Knowing the overall context can help you assure them this is ok to do, and they won't be judged – in fact all families are being offered this help right now.

Educators can sometimes feel the needs of children and families very keenly. We work with them every day and know them well, so we see the effects on children and parents or carers and also care deeply about them. It is easy either to feel helpless or to try to do too much. But, as we will see below, even if the part we play might feel small, it can make all the difference, just as a little bit of salt can transform the taste of a large bowl of soup. Early education settings therefore need to be involved in disaster planning and post-event support, and aware of their specific role within a coordinated response. If this is not possible for whatever reason, of course we can still be of huge help as long as we take our lead from children and families.

This section therefore sets out the core actions of psychological first aid as they apply in an early education context. Not every family or child will need all of these from you, or their needs might change over time. It is a normal human reaction to say one does not need help at first, for example. If we keep respectfully making it clear that help is available, families can seek it without feeling the need to climb down or admit they were wrong.

Supporting Parents and Carers

Contact and Engagement

In standard psychological first aid, this is all about how to approach people at the scene or in the aftermath of a major event. This might seem less relevant when families are coming to our setting regularly and we feel we know them. But the world has changed, and so have they. We do not know what they want from us. Some families might want our setting to be the one place in the world where the disaster in a sense "has not happened" - a space where they can step out of whatever is going on into our calm and ordered world. So these might not want our help, nor for us to talk to them about what is happening. Others might be the opposite. They are desperate for help and for kind conversation but don't know they can broach it, or that we are able and willing to support them in our role. And some might be at a stage where they are still reeling or not quite accepting either what has happened or their level of need. So while we might know, or think we know, what they need, they might insist that they need something quite different or even nothing at all.

A simple approach can work for all these varieties and as with most things in this chapter, it is just human common sense for how we start any conversation where we are unsure. We offer warm, positive, and reassuring body language, let families know we know what has happened, assure them we will do what we can to help and ask if they have any concerns right now they want to mention.

> Mateo's keyworker met his mother at the end of the session and shared what he'd been doing and how they had enjoyed it. "We have noticed he is a bit more tired at the moment?" His mother then shared that Mateo was getting later and later bedtimes and they weren't quite sure what to do. "Would you like to talk about that some more?" And she did.

> Ava's father was in a rush and not keen to talk. He seemed to know that the keyworker wanted to discuss her behaviour and was avoiding it. The setting decided to keep the drop-off and pick-up pleasant and low key for him, but to put a notice on the board giving information about how the recent accident might be affecting young children in the area. One day they noticed Ava's father reading it. "We've got a few children acting a bit differently at the moment". Ava's father then shared she had been difficult at home, and they'd thought it was bad behaviour.

Safety and Comfort

Providing a kind and open context in which families feel able to raise anything that is troubling them without being judged goes a long way towards helping them feel safe and comforted. People often play down their own reactions after a difficult event and it can help them to be reminded that it is normal and ok to have ups and downs for some time. There is no substitute for daily experiences of welcome and positive regard.

An early years setting has an additional role, simply by existing. For some families it might be one of the few, or last, places where the world is as it was. Our gentle and flexible routines create a sense of safety, as does being a place that parents and carers know their child will be safe and happy for a few hours. This is not just respite - it is a guarantee that whatever is going on elsewhere, their child's learning is continuing. We are helping the present feel safe by assuring them of the future and that neither they or anyone else is failing their child.

> Mateo's mother said, "I'm so relieved to be able to talk about this. We have been at our wit's end and so worried it would affect how she is here".
>
> Ava's father was surprised and delighted that instead of the expected conversation about how bad and naughty she had become, her keyworker started talking about how they were wondering if Ava was under any stress or if there was something (big or small) that was worrying her.

Stabilisation

Once people are feeling safe and have been able to receive some comfort, the next step is to stabilise. Sometimes this is about emotional stability, providing continued reassurance. But often more ordinary day-to-day aspects are more important since, unless these are dealt with, people cannot come to a sense of stability. Traumatic experiences and disasters can be very disorientating for a while as the mind struggles to update itself with what has happened and the new situation. People may have trouble forming plans, carrying them out and prioritising. Or they may even seem to lose skills that we know they have. Capable parents can become disorganised, or fall back on simpler approaches that don't work very well. Families might become temporarily more chaotic - not to mention that some events can have deep financial costs or remove resources.

An early education setting is ideally placed to help families stabilise, and can do this at three levels. Firstly, we are just there. As mentioned before, the fact that families can continue to know their children will be safe, loved, and cared for - as well as continuing the learning that builds their futures - is itself an island of stability. It does not matter what has happened, when, or to whom. We are still here, and here for them.

At the second level, we can have frequent and simple conversations that help them realise and continue to believe that what they are experiencing are normal consequences to a difficult event - be these financial struggles, not knowing what to do, or trying to carry on as though nothing has happened. Gentle enquiries as to how everyone is can be accompanied by respectful mentions of likely issues. "It can really throw you when something like this happens" "We know you need to prioritise X or Y right now, but we are always delighted when you can make it here" "A few families are telling us money is really short". These may open up a next step where we can signpost parents and carers to sources of support.

A third way we can help is by holding memories. At times of crisis it is easy to forget how things used to be - that one was a capable parent, or that one's child was happy and flourishing. People can start to believe that the present difficulties are all there ever was, and all that there will be. Our journals, apps, however we share information, can be a resource of past times and a source of hope. Also, traumatic reactions and consequences can come in waves. One thing is sorted, everyone improves, and then a few months later there is a different issue, or the same one returns. In between, families may not remember, or may not make the links with their past experiences. But we can, because we are not in it ourselves and because we know their children so well. "I noticed Rob is a bit upset at unexpected changes again - do you think it might be a left-over effect of the house fire?" "Remember when we all went to the park, and Amy climbed the steps for the first time? She's a brave girl!"

> Mateo's mother had made a reward chart for going to sleep and it seemed to be making things worse! Her keyworker said, "It can be really worrying when children have these issues - I've seen this a few times and it usually resolves with time".
>
> Ava's father shared that his business had been affected by the bridge crash and that he had been preoccupied with financial worries. "Well it sounds like you are sorting out your business for the sake of the family. I wonder if Ava is picking up on some of that worry?"

Information Gathering

Sometimes it is obvious what people need, and sometimes it isn't. In both cases we need to be careful not to make assumptions. We won't do much harm if we suggest or offer the wrong thing in a spirit of kind and respectful helpfulness, but we may miss an opportunity. Also, when difficult things happen around children, it is common for parents or carers to feel a degree of guilt or shame. It is their job to protect their children, how could they have let this happen? This can then make them resistant to help, or even resentful of it, since if they need help, they must really have failed in their first duty.

There are two ways round both of these issues. The first is to make sure we prioritise the stages above. Sometimes there are some obvious things to do - offer a refuge, a cup of tea, suggest contacting providers of financial relief. But whatever we do, it needs to be built on, and wrapped around with, promoting safety, stability, and choice. Secondly, and just as important, we can be led by families to prioritise what is most important to them even if it is not what we would do ourselves.

There is a balance here between finding out what we need in order to help, and being over-intrusive at a difficult time. If we meet defences - "we're all fine" - then it is best to go with that and keep letting families know they can raise things with us if they need. Again information boards and other general communications such as an email signature can be helpful in this; and we can use them to set out menus of what people might need so they can choose for themselves. For example, a display of options for financial support, or a poster about how to help children after a trauma, can help families choose without risking the humiliation of asking or being asked. When there is a large public disaster, it can be useful to offer a checklist to families so they can assess for themselves what the priorities are.

Practical Assistance

It is easy to feel helpless in the face of even small traumas, and even more so in times of public disaster. But there are three ways in which early educators can give families practical assistance. Firstly, as noted above, it can be a huge help to parents and carers just to know that their children are in a safe and loving setting some of the time, where they are looked after and their education can continue. Secondly, the chance for small chats and kind questions during routine interactions mean that educators can prompt families to think about what they need and gather the courage to ask for help - be this from a government agency or a grandparent. The same everyday conversations are opportunities for reminding families how well they are doing, considering the circumstances. Thirdly, early education settings are part of their community and can be a focus for mutual assistance. This might be at the very practical level of a clothing swap scheme, or a toy library, or at a bigger scale of being a place to meet and talk and consider collective action.

What makes the difference here is the actual help, but also the feeling of being helped. Even if we cannot provide families with everything they need, small offers of assistance can make a big difference.

> Mateo's setting had some books for children about safety in the home. They lent these to his mother to share with him at a good time to explain why he did not need to worry. He also spent some time in the setting each day dressing up as an emergency worker to explore this role in his play - this turned into a group endeavour to create a poster.

Connection with Social Supports

When difficult things happen, people often draw inwards both into themselves and into their core families. This is perfectly healthy as a response, but it can impede recovery if prolonged. At the same time, even quite small and brief interactions can promote recovery. As with practical support, early educators can help through the regular contacts they have with families. Making an extra effort to smile at and welcome a parent or carer at drop-off or pick-up can help maintain a sense of connection that might grow over time into a lifeline. And again, the setting can be itself a social focus and a place of connection. Organising some family events, such as "stay and play", or even better supporting parents and carers to organise their own events (how about a clear up of that corner of the garden?) can be very helpful in showing people that they are not alone and that, whatever they are dealing with, there is a place for them and life goes on.

> Ava's father just happened to be dropping her off at the same time as the mother of another child who had actually seen the bridge collision. The setting manager introduced them and they got chatting - realising that it was not "just us" who were having difficulties. They swapped some good ideas.

Information on Coping

Sometimes families need some specific advice or information on coping. This might be on how to re-establish a bedtime routine, or on any aspect of supporting children that they are feeling less confident with temporarily. It can also be useful to share simple information about how children respond to difficult events, and that these are normal reactions. They include what we saw as more permanent effects of traumatic memories in Chapter 2, with the difference that they reduce and pass over time (see watchful waiting, below):

- Changes in eating or sleeping
- Nightmares and terrors
- Being generally fussy (as a younger child)
- Other apparent regressions, sometimes just in the moment or more generally
- Aggression towards themselves - hitting, banging head, pulling hair, holding breath
- Taking undue risks or trying to put themselves in danger
- Aggression towards key caregivers (who should have kept them safe); this can transfer to other caregivers too
- Being highly aware of potential threats, constant vigilance
- Easily startled
- Frequent crying
- Fears of separation, even small ones such as toilet visits
- Tummy pains or headaches, or other odd pains
- Traumatic themes in play (see Chapter 3 for details)

Families can be reassured that they do not need to add worries about the children to an already stressful situation. By providing basic care and positive relationships, they will find a way through. It may help as well to share some of the content in the following section about supporting children.

Linkage with Collaborative Services

When disasters happen, people easily become overwhelmed with the many things they have to think about, and the routines that usually sustain them are disrupted. An early education setting can be a source not just of stability, as we will discuss below, but also a place to be reminded of support available, whether this be through information displays or hosting visits from other services in the setting. These might be legal support services, advice providers, local officials who can help with maximising benefits, as well as health or care professionals. Families may appreciate our help in approaching these services, or working out what they need to prioritise.

Supporting Young Children

Contact and Engagement

We might think we don't need to make much effort to contact and engage children who are coming to our setting. After all, they are here! But there are two things to bear in mind in the aftermath of difficult experiences. Firstly, that children may well be being brought to our setting, but their minds and hearts might be elsewhere. Perhaps they have worries about home, or loved ones. Or their heads are still partly in whatever the difficult experience was. So they may be present, but not quite with us. It might be that children are more engaged with us than they were - even "clingy". Or they may be more distant, less willing to accept comfort, help, or contact. Both reactions are quite normal, as is everything in between. What each needs is the same - patience and gentle responsiveness to whatever the child is needing from us. This is the foundation for providing the safety and comfort, as well as stabilisation, that will help them recover.

> Mateo used to really enjoy sitting in the corner with his caregiver for a story. He still comes and asks for this, but then seems to drift off, not paying attention. One time he even wandered off between the big bad wolf's "huff" and "puff". His caregiver realised this was not rudeness or a lack of interest - it was just that Mateo's head was elsewhere. Over time, he gradually sat for longer and before long was enjoying blowing down the pigs' houses.

Secondly, we have to remember the basic principle of trauma-informed practice, that the other person may not be experiencing a situation the same way we are, or the way we think or hope they are. We might feel we are in contact with the child, and engaged with them. But it might not feel like that to them. It is not that we are doing anything wrong. But the child has had an experience that may have created some ruptures, temporary ones, in their sense of connectedness, their trust of the adult world, or just their ability to hold attention for more than a short time. The result of all of these is that to them even the most beloved and trusted caregiver might feel distant or strange. We know what to do about this. It is all the things we would do if we were meeting the child for the first time. We can gently rebuild the connection through being available, following their lead, being alongside them - and waiting for them to offer contact and connection, responding warmly and calmly when they do.

> Ava always tends to need help putting her coat on for outside play. But she started angrily turning away whenever an adult tried to help with the buttons. Her caregiver realised that she was trying to be more independent and "look after herself" in response to her worries about her family, so they introduced some independence skills activities that Ava then enthusiastically engaged in.

Safety and Comfort

We saw in Chapter 3 that young children do not always have the capacity to generate a sense of safety by themselves. While there are ways to self-soothe that we can show young children (see Chapter 11), they rely more on being able to borrow our capabilities and on cues from the environment. Young children also have much less life experience than adults, so when a difficult event happens it can change their whole world view. What was a safe and kind world has turned out to be dangerous and threatening. The task in supporting recovery is to help them recover that sense of safety.

So we may see children who are more upset or fragile than they used to be. This might be in general, or it could be that small issues or setbacks that never bothered them before are now experienced as catastrophic. That can in turn be an additional layer of stress since it is frightening for a young child to feel very upset and not know why. Some children will start to self-manage their exposure to what they experience as difficult or upsetting, developing avoidances to apparently normal and benign things (see Chapter 3 for more on avoidance).

> It was a few days before her caregiver noticed that Ava, who usually loved to play at the water tray, was keeping away from it. She had also started to cry and run to her key-worker whenever one or her friends knocked something over.

It is for us adults to create as strong a sense of safety and comfort as we can, and to help children connect to this. There are three overall strategies that can do this:

Smooth the setting	• Be observant and aware of aspects of setting life and routine a child is finding difficult • Let them avoid this if they need to • If is something that has to happen, then provide lots of advance notice, comfort and support - give choices within the experience and keep it short • Increase the provision of whatever comforts the child - be it stuffed animals, stories, outdoor play, running around, or being quiet and still
Provide comfort	• Be aware and understand that the child may be less able to cope than usual • Offer levels and types of comfort that might suit a "younger" child • Notice the changing balance of support and space that a child needs • Move out of comforting into an activity the child usually enjoys
Help the child understand what they are experiencing	• Use narratives that label the feelings you see and connect to a solution. For example, "I think the doorbell made you jump! Shall we go and play where we can't hear it?" • Allow and support play that may be working out feelings or be a temporary regression - e.g., rushing around, tearing things • Work with families to help children understand what happened, how it is affecting them and why this is to be expected

Stabilisation

A child's world has been shaken by a difficult experience. Things which were certain are now unpredictable, major parts of their everyday experience might have changed. Early education settings can be a source of stability and predictability just by doing the day-to-day things well - and this a powerful aid to recovery for both child and family.

I'm often asked after a family bereavement, "when should the children go back to . . ." school or nursery or chess club or whatever. The answer is usually, "as soon as they can". This is because these things are important to children. They derive meaning and pleasure from them, as well as encountering supportive friends. But also, the tick tick of daily routines can give children a sense of normality even when around them everyone is struggling to get back to normal otherwise.

Within settings it can help to keep routines consistent, but with soft boundaries. The session or day needs a basic rhythm so that children know what is happening and what is happening next. The consistent sequence is soothing in itself, but also helps children gradually become more stable as the ground is no longer shifting under them. The soft boundaries to a routine mean that when a child has become engrossed in something we can let them carry on a bit longer. The focused engagement will be helping them and we do not want to disrupt this just because we normally sing a song at 11.30am.

There are also micro-rhythms to setting life that can be stabilising and soothing. These are the small rituals that often we do not even notice, but which can help children put back together their sense that the world makes predictable sense. For example, the way we put on our shoes before going out, or help to lay the table for snack, or the way an adult always starts a story in the same way, or that the pencils are always in the blue jar.

Finally, having some consistency and cross-over between home and setting can be helpful. These are the sorts of things we might have done to help children settle when they first came and includes common songs and stories, or having a transition companion such as a favourite stuffed animal or a photo of a pet.

Information Gathering

It is not usually helpful to ask children in detail about their experiences, and young children in any case are often limited in what they can tell us. But instead they provide abundant information through actions, expressed feelings, and sometimes what they say. In Chapter 3 we looked at some common manifestations of fight, flight, freeze, and flop in an early years setting. All of these are telling us about children's need for safety, comfort, and stability. And about their needs for what to do. We can find adaptive ways for them to do what they need to. If it is to flee, then we can play active games. If it is to freeze or hide, we can create calm spaces with soothing things to do, such as a den or a quiet corner.

When children have had difficult experiences then even more than usual we need to listen to behaviour as a communication of inner feelings or of thoughts about themselves or the world, and to respond accordingly.

> Mateo started covering his ears and screaming when the "tidy up" music started. His caregiver reflected on how he might be experiencing this. Perhaps it was the loud noise? So they turned it down. But he still was upset. Perhaps it was the transition from play to tidying? The setting experimented with an adult joining him and doing a "count down" together. Either this distracted Mateo, or he enjoyed it - but he started to manage the change better after this.

> Ava, usually a kind and careful girl, started deliberately running into people or else kicking or knocking over what they were playing with. Her caregiver reflected that this was a bit like re-enacting the collision - perhaps she trying to understand what had happened? They took this into some outdoor play and Ava had fun building and knocking over towers of pebbles.

Practical Assistance

Processing a difficult experience takes a lot of brain capacity for adults. The processing goes on even when children are not directly or consciously thinking about the experience. For children, with much more limited capacity, it can crowd out other functions such as attention or even motor skills. So it is not a surprise if, while recovering from a potentially traumatic recent experience, children temporarily seem to "go backwards" in their development or learning. If we do not anticipate this, and provide supports, it can then lead to frustration and further distress on the part of the children, their families, and educators - that then prolong or even halt the recovery process. Educators can be primed to notice if children become clumsier or find routine tasks harder than they normally do. This can be anything from forgetting how to do up a button, to losing the thread of conversations or forgetting simple instructions or behavioural norms. We know what to do. It is exactly the same as any child needs when they struggle with these things at first, but with the added element that we do not want children to feel stupid or incapable. "Do you want me to help you pour the juice today?" is more tactful and reinforcing of competence than "here, let me do it for you!"

Most of us who have experienced a bereavement will be familiar with this kind of presentation as we become more accident prone, absent-minded, or forgetful. We might also remember how tiring it is. Children recovering from a difficult experience face a double challenge. Processing the event takes a lot of energy, and then trying to do the usual things with reduced capacity is more tiring than it usually is. Plus, the family or other support contexts may themselves be less restful as the adults reel from whatever has happened; and sleep disruption at home is a normal part of processing a difficult experience, so children may be turning up for sessions already tired. Again, what they need from us is not complicated. A kind and restful setting, where adults notice when children are flagging (see above on listening to behaviour) or even better anticipate this and provide opportunities for rest and refreshment, is what children need. Even a small "stop, cuddle, and snack" can set children up for more play and learning, instead of what may seem like hours of grind and protest.

Lastly, learning is still going on. Children still need to develop new skills and find out new and amazing things about the world. This is where they find joy and fulfilment, and how they build their futures. There is sometimes an understandable instinct on the part of adults to think children shouldn't be trying to learn until they have recovered. But it is an unhelpful instinct from the child's point of view. While we want to be careful only to offer manageable challenge, continuing to explore, learn, and develop is part of what helps children recover - as well as being an oasis of normality in a world that has become stranger.

Information on Coping

This is another area where a common and understandable adult reflex can make things harder for children. It is natural to want to shield children from the stress of whatever is going on and that is surely right. But they also need to understand what is happening. For example, if a family member is sick, they need to know where they are and how they are doing. It is perfectly fine to err towards the optimistic end of reporting, but without clear information that they can rely on, children tend to fill in the gaps with imaginings or misunderstandings that are far worse than the reality. They also, for reasons we do not fully understand, have a tendency to assume that bad events are their fault.

The antidote to all of this is clear and reliable information at a level of detail and emotional content that children can cope with and process. A good mantra is that we should protect children *with* the truth, not *from* the truth. After all, they will already be experiencing upset adults around them, and if they don't know why the sense of threat can grow so that even small interactions or events can become traumatic.

> Ava's father got frustrated when she would not finish her dinner, and snapped, "when will you start to act your age?" He was amazed when she burst into uncontrollable tears on the floor. Reflecting, he realised that Ava had picked up on all the stress in the household. So he got down on the floor with her, rubbing her back - "I'm sorry, sweetheart. Daddy's been really worried about the accident, and it has made me all cross! Let's find something you'd like to eat, shall we?"

Education settings can help with this by making sure that they give children information when they ask for it, but that this is consistent with what parents or carers are saying and does not introduce new information without prior consultation. Children can seize on any differences and start to worry about those. "But mummy said we'd still be able to go to see grandpa". There are some cases where educators may be in a better position to give children information and answer their questions, for example when a parent feels unable to, or that they are still too upset themselves.

> Mateo's parents had explained to him what felt like a hundred times about how electric plugs are carefully tested and safe, but they couldn't quite keep the tone of exasperation out of it. His setting offered to do some learning with him about electricity, which he then came home and explained to his mother!

As well as having information about what it going on, children also need clear, simple and do-able guidance about what they can do about it. Without this, they may feel helpless and therefore even more frightened - remember that one of the three elements of a traumatic experience is feeling out of control. Alternatively, they may take on too much responsibility. This can be literally so, where children's attempts to help make life more complicated (setting the table resulting in a flood), or else in their minds as they take on the burden of solving things.

> Ava's father agreed with her that what she could do that would help them both would be to have a great time playing during the day and tell him all about it when she got home after putting her shoes in the cupboard. She also understood that if she was worried during the day, she could go and tell her keyworker (and the keyworker gave her the same information).

Settings can also help by building children's understanding about crises and recovery. This is not something they may know about. Adults have been through this pattern many times, from lost keys to the washing machine breaking down, to an unexpected bill, and as a result have an internal schema something like:

A. Things go wrong
B. We can do things to cope
C. Either they get better or we learn to manage

Even everyday play experiences such as making a mess and clearing it up, or not being able to find a resource and searching for it, or running out of bananas so everyone has to put up with stewed rhubarb today - all of these help to establish this pattern of understanding. So do ordinary learning experiences, if adults wrap some suitable narrative around them such as:

> "Oh, James can't get the top off the jar. He's trying really hard - nearly there? No. How about if I loosen it a bit first? Yes - done it!"

That might seem like an utterly trivial event to any adult, but for little James, it is creating, establishing, and reinforcing pathways that underpin emotional resilience:

> "I can manage problems and face them with help".

I cannot overemphasise the role of day-to-day achievements in supporting recovery, and there will be more on this with further strategies in Section 2.

Finally, a good source of coping schemas is stories! Nearly all of these involve the main character facing a difficulty, a fear, or messing things up and putting them right. Telling and re-telling stories again supports the development of information and understanding about what a disaster is, how people experience it, and that it can be overcome.

Watchful Waiting

It is important to be clear that "watchful waiting" does not mean doing nothing and hoping for the best (Dyregrov & Regel, 2012). Instead it is providing the immediate help in the expectation that people will recover over time, while keeping an eye in case problems persist or worsen (NICE, 2018). A good rule of thumb would be to seek further advice, or encourage families to do so, if difficulties persist more than a month or so after the event, or it they return at any point afterwards.

Do and Don't!

The content of this chapter can be summarised as some "do and don't" recommendations for supporting children and families. Firstly, here are the things that are worth trying and usually help most people.

After an event, do:

- Use the principles of psychological first aid
- Consult with children and families about what they need
- Help people feel in control of what is happening to them even in small ways
- Listen to whatever they want to tell you about without judgement
- Make sure families can contact sources of help
- Make sure a child knows who can help them right now
- Help children and families reconnect with normal life and routines
- Support existing friendship, family, and community networks
- Offer positive experiences of fun and nurture

- Comfort children whenever they need it
- Meet the needs of helpers and caregivers
- Encourage helpers and caregivers to look after themselves so as better to support the children

And there are some things that can easily happen, but usually do not help in the long term:

After an event, do not:

- Make people talk about it in detail beyond what is needed
- Assume people won't cope, or communicate this
- Focus solely on the children and forget the support networks
- Minimise or dismiss any stress-related response
- Forget that young children's main communication channel might be through behaviour
- Allow children to feel they are to blame for events
- Allow families to feel they are to blame for their child's reactions
- Ignore or neglect your own distress and needs

Closing Reflections

This is, in some ways, a heavy chapter, as we have been thinking about how to respond to known traumatic events or disasters. It is not easy to consider how bad things can happen, but the truth is that they are certain to - the only question is when and to whom. It is quite likely that any given early educator will encounter such needs several times in a career. For who work with particular populations, it may even be a matter of routine.

My promise in this book is to make the content as in depth as it needs to be, but as comfortable as possible to learn about. So I want to offer a final Reflective Activity to conclude this chapter. This has two purposes. Firstly to reinforce the confidence that the main needs described here are things we are already pretty good at meeting, and secondly to end on a positive note.

So, if you'd like to do this, take ten minutes or so with the following - write it down or draw if you prefer.

Reflective Activity

Think of a time a friend or a colleague had a very minor mishap. Perhaps they were late for work, or forgot their lunch! Nothing more serious than that.

What did you do to help them that was something like any of the following:

- Contact and engagement
- Safety and comfort
- Stabilisation
- Information gathering
- Practical assistance
- Connection with social supports
- Information on coping
- Linkage with collaborative services

Chapter summary:

- Most people recover, with kind support, after difficult experiences
- Psychological first aid provides a map for what people might need to recover
- Settings have a key role in supporting children and their families

Practice points:

- Use the elements of psychological first aid to plan how to help
- Consult with children and families about how they want you to help
- Seek further advice if significant difficulties persist for more than a month or so

7

What Traumatised Children Need Help With

This chapter will provide:

- A detailed account of the range of needs that can result from childhood trauma
- A map to help make observations, assessment, and planning manageable
- A positive approach to difficulties aimed at creating coping and flourishing

Reading through Section 1 on Understanding Trauma, it is easy to feel overwhelmed. Early trauma is so common, and its effects can run so deep in children's development. There seem to be a bewildering range of things to think about, and feeling helpless from time to time is understandable.

However, we have also seen some principles that can guide us. We have a simple way to understand complex behaviour. If we see something with elements of fight, flight, freeze, or flop, then it is a good first assumption that 1) the child is not feeling safe and 2) their developmental capacities are not up to dealing with it.

This chapter gives a map for understanding 2). Every child will be different, but having an outline of the main developmental areas we might help them with provides an orientation. The following chapters are about how we help.

Overall, trauma impacts on two clusters, both of which we have already seen. Firstly, our sense of safety can be disrupted or unreliable. And we might have difficulties coming to feel safe, even in safe situations. Secondly, our sense of self can be disrupted. A child who meets a trigger suddenly experiences themselves doing and feeling things that are a sharp break from their usual. A child who has experienced a chaotic and unstable world may have developed a chaotic and unstable inner experience in order to match it.

There are many ways to categorise the resulting needs, and to break them down into different levels of detail. The approach used here is simply a heuristic – which means a way to set out a complex reality in a way that is simple enough for action, but nuanced enough to help focus that action. This and the following chapters will therefore follow the same structure. With the caveat just given, children need our help to develop:

DOI: 10.4324/9781003563808-11

Developing safety	*Developing a self*
Coping with sensory input Tolerating affect Calibrating stress (getting the right level of response) Creating a sense of safety Emotional regulation Assessing and managing risk	Core self Cause and effect - a coherent world A capable self Motor coordination Language development Executive function Social schemas An effective self A worthwhile and wanted self A self in relationships
Curiosity and Joyfulness	

Developing Safety

The foundational intervention for people of any age who have experienced trauma is to help them find ways to feel safe. We also saw in Section 1 how one of the impacts of traumatic experiences is that people sometimes do not feel safe even in apparently safe situations. For simple trauma, this might be a matter of a few trigger experiences. For people who experienced developmental trauma, their whole stress system might be primed for danger. The same principles apply for young children but we need to remember three further aspects. Firstly, that children, whether or not they have experienced trauma, are more easily overwhelmed than adults. Secondly, while most adults can generate their own sense of safety, young children's stress systems are still developing. So children rely more on the people and relationships around them both to feel safe now and to develop their abilities to cope. Thirdly, as we saw with the example of the two very different islands in Chapter 4, if a child is accustomed to a world of difficulty and danger, they will not always benefit immediately from being in a safe and nurturing setting. Sometimes developmental changes will need time, even a lot of time. But everything we do to promote children's sense of safety will assist in their education now, and create foundations for long-term progress.

Of course this can only be effective if children are actually and really safe in all areas of their lives. So before we think about anything else, we need to be sure that children are not currently in danger or at risk of it. This might sometimes be a matter of carefully following local safeguarding approaches. Since these differ across countries and localities, this book will not provide detail on these, but there will be some coverage of the principles in Chapter 15 on the wider context in which we work.

Coping with Sensory Input

We tend to be taught early on that we have five senses, but of course we have many more. Some of these are internal senses, and not all of them are ones we are consciously aware of. For example, you have an internal sense of where you are in space, and that your hand is yours and not an object separate to you, or for that matter somebody else's hand. More obvious are our senses of pain, of being too hot or too cold. And then there are the external senses we know well.

Trauma can impact on sensory processing in different ways and with different degrees of depth (Lloyd, 2020; Matson et al., 2024). For children with only one or two simple traumatic memories, this may be limited to a few sensory experiences that act as triggers, or it can be a general state of higher, or lower, responsiveness. Developmental trauma can affect how the whole sensory processing system develops.

Consider an infant exploring their world. They encounter a new sensation - what does it mean? Initially babies have a very broad assessment, basically categorising as ok or not-ok. As they experiment more, their sensory system learns from what happens. Maybe nice things happen. They are cold, and someone comforts them and wraps them up so they feel warmer. Gradually, the feeling of cold becomes easier to bear. The baby becomes the young child splashing into the pool with delight, and the teen walking through the rain anticipating the warmth of home. Maybe worse things happen, in which case, "feeling cold" becomes classed more as a difficult, or even very difficult feeling. And there are two ways to cope with that - either ramp it up to a fight/flight/freeze/flop level response, or else numb it out. And then any new sensation might be more likely to be a bad one too, in which case it is best avoided. This reduces not just exploration, but also any chance that the new sensation might get re-classified as ok, or even good.

Through these kinds of experiences, or lack of experiences, children may end up with any or all of the following issues:

- Aversion to particular sensations. Could be external such as touches or textures, or internal such as hunger, cold, or even joy.
- Overresponsive, either to sensation in general, or to particular sensations. Again can be almost any, including sound, smells, clothing, minor pain.
- Underresponsive, appearing not to notice, or not to the degree expected, warmth, cold, hunger, sounds, pain, fear. Might present as risk taking or dissociation.
- Proprioception. Knowing where they are in space, where their body is, or what it is doing. We might see lack of coordination, clumsiness, or lack of control such as pushing when they meant to join in.
- Vestibular. Linked to proprioception, but more about balance and fluent movement. Might lead to avoidances of running, swinging, etc. - or else seeking it as an attempt to develop balance.
- Seeking. Children with few other coping resources may use sensory input to manage stress, including flapping, spinning, head-banging, repeated actions (e.g., rolling a car back and forth).
- Filtering. In a busy or noisy environment finding it hard to focus, or filter out distractions, or choose what to attend to (including our attempts to help them).

Affect Tolerance

Even small amounts of emotion or arousal can be hard for children to cope with. This is obvious for negative feelings, like fear or uncertainty, but is also true for positive ones such as curiosity or joy. Even simple trauma can lead to happy feelings being a trigger if, for example, the difficult experience happened just after the child was feeling particularly happy.

This is an essential practice point since the main intuitive thing we want for children, especially distressed ones, is for them to feel happier. We might aim to fill their lives with positivity, or emphasise the upsides and enjoyment of an experience. For some, this will be great and just what they need (see above on joy and curiosity), but for others it might make life more difficult as these are emotions they cannot easily cope with.

The other effect we might see is that what seem to us to be low key experiences with acceptable levels of risk or uncertainty might be experienced as highly stressful by the children, not because they can't cope with that amount of stress but because the experience of stress of any kind is hard to tolerate. In terms of practice, this means that we need to sensitively adjust the levels of arousal created by the environment as well as for any particular experience. If we do this, children will be operating within but towards the edges of their zone of tolerance and thus over time expanding it. I've used the word "zone" there deliberately to make a link to what we know about the "zone of proximal development" in learning. It is exactly the same idea, in that by supporting children to manage at the leading edges of their capabilities, we gradually expand them. There is much more practical detail on this in Chapters 11–13.

Stress Calibration and Emotional Regulation

We saw in Chapter 1 how the adult brain is constantly tuning our responses to what is going on. Initial options are adjusted by a cascade of brain systems that add further information and judgements to create a coherent response. In Chapter 3 we saw how these systems differ for young children in three main respects. Firstly, the response range is simpler (big or small), the regulating systems are not yet developed, and thirdly, there is a smaller range of possible reactions.

> Alice runs up behind her keyworker, Jeff, and shouts "boo!" Jeff is startled, but quickly realises it is Alice and her joke, turns and says "boo to you!"
>
> Alice runs up behind Josh, another child in the setting and shouts "boo!" Josh is startled, turns round and pushes her. Two seconds later he realises it was only a joke, and that he shouldn't have pushed, and feels ashamed.

There is also of course a fourth key difference, which is that young children also have sensitive and responsive adults around who can do some of these impossible tasks for them. These include 1) realising it is not a huge disaster, 2) managing and soothing the strong feelings, and 3) being able to do something to solve it other than fight, flee, freeze, or flop.

> Jeff sees all this happen and comes over smiling. He crouches down to the children's level, with a hand on each child's shoulder. "Oh dear, that was a joke went wrong! Alice is sorry and Josh is sorry too. Let's go outside!"

For any young child, therefore, a lot of the work of self-regulation and soothing is done by the environment and the people around them. This means that for children with simple trauma, the need is to both smooth the environment around them so they encounter fewer triggers, or more manageable ones; and to provide higher levels of adult support to manage feelings, soothe them, and work out what to do. Note that is not something particularly different to what any child needs - it is just more of it, and more focused onto experiences we know they might find difficult.

Developmental trauma presents what is at first sight a deeper challenge to children and to educators. Children are on the way to developing a stress and response system tuned to a difficult and dangerous environment. Those brain areas we saw in Chapter 1 (Amygdala! Orbito-frontal cortex!) are different than they might have been. For these children's brains, adaptive self-regulation means creating fight, flight, freeze, and flop responses as quickly as possible, and they are developing around that priority.

I said "at first sight" because despite the involvement of complicated brain systems with long names, what children who have experienced developmental trauma need is in principle quite simple. It is exactly the same as what any child needs, just more so. The children need to shift the course of their developmental adaptations. So we need to give their brains clear and consistent information about what the world is actually like. There are two parallel strategies to doing this, although we will fill in much more detail in Chapters 8 to 10. Firstly, we can find outlets for the adaptive actions that the brain feels it needs to do. Need to flee? Fine, let's go outside and run around a lot! Need to hide? Fine, let's learn to come to a keyworker's lap for a cuddle. Need to fight? Fine, let's find some things to carry about or even throw as part of a game of catch or skittles. Secondly, we can provide wrap-around, consistent, obvious, constant, unarguable, clear messages about what kind of world this actually is. Not a difficult and dangerous one, but a safe one that has manageable challenge and even the prospect of joy and exploration.

In early education we should only expect partial success. Changing the course of development takes time. We can lay the foundations, without which it won't happen at all, but may not see final results until long after the children have left us. For this reason, working with families in a trauma-informed way is critical so that they and we (and the children) can see the progress they *are* making without being downcast and disempowered by a sense of the progress they *should* be making. We will consider this further in Chapter 16. Finally, we also need to remember that while we are providing a safe and interesting world, many children will still be living as well in a world that seems to them difficult and dangerous. This will not only be confusing, but means we should not expect rapid adaptation to our settings, even if some things can get easier more quickly.

Judging and Managing Risks

Given one of the main effects of traumatic memories, or developmental trauma, is an alertness to danger even in apparently safe situations, it is no surprise that children who have experienced trauma often need help to develop judgement of risk. This can go both ways. One might think immediately of children who are over-fearful or withdrawn as a result of feeling scared, but the need is equally great for those who are over-adventurous and tend to overreach.

We saw in earlier chapters how trigger experiences, or the anticipation of them, can raise levels of arousal so that children will feel strong impulses to fight, flee, freeze, or flop. Sensitive accompaniment from adults can instead make these experiences of coping and managing. As we saw in Chapter 3, one can regard the adult/child stress systems as interlinked. In the same way as we support children's learning through careful interactions, we can support their managing of trigger experiences and thus gradually develop a child's sense of scale for what they can cope with. We will look at practical detail on this in Chapter 9. But the background ethos of the setting and its environment is equally important. If there is a general sense of higher risk - whether this be due to high stakes approaches to learning or behaviour, other things going on, stressed staff, or any other cause - it will be harder for children to adjust their judgements for particular scenarios.

> June would do anything rather than go outside and play. The setting staff could not puzzle out why, but decided to back off urging her for a while. When she stood at the door looking out, they did not respond beyond smiling. One day, she just went out, and stayed out until the end of the session.

> Jane would do anything rather than go outside and play. Staff were under pressure to implement new guidelines on outdoor education, and were disagreeing how to approach the issue. They gave her lots of encouragement, especially when she went near the door. No change.

One thing it is easy for adults to forget is that every new learning involves an element of risk. We are not usually thrown by being handed a new book - but to a young child the experience of wondering what is in it is also has uncertainties that might be uncomfortable. Helping children discover how to work out when things are ok, and when they are not ok, actually helps everyone learn better.

The issues are more fundamental for children who have experienced developmental trauma. As we saw in early chapters, their brains and bodies have started to develop in order to adapt to a difficult and dangerous world. This might lead to either excessive fearfulness, excessive fearlessness, or a more disorganised flipping between the two. All of these are helped by a predictable environment and predictably sensitive and responsive adults. Children who are more fearful might need very low levels of challenge and high levels of support. Children who are more fearless may in addition need some outlets. They have grown used to a world full of challenge and may feel so uncomfortable without this that they will start to create it for themselves.

> Akoni seemed out of control. He would climb on furniture, jump off regardless of what or who was in the landing zone. Outside he would find the largest stick, waving it around. Then, as if a switch was flicked, he would glue himself to the nearest adult, hiding his head and wanting to be cuddled.

These developmental pathways are established early and they are, for good reason, slow to change. By providing the environment, the relationships, and the stimulation that can show the developing brain that this is a safe, helpful world with manageable challenge and interesting things to do, early educators are key people to start this process.

Developing a Coherent Self

On the whole, you probably know which person is you. There is a sense that "you" are you, and that this is the same person from moment to moment. Life unfolds as a relatively smooth movie. We saw in Section 1 how even simple trauma can create bumps and gaps in people's experiences of the world around them. This is also true for their experiences of themselves. For people who have experienced trauma, the memories themselves can often feel "ajar" from the main story of their life. Trigger events feel unconnected to what came before or what came after. As we saw in Chapter 2 this can lead to dissociation, a sense of not being really there, of not being real. This sense of self is not quite the same as self-esteem or other ways we see ourselves, covered in the next subsection.

We don't know what this is like for young children as it is hard to research and it is hard to imagine what it feels like to have a fragmented sense of self. We can see it in behaviour where children appear to be disorganised or inconsistent in their responses to what happens, as though they are different people at different times. Alternatively we might encounter children who have difficulty knowing what they like, or who default to simple, repeated choices in order to simplify this experience. Or they may be inconsistent in learning - appearing as though there were not "there" yesterday when we explained the new rule for handwashing, or struggling to take pleasure from a story.

To see what children need from us, imagine for a moment that you have a really peculiar day. Everyone you encounter treats you slightly differently. The barista completely ignores you as you ask for your order, so does the person who slams the door in your face as you try to go out. Some people notice you, but treat you with impatience, while others go out of their way to be helpful, even to the point of being embarrassing. You might well wonder what's got into them all, but you also might if this goes on for days start to think "is it me?" You'd become uncertain, and inconsistent yourself. Even adults can have their sense of self disrupted in this way. Developmental trauma can fundamentally disorganise the process for young children. What they need from us, to build or rebuild, is to be noticed, seen, and heard. It's the opposite to that barista. Children then experience themselves as a self because they experience our treating them as a self. And they need this to be consistent, as do we, so that the self in different times and with different people is always the same self. This can take years, but in early education, we can give it the best and most hopeful start through consistently positive, responsive, and loving relationships within an ordered and interesting environment.

Core Self

This is a difficult concept to describe because it is entirely pre-conscious and pre-verbal. Deep in our brains are stored some basic rhythms that provide pattern and order to our experience of the world and of ourselves. These are the templates that link sensations to feelings to actions, and the smooth operation of these are what give us the foundational sense that "I am me" (Seth & Tsakiris, 2018).

It is no accident that a lot of early infant experiences involve rhythm and repetition. This can be literal, as we watch a baby try something over and over, or shake something up and down, up and down. Or it can be relational, in the back and forth of a two-way interaction, be this peekaboo or a simple chat. Or it can be more about the regular patterns of need-solution, need-solution that are part of everyday sensitive and responsive care. Watch a parent feeding a baby, and you will see patterns of suck-suck/jiggle-jiggle (Kaye & Wells, 1980).

Children who have simple traumatic memories have this basic sense of self, but triggers disrupt it temporarily. It can be frightening to suddenly feel full of urges to fight, flee, freeze, or flop, and strong feelings of terror or rage. Suddenly I am someone else. Children who have experienced unstable and even dangerous worlds may not have built the basic sense of self in the same way. Instead, they lack inner coherence - we may then see random, disorganised, or catastrophic reactions to even minor stressors. This then reflects on how easily they can make sense of the world around them (Lloyd, 2023) including things we try to do to help them.

A Coherent World - Cause and Effect

Nearly all young children find life baffling from time to time, and have a shaky grasp on what causes what. Events can feel random and disconnected to them. This is even more so for children who have experienced trauma. In the case of simple trauma, the daily experience of the world as predictable, and predictably safe, has been disrupted. Bad things, it seems, can happen randomly and out of the blue - rather like the way adults remember events in those strange dreams we have sometimes that make no sense. For children who have experienced high levels of trauma, the usual course of development of understanding of cause and effect can be disrupted since very few things in their world seem to be predictable or reliable.

The day-to-day impacts can be profound, and very noticeable to adults. Children need us to understand these impacts for what they are. For example, it is our basic sense of how one thing follows on from another that means we do not have to consciously think about "now and next". A huge amount of an adult's sense of security comes from this, the steady tick, tick of an ordered life. We do not worry about our cup of coffee suddenly turning into a bouquet of flowers and would be surprised at anyone who did so worry to the extent that it distracted them from what they were doing or from managing their behaviour. But this is what life can be like without a deeply internalised sense of cause and effect. It also goes without saying that learning any skills or knowledge without this becomes much harder - be that science, following a story, or problem solving.

The key word in the paragraph above is "internalised". Cause and effect is one issue that shows that trauma-informed practice, if it is to be effective, needs to be more than teaching children skills. The regularity of the general environment, the reliability of the people in it - all these, and similar patterns, are how the young brain develops understanding of cause and consequence. Without these, children won't benefit so much from anything else we offer them.

A Capable Self - Addressing Developmental Gaps

Children respond to simple or developmental trauma in adaptive ways. Their brains are agile at adjusting to help them do as well as they can in their contexts. But this does involve choices and trade-offs. There is only so much resource available for development, so more of one thing (quick to act) might mean less of another (thinking and wondering). In addition, development happens as a complete package. An ability to be lost in thought about a particular stimulus (otherwise known as concentration and focus) is not compatible with a need to react fast and flexibly to unstable threats.

There are some common gaps or developmental differences for children who have experienced developmental trauma. These are relevant for educators for two reasons. Firstly because, according to the theme of this book, we are very well placed to be able to support children to address these gaps. But secondly, because the key aspects of development influenced by trauma turn out also to be the key aspects of development most important for lifelong learning. So if we want children to benefit the best we can from our educational efforts, being trauma-informed is an effective way to do this.

The particular patterns of strengths and gaps is going to vary for each child, and indeed may look different in different situations. But on the whole, we might want to be observant of how children do with the following aspects of development. For more detail on what each is, and how we can support them, please see Chapter 13.

Developmental aspect	*Impact of developmental trauma*	*What we might see (includes)*
Language	Prioritisation of action over talking and listening Reduced experiences of language and two-way interactions	Language delay Difficulty following instructions Higher frustration Difficult behaviour
Motor coordination	Priority given to easily produced simple actions rather than smooth or complex sequences	Rigidity or poorer muscle tone, difficulties judging force and pressure Uncoordinated or disorganised movement, collisions or accidents
Executive function	Vigilance leading to switching rather than focused attention Rapid responses reduce inhibition and waiting Instability leads to reduced forward planning and/or consequential reasoning	Flitting about Difficulty with changes and transitions Hair trigger responses Poorer reasoning Disorganised behaviours
Social schemas	Relational templates designed for fear and threat Reduced learning of social norms Experience of control rather than cooperation	May struggle with peer interactions Or adult interactions Inappropriate responses to normal situations Difficulty with "no"
Learning how to play	Reduced appetite for new experiences Reduced experience of social play Prioritisation of self-soothing play	Clumsy attempts to start play (hitting, etc.) Unimaginative play Difficulties sharing Reduced exploration Repeated sensory play, or activity that provides sensory experience

What has been said thus far in this subsection applies mainly to children who have experienced developmental trauma. For children with simple trauma, we need to remember that trigger experiences, or the anticipation of them, can mean that they temporarily "shed" skills, so may present with any or all of the effects above in a more limited way or only in certain situations or contexts. Or, if their experiences have led them to be hypervigilant a lot of the time, they may have missed developmental and learning opportunities.

An Effective Self

Over the last few decades there has been a lot of attention in education and elsewhere on building children's self-esteem. This is an important set of beliefs that they are good people and are valued by others. Just as important, and less often talked about, however, are self-efficacy beliefs. These are about our sense of our ability to get things done, to change things, to influence the world around us and what happens to us. People naturally vary in their self-efficacy beliefs. Most of us have friends or relatives who we think are a bit passive and "helpless", and others who we think are rather too busy and "pushy".

Self-efficacy is hugely important for our wellbeing and resilience. We do better if we have some sense that whatever happens next, there is probably something we can do about it, or at least to survive it. One reason experiences like airport delays can be upsetting out of proportion to the actual danger is that feeling of being unable to influence events. But also, self-efficacy out of proportion is bad for our wellbeing. I used to be scared of flying and realised that I was unconsciously "willing" the plane onwards - it got better once I realised that the pilots would fly the aircraft perfectly competently without me.

Children who have experienced trauma can present at either end of the extremes, or sometimes flip bewilderingly between them. We saw earlier how one key aspect of the trauma triangle is that "I can't control what is happening". Trauma for adults disrupts this belief that we can determine our fate and cope with what life throws at us. For developing children, even a simple trauma can provide an early lesson that they are helpless and whatever they do won't make much difference. In more developmental trauma, children start to develop brains and bodies adapted either to be very passive (don't make it worse) or very active (deal with it!).

We can see both of these in our settings. Remember that all young children are still working out their self-efficacy beliefs so will sometimes give up too soon or else overreach. This is a normal need to help them develop a realistic sense of competence. But children who have experienced trauma may also show a need to work out what they can control and what they can't. For some that will manifest as a need to be "in charge" of even tiny details. For others, it will show as struggling to cope with any choice or any lack of determination by another. It can be equally frightening to feel controlled as it is to feel out of control. There is no substitute for knowing each child as they are - and once we do this, there is lots we can do to help them.

A Worthwhile and Wanted Self

We saw in Chapter 3 that even after a simple trauma, young children often will blame themselves for what happened even when it cannot possibly have been their fault. If they struggle with trigger experiences, then without a trauma-informed understanding, adults may naturally see this as just bad behaviour and respond accordingly. This only reinforces the child's developing belief that they are a bad person with two effects. The first is a powerful cognitive bias where we tend to see evidence of what we believe and ignore evidence that says something different. So children will start to focus more on things that show they are bad (a minor incident at breakfast) and less on the opposite (praise for being kind to the puppy), further confirming their poor self-image. Secondly, we all have a tendency to behave and react in ways that fit our self-image - it is the best way for the world to make sense. So children might start to live out their mistaken belief that they are a bad person and recruit the rest of us into the same script. Developmental trauma adds further layers of complexity.

Because the children are young, these are not yet well-formed and founded beliefs about themselves. This is hopeful in the sense that we therefore have much more chance in early years of helping them shift to more positive beliefs. It makes things harder too, as it is not likely to shift through reasoning and conversations. Nor will it give way to occasional positive experiences. Children need a wrap-around experience where every interaction, every aspect of the environment tells them that they are good to have around, are positive contributors to the world around them and to our lives too. Once again, it starts with the basic ways we organise our setting, through the positive relationships we provide, before any kind of "self-esteem" boosting activities will have any effect.

A Self in Relationships

Trauma can disrupt positive relationships in two stages. Firstly, there is the impact of the trauma itself. We have seen how living with memories even of simple trauma can mean children at some level blame themselves. They might also blame others:

> Matty started playing up when his mother got home from hospital after recovery from a sudden illness. He would run away from her, or become furious during bath or bed time. He started trying to do everything himself.

It's reasonable to see this behaviour as communicating both Matty's anger with his mother and his realisation that he can't for the whole of his life rely on a parent to meet his needs. We all come to this realisation in time, but for most of us it is through the turbulent approach to young adulthood rather than in our early years.

Simple trauma can therefore change children's views of the adults who care for them though this is often in a limited way. Developmental trauma has an impact on the basic schemas, or patterns, out of which children form their relationships. Remember from Chapter 4 that this is an adaptive process. Perhaps the child's experiences have convinced their brains that the best way to do well is to develop high levels of self-reliance. Or alternatively that only by getting Velcro-close to the powerful adults can the child be truly safe. Or perhaps, in a chaotic world, that flipping randomly between these alternatives is most likely to sometimes work out to be the right response. If these sound like the classic "attachment styles" that is not an accident. It is the same thing and the same processes. However we describe it, though, these are not always the most adaptive patterns for relationships in most societies today.

Which leads to the second stage of trauma's disruption of positive relationships.

> Matty's mother found all this very difficult to cope with. She started leaving the routine tasks to her partner, and avoiding playing with him. Watching a TV program on parenting, she learned about the "naughty step" and started putting Matty on it whenever he was upset.

It is nobody's fault, but trauma-caused fight, flight, freeze, or flop responses are easy to see as bad behaviour or hostility, or at the least something to be corrected. A natural unreflective response is to punish, or to start to see the child differently, and this can extend across a whole system. We now label people who experienced early trauma, for example, as having a "personality disorder" or a "conduct disorder".

All that can be prevented or reduced by being trauma-informed.

> Matty's mother had a chat with her health visitor, who showed her some materials about childhood trauma. She realised that Matty was lonely, frightened, and angry. He needed information and comfort, not punishment. So she spent more time with him, helped him to manage the feelings he had, and built up a story to help him understand about her illness and recovery.

The bottom line is that for children who have experienced trauma, at any depth of impact, we have to do a larger share of the work of the relationship. We also have to remain the adult, by which I mean remembering what is really happening and not getting pulled into the trauma's scripts. In order to do this work, we need to be in a context that acknowledges and supports the impact on us. There is material on this in Chapter 17. But also we need the setting to have an environment and an ethos that makes this work possible. A lot of what children need in terms of positive relationships is embedded in the policies and routines of the setting. Or not, or even its opposite. We will look at this in Chapter 15.

Joyfulness and Curiosity

Trauma and its impacts can dominate children's experiences of life. It can also dominate how we think about children and how we plan for them. The focus can appropriately be on helping them recover, and to develop the resilience that they need for the future. Or the preoccupation can be with managing and preventing behaviours that are causing problems for us, the child, or their family. Yet if children are to make progress, they need what all children need, which is a range of experiences that give pleasure and arouse interest in the world and the people around them. This can help by making life gradually "bigger" than the trauma, but also because it contains the affordances out of which children can build safety, hope, and self-efficacy.

Some children will have a reduced ability to feel positive emotions such as joy and curiosity. For some children, these feelings may themselves be triggers. Others may find joy in apparently "younger" experiences, such as touch and textures. What all these children need are low key experiences that can excite gentle amounts of pleasure and interest they can recognise and cope with.

A Framework for Helping

The next six chapters set out how we can help and support children in all of these areas. While it may seem at this stage as though children who have experienced trauma may have a wide and bewildering range of needs, intervention can in practice be quite simple. The foundation of any successful work is the development and maintenance of positive relationships. These not only help children feel safer, and therefore more able to take on what we might want to teach or show them, but also are the main means by which they can start to develop their own capacities to cope and flourish.

The first three chapters therefore look in detail at what these positive relationships are, what we can do to create them, and how we can make them effective and do-able. The following chapters then build the rest of resilience on that foundation as we look at particular strategies and experiences that can help.

Chapter summary:

- Trauma can impact on a wide range of developmental and other issues for young children
- This can be different for each child
- Using a framework such as in this chapter can help us provide support without becoming overwhelmed

Practice points:

- Consider possible impacts of trauma across the whole range of children's development
- Use the framework to focus and to plan how to respond
- Remember the big impacts that even small changes can have within a positive relationship

8

Positive Relationships 1 - The Building Blocks

This chapter will provide:

- An account of mind-mindedness and co-regulation as the building blocks of positive relationships
- Practice examples to illustrate the concepts
- Application to children who may have had traumatic experiences

A Grand Day Out!

This is a grand day! We are taking the children to the beach, thanks to a donated coach hire and some parent volunteers. It is a lovely sunny late morning when we arrive, with a gentle breeze. The waves on the ocean are not too big for paddling, although the water seems a bit cold at first. Most of the children potter happily about, digging things up, splashing in the waves, running up and down. Some do more unexpected things:

> Martha squats down and starts eating the sand
>
> Jonty rushes off into the waves without apparently thinking about whether they are too big for him
>
> Aarya stays close to an adult, sitting quietly, with her arms round her knees
>
> Cal starts digging a huge hole in the sand using his hands, then gets it in his eyes when he rubs them and starts to cry
>
> Oleksandr stays close to an adult, sitting quietly, with his arms round his knees

There is a lot going on! The practitioners have their work cut out and need to make some rapid decisions before it all gets out of hand. The concept of mind-mindedness provides an easy way to do this and come up with solutions that are worth trying. I will describe it in practice before giving a more theoretical account.

DOI: 10.4324/9781003563808-12

The key step is the trauma-informed one of reflecting what might be going on in the children's heads. We have a map to help us from Chapter 1:

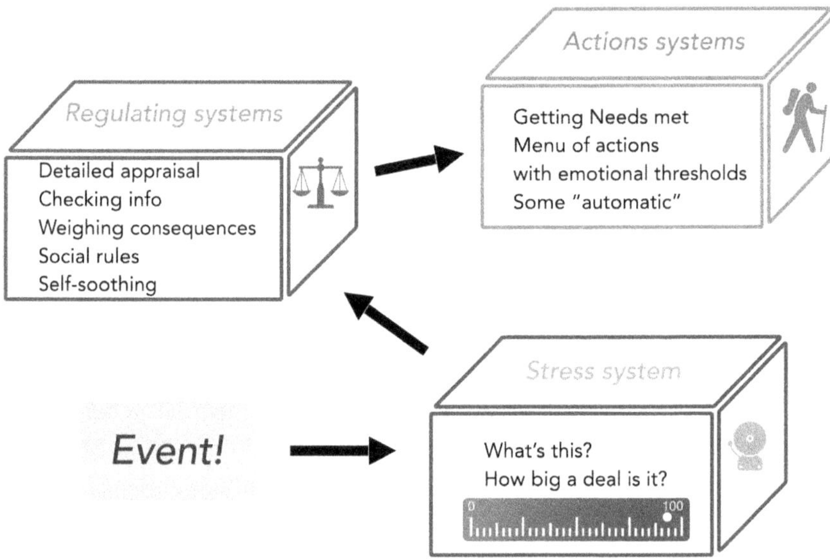

Figure 8.1 How the brain decides what to do

When we encounter an event or a stimulus, recall, our stress system gives a rapid initial response about what is going on, whether it is a good or a bad thing and how good or bad that is. Our regulating systems then take a closer and more detailed look, checking for other information, judging the possible consequences of actions, and applying social rules, etc. The joint judgement of these systems is used to choose from our menu of actions a response that fits the needs of the situation as we see them, and then the actions systems get that done. You might wish to review the first sections of Chapter 1 as a reminder at this point.

We can apply this map to what we are seeing. Starting with Aarya, staying close to the adults, and wrapping her hands round her knees, this looks like a flight or freeze response. So we know what that means - Aarya is not feeling safe. Something about the beach experience is frightening for her. In terms of the map, we might imagine something like:

Aarya	
Stress systems	Terror and fear
Regulation systems	You're right! Loud noises, huge space, far from home
Action systems	Freeze!

We can also consider some possible responses the adults could try. Firstly, the one my mother always tried whenever I was reluctant to do something new:

> Look what fun everyone is having! Let's go and paddle in the waves!

This is those mainstays of behaviour management in early years - encouragement and distraction. Excellent strategies, often, but how well do they match Aarya's experience of the situation? I will ventriloquise this using words she might not use herself, to give a sense of the effect:

> Waves? Those are huge! Does that sea ever end, it's so much bigger than the pond in the park. It has a life of its own, so noisy! This place is even more scary than I thought! And the others are enjoying it, there is something wrong with me, I am disappointing everyone, I might be punished.

What we've done, without intending to, is highlight even more the potential threats, confirming what Aarya's stress system was already telling her. And we've added an element of shame too. It was a perfectly good idea, but it did not match where she was. So what would? Thinking about what the situation is like for Aarya, and how that plays out in her young brain, gives us some options. She is terrified - so what do frightened children need? The intuitive answer is, as we will see below, often exactly the right one. In this case, Aarya needs to feel safer. So perhaps we can let her sit with us and make it clear that is ok. In fact, we like having her company. We can watch for small signs that the freeze response is starting to unwind and talk about what we can see and hear, explaining what it is. Or we might model some gentle soothing activities, such as feeling the sand as we dig our fingers into it. The list is potentially endless, and also anything that is "in tune" with Aarya's internal experience is going to be right.

In fact, there are very few "wrong" strategies, which is one reason why trauma-informed practice can never be a tick list of actions or a simple set of things children need. To show this, let's reflect on one of the other children we saw:

> Oleksandr stays close to an adult, sitting quietly, with his arms round his knees.

When you first read that, you might have wondered if it was a typo as I seem to have put in the same child twice! But it is not. We have the same apparent behaviour and a different child. Oleksandr is experiencing the same situation very differently to Aarya, as we can see from our brain map:

Oleksandr	
Stress systems	Wow! Amazing new place
Regulation systems	Hang on, I have no clue what to do here
Action systems	Best avoid getting it wrong See what my keyworker does

This young boy is not scared by the beach. He is amazed by it! This is a completely new experience for him so he does not have anything in his actions menu that matches it. To be sure he knows how to run around, dig, etc. - but not that these are the things to do on the beach. He is not sure the other children are doing the right things, confident as they appear. So he comes up with a sensible solution. If in doubt, do no harm, and take your lead from the grown-ups. So here he sits with us, hugging his knees to stop himself doing anything impulsive.

A "right" strategy for Aarya was maybe to let her have space and come out in her own time with gentle encouragement. This is a "wrong" strategy for Oleksandr who will thus be left mystified and with the idea that sitting doing nothing is the right thing to do. A "wrong strategy for Aarya (cheerful proposal of something to do) is by contrast a possible "right" approach for Oleksandr.

When I talk about this with early education practitioners, a common reaction is "well, obviously!" This is indeed not rocket science, but it is developmental science. It is also one of the most powerful ideas that research has to offer for the development, learning, and wellbeing of everyone in the setting, including the staff. The next section discusses the concept more theoretically.

Mind-Mindedness

One of the mysteries of child development is sometimes called the "transmission gap" (Fonagy & Target, 2005). We know that secure attachment is important - but why? And what exactly is it that parents and other adults do that leads to this security? As with any aspect of human life, the answers are complex and not fully understood. But one key component is carer "mind-mindedness" (Meins et al., 2003). Although it has a somewhat unappealing name, the concept is itself quite simple and intuitive. There are two parts:

- Seeing children as having minds - thoughts, feelings, and plans, etc.
- Responding to these with actions and words that fit with them

The first of these might seem so much common sense that it hardly needs stating. But people do vary in how far they think of children in terms of their thoughts, feelings, and plans. Let's consider how we might think about Jonty at the beach. He rushed off and threw himself into some rather large waves, and we need to do something about it. Here are three different ways of thinking about the same event from three practitioners who are about to deal with it:

Angie thinks . . .	*Bob thinks . . .*	*Cassa thinks . . .*
Jonty's going to be washed out to sea!	Jonty is always flying off into the distance!	Jonty's really excited to see the waves!

All three might well be right. Jonty may well be in danger from the waves, tend to have difficulty controlling his impulses, and is highly likely to be very excited about the visit to the beach. The issue is not whether anyone is wrong, but the responses do differ in how "mind-minded" they are.

To show this, consider a parallel case where the children are playing with a frisbee. A gust of wind catches it and carries it out over the waves. The children look expectantly at the adults to go and get it back for them. Here are three ways of thinking about the frisbee:

Angie thinks . . .	*Bob thinks . . .*	*Cassa thinks . . .*
The frisbee is going to be washed out to sea!	That thing is always flying off into the distance!	The frisbee is really excited to see the waves!

There is something quite understandable about the first two reactions, particularly Bob's if he has spent a wet morning retrieving frisbees from the ocean. But Cassa's thought strikes us as odd! Frisbees don't get excited, or care one way or the other whether they are at the beach or in the park. But children do - and that's the key difference I want to bring out. Angie and Bob are not wrong, but what they are thinking could also be applied to a frisbee. Cassa might not be right (we will see in a moment) but what she is thinking can only be applied to something with a mind. That is mind-minded thinking. And we can see that our normal adult responses to what children do vary in how mind-minded they are.

Does this matter? Sometimes it doesn't at all. Jonty might not be in actual danger, but he is at increased risk, so whatever he is actually thinking we need to reduce that risk. Here are some options for what we might do in that situation:

Run down and lift him out of the sea
Call out to him about the interesting shell we have found
Get into the waves with him, start splashing around, and tempt him to shallower ground
Talk to him about the dangers of the sea

There are many more ideas, and probably better ones, but let's look at some possible outcomes for each if Cassa is right about Jonty being overwhelmed with excitement about the waves:

Strategy	*Possible result*
Run down and lift him out of the sea	Resistance! And he might run back in once we turn our backs
Call out to him about the interesting shell we have found	Takes no notice at all. Who cares about boring shells with these waves?
Get into the waves with him, start splashing around and coax him to shallower ground	He starts joining in with us, and follows our lead into less risky depths
Talk to him about dangers of the sea	Only half listens and goes back to the waves

These are all right things to try, and if Jonty really is at risk, the first one is the only one open to us of course. It is always right to take action in situations of risk. But the question is - what action will make the most long-term difference? Jonty is still excited about the waves, so stern sermons from us about danger might not land.

What's different about the successful approach? It's more fun, but that's not it. The difference is that it matches what is in Jonty's head. The waves are a wonder for him, not a danger. We want him to also realise they can be a danger - but we can only get there if we join him in the wonder first. Once we are "on the same page", he might well be able to hear and listen to our guidance, and be able to accept and follow some limits on how far he goes.

Reflective Activity

Think of a time when you responded effectively to children's unexpected or difficult behaviour. In what ways did you reflect on how they might be experiencing the situation? How did that give you ideas for what might help?

How can we be "mind-minded" when we are under pressure to just "stop it happening"?

"On the same page" is not the best metaphor for this. Being "of one mind" is better – we are mind-minded with children when we consider their thoughts, feelings, and plans, and provide responses that tune into these. What is going on in our brains is then something quite profound, which we explore in the next section. Before we do that, I want to emphasise that mind-minded thinking and practice is not just a "nice thing", but that it has significant impacts on children's development (Aldrich et al., 2021; Bernier et al., 2010).

Co-Regulation

I'm going to demonstrate co-regulation using practical examples rather than theory (for this, see Bornstein & Esposito, 2023; Feldman, 2020; Silkenbeumer et al., 2018). This is for a couple of reasons. Firstly for those unfamiliar with it to show how it is not a different or new set of processes. It's what we do already, perhaps without realising, when we do effective learning with the children about anything from numbers to woodwork. Secondly, because it is easy to pick up the impression that co-regulation is all about calming and soothing children's difficult feelings. That can be so, but it is also much more (Kurki et al., 2016). Let's look at this using a different experience, with literacy.

What Is Co-Regulation?

We've looked at how mind-minded thinking can open up understandings about how children are experiencing a situation and can suggest ways to respond that match this experience. We saw that when we tune in to children's feelings, thoughts, and plans, and respond in a way that matches them, then not only might we solve situations but we can get better short- and long-term outcomes. This is a book about trauma-informed practice, so we naturally tend to consider behaviours or situations that are a problem. But co-regulation is a part of all effective learning, so let's start this section with an ordinary example.

> Marlee (just 3) is reading a picture book with the help of Joseph. They have found a quiet corner of the garden and are sitting together on a blanket. Marlee is entranced by the book, and is insisting on turning the pages, even if her grasp is not quite up to it. So Joseph "helps" her. She points at a picture and Joseph talks about what it is, and describes a story about it. He starts to turn the page, but Marlee puts her hand on it, so he says "you want more about the elephant? Well, look at his big grey ears!" Marlee looks up. Joseph laughs, and says, "yes, they are funny big ears!" And Marlee laughs too.

It's a lovely scene, and a common one in our settings (or if not, it could be – see Chapter 15). It's nothing particularly unusual in this moment of developing literacy through joint storytelling. But it is something pretty special, as indicated by that word "joint". Let's see what Joseph is doing to help Marlee:

- Sitting together with her
- Helping turn the pages
- But not helping too much
- Talking about the picture
- Making a story
- Responding to Marlee's lead

- Expressing Marlee's wish in words
- Laughing

As I say, this is so routine it is easy to miss what is really happening. If we consider what Marlee might be learning from this, however, we can see the depth of the encounter:

What Joseph does	*What this shows Marlee*
Sitting together with her	It's safe and cosy so I can relax and learn
Helping turn the pages	People help me
But not helping too much	Some things I can manage and some I can't!
Talking about the picture	We use words to express thoughts and feelings
Making a story	How to make meaning; things have beginning, middle, and end
Responding to Marlee's lead	I can change what people do; what I want matters to them
Expressing Marlee's wish in words	If I want something, I can say it and this is how
Laughing	This is a really great moment!

This ordinary event is actually quite a profound experience for Marlee. There is a lot of fundamental learning going on, about herself, about other people, and about the world around her. We can connect this to what we saw in Chapter 4 about the general processes of child development, and how these come down to two basic questions:

- What kind of world is this?
- What kind of brain and body do I need to develop to flourish?

With respect to the first question, Marlee is finding out some very useful information about what kind of world she is growing up into. It is a world where we do things together, where adults help, where there are interesting things, where things can be puzzling at first, but this is ok. What is more, we can come to understand them, and there are people who help us do that. More, there is such a thing as calm, gentle fun, and we can get this from reading together. A big part of this seems to be talking, and this makes sense because the world seems quite orderly – it kind of stays still while you are talking about it. Astonishingly, although adults are large and powerful, they also sometimes do what I want, and I can influence this just by letting them know what that is. Oh, and elephants have HUGE ears!

So, for the second question, what kind of brain and body is best to develop so as to match this world and do well in it? Language, for one, so as to be able to have even more of these conversations, and one day be able to enjoy books without needing an adult. Meanwhile, to get there one needs a degree of curiosity and determination, and an understanding that when problems arise they are almost certainly solvable. But is it also a good idea to develop some ways to get help for those things that are too hard for me alone. And since it all seems stable and predictable, then an ability to understand how one thing follows another in sequence will be useful. And so on.

Co-Regulation and Trauma

We can see here how co-regulation helps everyone. We don't know anything about Marlee's past and present life. Perhaps she has these kinds of experiences all the time, in which case, this enjoyable time with Joseph and the elephants is simply what it seems – an effective way to bring her into independent literacy. And it is also reinforcing the development she has had to date in creating stress tolerance and curiosity. It's just good practice for learning and wellbeing. Anyone will be more resilient for future troubles if they have lots of experiences like these. But if Marlee has so far experienced a very different world, exactly the same apparent activity is actually for her a world-changing experience. If it is reliably repeated, and accompanied by many others with the same kinds of messages, then it is also life-changing. So the same approaches to learning can be for some children just good education and for others trauma-informed practice. We don't even need to know which of these children is in which category.

Trauma-informed? But all Joseph was doing was reading a book with her! Let's be clear about what is going on. My metaphor about finding out what kind of world this is might mislead us into thinking this is like finding out what is the capital of Peru, or how to make a sandwich. A parallel adult example might be when I ask where in a huge department store I can find the exit. I didn't know, and now I do. Marlee is not experiencing just this kind of learning - for example that elephants have ears. What is going on is changes at the level of brain systems. Marlee's brain will develop differently because of her experiences with Joseph. Although I don't like comparing children to machines, one way to understand this is that learning that elephants have big ears is like software, while the other kinds of learning going on are changing the underlying hardware. She's not just learning new words and sentences, she is creating the neural structures for those to live in; not just being made to laugh, but developing the capabilities to understand humour and its limits.

The following table shows some of the brain systems being changed by Marlee and Joseph as they explore together.

What Joseph does	*Coordinated brain systems*
Sitting together with her	Stress
Helping turn the pages	Action
But not helping too much	Regulation
Talking about the picture	Action
Making a story	Regulation
Responding to Marlee's lead	Regulation
Expressing Marlee's wish in words	Action
Laughing	Stress

The second column says something essential. We can understand that sitting together with Joseph might be calming for Marlee, but this still understates what is going on. If we could look inside their brains and bodies with some kind of portable scanner, we would see something extraordinary. Marlee is a bit hyped up and fizzy. Joseph is really calm. Marlee's stress system is not at full alert, but it is certainly high enough that it could be tricky to sit still. Joseph's stress system is not at zero either as it is a busy session in the setting, and he is worried about a conversation with a parent later. But Joseph's regulating systems are doing their job well, reminding him that he's had many difficult conversations in the past that have gone well, and transforming his sense of "too much going on!" into a feeling of happy engagement in a job he loves. Marlee's regulating systems are wondering when lunch is.

Co-Regulating Relationships

We can see how this is *co-regulation* rather than just helping or scaffolding by considering whether Marlee could do any of these things by herself:

- Sitting quietly for 15 minutes
- Turning the pages
- Focusing attention for a long period
- Understanding the text
- Knowing what an elephant is

The answer to these is probably not, or not so well and successfully. But Joseph can, and it is this ability that she "borrows" from him. Putting this in terms of the underlying brain systems, we might see:

	Marlee	*Joseph*	*Marlee-with-Joseph*
Stress system	Not sure about this!	Calm and anticipating enjoyment	Sitting quietly for 15 minutes
Regulating systems	What's for lunch?	Sitting together is soothing; talking to maintain interest	Focusing attention for a long period
Action systems	Fumbling pages, puzzling over text	Able to read text, share knowledge	Understanding the text; gaining info

As her brain systems develop, Marlee will gradually be able to do more of this herself. This is the fundamental developmental pattern of co-regulation, that might be summarised thus:

> I do it for you . . . I do it with you . . . You do it with me . . . You do it!

And there is some traffic the other way too. Joseph is also getting some of Marlee's enjoyment and wonder. It's one reason why working in early education can be so rewarding as we get to share the "first time wonder" experiences over and over with different children. Of course we also experience the downs, especially with children who fall into fear and terror and fight/flight/freeze/flop responses. We feel those too, and they can be difficult to manage. For this reason, how we respond habitually to these moments in ourselves is really important, so we will spend a short diversion considering reflective practice.

Being a Reflective Practitioner

We are not machines, and that is a good thing. Children do not need perfection, they need people. There is a lot written about reflective practice in early education, and many approaches to it, but they all come down to the same quite simple principle. This is to be mind-minded for ourselves in the same way as we try to be for the children in our care. So to notice what we do, or feel like doing, be curious about the feelings and needs that are driving it, take a compassionate and kind stance towards this and then make a considered choice about how to respond (Brunzell et al., 2016).

It is not just good for our wellbeing, it can be transformational for us and for the children. Here is an everyday kind of example to illustrate.

> Mia (4) is wobbling across the setting floor with a tray piled high with loose parts. She is nearly at the table, when two other children bustle past carrying a large box. The corner of the box nudges her elbow and acorns, twigs, and small pebbles fly everywhere. Jan, an experienced educator, opens her mouth to say . . .

Assuming we can cope for now with the mild suspense of this cliff-hanger, let's consider what Jan might say. Here, first are some of the things we might hope to say in those circumstances, in the light of what we learned about co-regulation in Chapter 10:

> Oops, it's only an accident
> Well done, you nearly got there
> Mind your feet!
> Oh dear, shall I help you pick them up?
> Are you ok, Mia?

There are many alternatives and other versions, and you might already be thinking of some better responses that those. Here we need to remember that Jan is a grown adult, and so knows a lot of other things too that she could say in these circumstances, such as:

> I give up!
> STAND STILL!
> I've told you not to do that!
> Clear that up!

So, how come she doesn't? (We'll look at the understandable case that she does in Chapter 17) We have met this question before, in Chapter 1, when we were considering how my brain manages in only half a second to create an appropriate and organised response to the appearance of the Loch Ness Monster. Jan would not be human if there were not somewhere in her stress system a little flash of annoyance, surprise, or irritation at what has just happened. But because she is a capable adult, the stress system just creates a little flash because it knows this is no big deal. Her regulating systems soothe even this little twinge, which allows her to draw on her reassuringly extensive range of actions to find what might help.

So far, so easy? This kind of self-regulation happens so many times a day that it is easy to forget that it comes at a cost. We will look at this impact on the practitioner and how we can look after our wellbeing in Chapter 15. These kinds of events are also so routine for skilled adults that they probably are not aware of how hard their brains are working for them. Reflection requires honesty, which requires a compassionate and kind attitude to ourselves. And this can only happen for most people in a working setting that feels emotionally safe.

Co-Regulation in Practice

If we are mind-minded about children, then we start to see not just their amazing developing capabilities but also where by co-regulation we can help them do more than they can by themselves. This pattern of noticing and responding not only enhances the moment but is the same pattern that builds the brain systems that underlie managing for themselves. The same applies whether it is managing a difficulty, or learning a new skill. At its core, we are using our adult brain with all its abilities to help the young brain by providing at least one of the following:

- Soothing stress reactions
- Managing feelings and selecting actions
- Knowing what to do and how

For some examples of each of these, we can revisit that trip to the beach. Aarya was staying close to the adults, wrapping her arms round herself. We could understand this as a flight/freeze response, which tells us that she is not feeling safe. The "picture" of her feelings and thoughts was:

Aarya	
Stress systems	Terror and fear
Regulation systems	Too right! Loud noises, huge space, far from home
Action systems	Freeze!

One of the adults, Bethany, realises this, and brings her own brain along to help. She sits close to Aarya, talking gently about what is happening, mentioning the shiny stones. She puts some of what Aarya might be feeling into words that she can hear:

> "What big noisy waves. I'm a bit scared of them! And a huge beach, I'm not sure what to do".

But Bethany is careful not to come across as trying to "get" Aarya to unfreeze. She is just letting her know that she's there, she understands how Aarya is feeling, and that this is ok. So most of the time, Bethany is just "there" - enough that Aarya can feel it, but not so close that she might go further into her shell. After a while, Aarya looks up at a passing bird. Bethany looks too - "it's a seagull! Enjoying the wind!" Small smile from Aarya. Bethany says, "shall we sit here for a while and listen to the wind?" Aarya nods.

We are still some way from Aarya skipping confidently across the beach, but we have, in trauma-informed terms, travelled a huge distance. She has started to come out of the freeze. With Bethany's help she is noticing more around her than threats, and beginning to see some of those threats, such as the loud wind, differently. Even if this is as far as they get, this is significant learning. How significant, we will see in the next chapter. It's happened because Bethany has used her own calmness and ability to regulate, as well as her knowledge of what it all means. She has done with Aarya what Aarya could not do alone:

Aarya		*Bethany for Aarya*
Stress systems	Terror and fear	Being there to provide a safe base
Regulation systems	Too right! Loud noises, huge space, far from home	Acknowledgment of feelings, gentle explanation
Action systems	Freeze!	Things to do that Aarya can manage

You might notice that there is an order here. Saying "look at the seagull!" while Aarya is locked up in her freeze might work, but only if she is already feeling safe enough to be able to look up and take it in as something other than another threat. Good old distraction, that mainstay of behaviour management, has its limits here. Instead, Bethany works skilfully to help Aarya's stress system realise that while it is still all scary, there is another thing in the equation - namely Bethany - that provides some security. But Aarya still can't quite pull herself out of the freeze, so Bethany meets her halfway, offering regulation by recognising and labelling the feelings, and putting them in a different frame. Only then can the actions systems start to contemplate doing something other than freeze, and can put together a peep at the seagull.

It's exactly the same order as Joseph followed with Marlee in their shared reading. First came the cozy blanket and the physical closeness. Then the help to engage and focus on the book. Then the informational exchange (teaching!). There are two observations to make here. Sometimes it does not take very much to bring children into a sense of safety and self-regulation. Joseph has not done anything that anyone else wouldn't. But also, this is a fundamental step for how things turn out. Marlee might not have engaged so deeply or for so long if he hadn't spent that small effort on co-regulation.

What should be clear by now is that providing positive relationships through mind-minded co-regulation cannot be boiled down to a list of strategies. What we do depends on understanding each situation as each child is experiencing it. This can only be built up over time as we get to know the children and they get to know us. A lot of the time we may well misread what's going on and have to adjust. That is the nature of human relationships. In everyday life with other adults, we make mistakes and correct them all the time. I make a joke in a meeting and nobody laughs, so I realise this is a serious occasion and adjust my approach. Someone calls me, and realises from my response that I'm in the middle of something, so offers to call back later. In fact, getting it wrong and adjusting is in a sense one of the most important things we can do for children, as we will see in the next chapter where we connect mind-minded co-regulation to trauma-informed practice and ideas of "rupture and repair".

Aarya may just be shocked by a new experience; Oleksandr just doesn't know what to do. We have the same apparent behaviours, but a different reason. This is why being mind-minded is so important. It includes reflecting and learning from how children respond to what we try.

> Aarya stays close to an adult, sitting quietly, with her arms round her knees
> Oleksandr stays close to an adult, sitting quietly, with his arms round his knees

So it might be a fair assumption that the two children are having the same experience. We try with Oleksandr what worked for Aarya, but he doesn't seem that interested. He looks politely at the seagull and starts fidgeting. We realise the last thing he wants to do is sit with boring old us, but he is ending up doing this because he is out of other ideas. By responding sensitively (but wrongly) and being mind-minded about why it didn't work, we have got to the right picture of what's going on.

Oleksandr	
Stress systems	Wow! Amazing new place
Regulation systems	Hang on, I have no clue what to do here
Action systems	Best avoid getting it wrong See what my keyworker does

He is fine - he just doesn't know what to do, as he's never been to the beach before! Why doesn't he just copy the other children. Well, given that one is setting off across the ocean, another is eating the sand, and a third has got it in his eyes, Oleksandr is actually making a sensible choice! He still can benefit from co-regulation, though. It's just that he needs it for the action systems - some suggestions what to do, and some guidance and demonstration to help him get the hang of it, or try out to see what he enjoys.

We can see the same processes at work in a successful response to Cal's adventure with the sand. He has got stuck straight into it, digging with his hands. Now he has sand in his eyes and is crying. Let's consider some possible adult responses:

- "I told you not to use your hands and now look what's happened", *or*
- "Come and sit here with me", *or*
- "That looks sore! It'll be better soon. Come and sit here with me", *or*
- "Use your words and count to 10", *or*

In the spirit of the section above on reflective practice, there is nothing wrong with a practitioner occasionally getting exasperated and saying something like the first thing, or needing to resolve a situation quickly and using the second just to get it over with. This isn't about being right or wrong. But it is an invitation to consider what Cal's brain will learn about himself and about the world if some of these responses become part of his normal "diet" when things go wrong. Obviously with a single incident, the table below is a ridiculous exaggeration, but if this is the consistent experience over time, these are possible trends:

Response	*What does Cal's brain learn about the world?*
"I told you not to use your hands and now look what's happened"	I get things wrong, and people are angry with me. I deserve this pain.
"Come and sit here with me"	I've been bad and must be punished.
"That looks sore! It'll be better soon. Come and sit here with me"	People understand, help me make sense of what's happening. Being close to people helps.
"Use your words and count to 10"	There's something I am meant to do, and I can't do it. It's up to me to solve things.

The point here is that co-regulation is also about anticipating the brain states of children. Cal is in pain, for sure. Is he feeling unsafe? Possibly not. But looking at the responses above, which are more likely to make him feel safe, and which unsafe? Part of providing a positive relationship to a child is realising that what seems to "work" from an adult point of view may not work for the child in terms of meeting the actual need. If so, then we not only store up more problems for the future but we miss a key moment of education. In the next chapter we look at how to spot these moments, how to use co-regulation to intervene, and how these can build the learning and skills that all children need, but which are especially essential for those who have experienced trauma.

Chapter summary:

- Mind-mindedness is a useful concept to help us consider how children experience what is happening
- Co-regulation is the first step, and foundation, for any response we might make
- Working in this way can help simplify complex situations and give ideas for what to do

Practice points:

- Consider a situation in terms of children's feelings, thoughts, and experiences of it
- Use co-regulation to meet children where they are as a first step
- Reflect on and manage your own responses to whatever is happening

9

Positive Relationships 2 - Establishing Safety

This chapter will provide:

- An intuitive account of the aspects of positive relationships that make a difference
- Practical details of each of these applied in early education settings
- Guidance on using positive relationships to help children cope with triggers and avoidances

A few years ago I worked in a very friendly office where we took daily turns to make the mid-morning drinks. Although there were only ten of us, the different requirements were very complicated. Tea, herbal, or coffee, caff or de-caff, milk (different amounts), sugar (ditto) - everyone was different, and some even had daily variations. We had a notice pinned up by the kettle listing the preferences, and the main problem was to remember which mug went to whom. Anyone who has cooked for a large family knows a similar set of problems. Some love sprouts, others hate them, or only have them with gravy; others are vegetarian unless it is chicken, and so on.

Providing positive relationships for a group of children is no less complicated. In principle it is simple, so simple it can be reduced to ideas such as love, attachment, positive regard, and so on. But that is like saying "morning refreshments". In practice, each child needs a different mix of ingredients in terms of what we do. And this mix changes depending on what is going on, and how the child is feeling, sometimes from minute to minute.

We can reduce the complexity, and make it manageable, by being clear about what the ingredients are. Then rather than having to create a response in real time, or plan support in advance from scratch, we can think about the basic mix that a child tends to need - just as we can know that a given colleague prefers tea to coffee or doesn't take milk on a fasting day.

The Ingredients of Positive Relationships

Anticipating the possible refreshment requirements of all adults is impossible (just think of all the kinds of tea) but having a basic stock of items means we can cope with most.

DOI: 10.4324/9781003563808-13

Similarly, one could spend chapters and books on the complexities of adults' relationships with children, and the factors that make them positive - let alone trauma-informed (for a good discussion see Williams, 2023). However, there are five essential ingredients that provide what nearly all children need. In different amounts, and with varying levels, children need us to be:

Attuned
Interactive
Available
Approachable
Meaningful

We explored mind-mindedness and co-regulation in the last chapter in some detail and we will apply these to trauma below after sketching out the others above.

Attuned

This is in some ways an out-of-date metaphor, as it refers to being tuned into a child in the same way that we tune in to a station on an old style radio (or "wireless" as my grandmother called it). A better metaphor is to think of two people playing musical instruments. We can tell when those are tuned to each other, and certainly when they are "out of tune"! Applied to children it means that we are providing responses in words and actions that fit what they are thinking and feeling (Atkinson et al., 2016). For example:

Action	*Internal experience*	*Attuned response*
Finn is rolling a car back and forth	Interested in the wheels moving	Do nothing - he's happily absorbed
Gianni is rolling a car back and forth	Not sure what else to do	Start playing alongside with cars and wheels to model
Hamish is rolling a car back and forth	Blotting out difficult feelings, e.g., a noisy background	Being quietly alongside, offering company and comfort

You can see here why being mind-minded is so important. We tune in, not to what a child is doing, but to their internal experience. How do we know, and get this right? The first answer is that we gradually get to know each child. So we learn over time that Gianni likes to have a demonstration to build confidence, while Hamish often needs to block out noise if things get busy around him. The second is by paying attention to the next ingredient.

Interactive

Children are not little machines but interacting human beings. An important way of being attuned is to respond to what they do, having reflected on what it means. This sounds technical and difficult, but it is a normal part of everyday life. Suppose you are in a queue for the bus, and someone joins it next to you. Perhaps you smile and say something about the terrible rain. They smile too, and say how wet they got earlier that day - and you are into a conversation! It turned out they wanted to talk. Or suppose they respond differently, with a nod, and then get busy on their phone - so they don't walk to chat! We learn from how people respond and "re-tune" our responses accordingly. Here's how it might go for Iain, who is the practitioner noticing Hamish rolling the car back and forth:

Thought	*Response*	*Result*
"Hamish is not sure what else to do with the car"		
	Models driving around, "brum brum", etc.	
		Hamish turns away, with lowered head, and carries on rolling
"Ah, now I see, he's doing his blocking out thing"		
	Sits quietly near Hamish, "I'm here buddy"	
		Hamish carries on, knowing Iain is with him

Note that from the face of it, nothing has been solved here. Hamish is still doing what he is doing, and this might be either concerning or convenient. But it is a completely different context. Now there is an attuned adult with him, which as we will see, might make all the difference. By showing attention to Hamish and his emotions, Iain deepens the extent to which he himself is a source of safety to the child (Alamos & Williford, 2020).

Available

First, let's notice something important about what Iain has done here. He has not scooped Hamish up in a big hug, or even touched him. Iain is just nearby, and has let Hamish know this. In other words, Iain is being *available* (Biringen & Easterbrooks, 2012). If this wasn't a book about trauma-informed practice, I might have just called this being "a secure base". But Iain is not doing any comforting, and Hamish is not looking to him for comfort.

Instead, Iain is right where Hamish needs him right now in a balance of being "there" but not "too close". Sometimes, readings of classical attachment theory emphasise closeness and comfort, but a key part of attachment relationships is giving space to explore. It is rather like a stretchy rope connecting child and caregiver. When a child gets too far away - either literally, or in emotional terms - the attachment relationship pulls them back to safety.

This is how it works a lot of the time for a lot of relationships. However it is also too simple for two reasons. Firstly, we all differ in the balance that we need. Or to put it more accurately, we all have different comfort limits of nearness and distance in relationships. And these can change with situational demands. Some people when they face a challenge like to have all their friends around them, on the sofa, making cups of tea and so on. Others want to be left alone to get on with it.

Children are no different. Some want a big and close hug to manage difficult feelings, others need us to give them room. But both groups need the adult to be "there", to be available - just at different distances. If we are too far away (again, either literally or emotionally), they will produce behaviours designed by nature to bring us closer. We've all seen these many times, from crying to tearing things up. If we are too close, they will produce behaviours designed to introduce distance. This might be, as with Hamish, turning away - or even running away - or else wriggling and pushing.

The second reason is that children who have experienced developmental trauma might have quite different scripts and expectations of what a positive relationship looks like. We will explore this in more detail in the last section of this chapter, but one example might be that a child with a lot of experiences of adults as sources of danger might interpret closeness as threat. They are then faced with a catch-22 situation, and so are we. They need us to be closer in order to help them manage a difficult feeling, but the closer we get, the stronger those feelings become. This is solvable, and we will see how below. For now, what we can say is that a key part of providing positive relationships is to realise that what these actually are varies considerably from child to child.

Approachable

As well as being available, children need us to be approachable. In our example above, Iain has let Hamish know that he is there if wanted. There are many ways that we can seem approachable to children, but getting this right relies on two principles. Firstly, that it lies in the eyes of the child, not in our intentions. It is possible to seem too approachable, in that what we intend as an invitation comes across as an obligation. The child feels a loss of control. So some children need the full smiles, body language, cries of "let me help you"; while others might find this too much and need space (Southall, 2024). Secondly, it can't be a means to an end. It's not going to work if we are providing a relationship in order to "get" the child to do something. Children will approach us to meet their needs, not necessarily to follow our agenda. It is, for sure, how we get there, but not if we are using being approachable effectively as a lure.

Here are two scenarios that show the difference. It is really important that Jack puts his coat on to go outside, but he is hanging back. June knows that Jack really loves Fred the Ted, so she starts playing with Fred hoping that Jack will come over.

Scenario 1	Jack comes over and reaches out for Fred the Ted. June takes advantage of him being close to flip the coat over his shoulders and right arm. A struggle ensues over the left arm, and Jack gets away again
Scenario 2	Jack comes over and reaches out for Fred the Ted. June hands him over and they play for a few seconds. June says, "I wonder if Fred wants to go outside on the swings". Jack thinks he does. "Shall we help him put on his coat then?" So they pretend to do that. "Shall we do yours too?" Yes, ok.

We haven't tricked Jack here. We've used the approach to help him feel connected and comfortable. That was his need and agenda. And now he can follow ours.

The key element for being approachable is whether we feel safe and calm to the child. This includes smiling and so on, but the foundation is in our own feelings. An essential part of this is the reflective step of becoming aware of how we are experiencing the situation ourselves, noticing without blame any negative feelings (irritation, boredom, panic) and using our adult abilities to regulate those emotions so that we come across as safe and calm, with all the time in the world should that be needed.

Meaningful

When we talk about positive relationships with children we often focus on the emotional elements, such as the way it feels. But there is another important aspect, which is in some ways the most important. This is the informational content that relationships have. Put less coldly, it is the way positive relationships involve meaning, making both events and the relationship itself meaningful. Children do not necessarily know from the outset what an experience means. How we react and respond will give them important information about this that can, over time, have long-term effects.

> Yara has knocked a jug of apple juice off the snack table and caused a small flood just as the other children are approaching. They start treading in it and spreading it round the setting leaving sticky footprints everywhere.

It's the kind of event that is amusing a few hours or days later when we tell people about it, but at the time there is some pressure on practitioner Scott to stop the mess escalating, clear up the juice and reset the table. But there is something much more important to think about first. Yara is waiting to find out what she has done and what it means - she will use Scott's reaction to help her learn this. Consider two possible responses, and what these might convey to Yara:

Scott's response	*Yara learns . . .*
Scenario 1 Tenses up, frowns Starts speaking loudly. "What have you done? You've made a mess. Just step back, you are making it worse" Starts mopping	I make a mess of things. It is all too hard here. The adults don't help me. I am always in trouble.
Scenario 2 Stays calm, makes eye contact with Yara and gives a small smile "Oops, what an accident! You ok? Did you get any on you?" "Why don't you pick up the jug for me, and I'll just get everything ready?"	Things go wrong sometimes and it is ok! Adults understand me and help me. I can solve problems.

How we relate to children therefore obviously contains vital information when events happen. But this illustrates how meaningfulness is part of a positive relationship all the time. We are never not conveying information to children about us, them, and the world, whenever we interact (or don't interact) with them. Being meaningful is about being purposive about this and reflecting on the messages we are giving.

One of the most powerful ways we can do this is in commenting on children's play in a mind-minded way. So we might talk as we observe or interact, just saying what we see.

Adding commentary about thoughts and feelings in the course of the play adds meaning and depth for the children. For example:

> Emotional commentary:
> "You are loving the feel of the water!"
> "Yuk, it's all wet and makes you feel cold!"
> "I think you are a bit scared of the big tree"
>
> Intentions and desires:
> "You really want to go outside today!"
> "I can see you are trying to build a big tower"
> "I wish we didn't have to stop now, and I think you do too"
>
> Thoughts:
> "You're puzzling out that jigsaw!"
> "I can see you thinking really hard!"
> "You've made a good plan"

As we will see in the next chapter, using this kind of meaningful communication in a positive relationship is one of the most effective ways to help children recalibrate their stress system and develop self-regulation. Of course they can only do this in a context that feels safe to them, so before then we will look at how positive relationships can help with triggers and avoidances, as well as start to change the outcomes for children who have experienced developmental trauma.

Reflective Activity

This can be either an individual or a group exercise if everyone is comfortable to do it. Either consider your own ways of relating with children - in what ways do children experience you as Attuned, Interactive, Available, Approachable, and Meaningful? How do they show you this?

Alternatively, take a few minutes observing each other in pairs. With *positive* feedback only, what elements of being Attuned, Interactive, Available, Approachable, and Meaningful did you see? What were the effects?

Which do you want to develop to do more of?

Managing Traumatic Triggers

Let's apply these core ingredients of positive relationships to helping children manage trigger experiences. In Chapter 2 we looked at how traumatic memories even from long ago can be triggered in the present by events and experiences that provide reminders of the original trauma. When triggered, traumatic memories can come back with all their force, with strong feelings of terror or rage, shutting down thinking and planning. Often they become visible to others when we observe people doing, or trying not to do, various versions of fight, flight, freeze, and flop behaviours.

While we can't predict what might be traumatic for any given person, or whether they will develop traumatic memories after it, we did see that there are three basic elements that make this more likely, which I have called the "trauma triad".

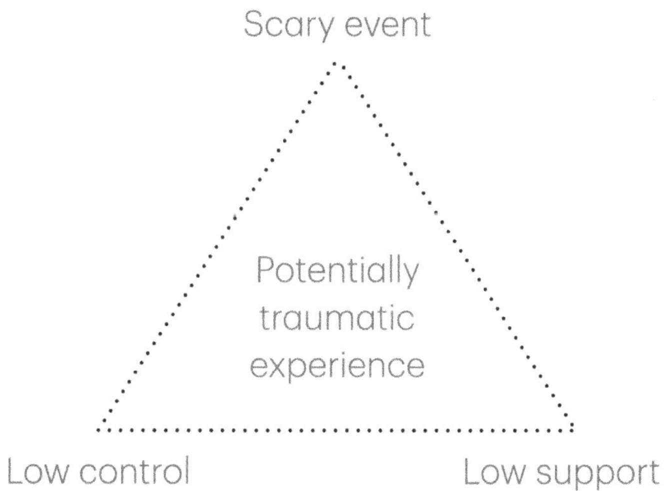

Figure 9.1 The trauma triad

The three elements start with a scary or difficult event. Something is happening that our stress systems read as a significant threat. Recall that this does not have to be something that is objectively life threatening - it is how the person experiences what is happening that makes the difference. A difficult event we can do something about is obviously less threatening than one where we are helpless, so having a sense of low control increases the risk. And if help is available, the event is soon over or more easily dealt with, so ironing fight/flight/freeze/flop responses into a memory is less necessary.

When a traumatic memory is triggered, it feels like it is happening all over again, and the details get "painted" onto the present. We saw this in an example in Chapter 2 over the staffroom coffee machine, but here is a short recap using an early education example. What was happening was that the practitioners would gather a small group of children together as part of a well thought through programme to build vocabulary. The session always started with a song to help the children transition into the activity. As soon as the song started, Lucas would get up and wander off. Let's suppose just for now that we know everything about Lucas, including his experiences of the past and the present. He does in fact have a traumatic memory that is being triggered:

Traumatic memory	*Trigger*	*What it's like*
When Lucas was 3, he and his family got briefly stuck in an elevator between floors. One of the adults screamed.	Lucas is asked to sit in the group of children for a story; it opens with a song	When the song starts, Lucas suddenly feels afraid. That adult is screaming again. He has to get away!

While it is hardly polite to compare his beloved practitioner's singing to an adult screaming in a lift, there is enough similarity for the starting song to be a traumatic trigger. Lucas immediately feels trapped, and his young brain and body do what they are meant to do in order to reduce the perceived danger - flight! Once we recognise this, we know exactly how to help Lucas, having spent that exhausting chapter on the beach looking at mind-mindedness and co-regulation. And we have the ingredients of this chapter to help us do it.

The essential strategy to help children manage trigger experiences is to make them as unlike the trauma triad as we can. There are therefore three lines for intervention, all of which can be used, and which can interact with each other:

Traumatic element	*Adaptations*
Scary event	Can we adapt it to make it less threatening? Or even avoid it altogether?
Low control	Can we introduce more choice and control for the child? But not too much - is the experience actually too open-ended for them?
Low support	Can we make adult support more available? Does the support we are providing match the experience?

Setting it out like this gave lots of ideas for helping Lucas to try, including the following:

Reducing threat:

- Leaving out the song and using a different transitional cue
- Doing some quiet singing with Lucas at other times so he gets used to it
- Giving Lucas the storybook to look at to reduce attention on the song
- Keeping Lucas busy and bringing him in after the song is over

Increasing control:

- Using a song with some actions that Lucas can join in
- Asking Lucas to choose the song
- Letting Lucas choose how close or far away to sit

Low support:

- Having an adult sit close to Lucas
- Offering a hand hold, or a hug on the lap
- Chatting gently to Lucas about how the song will soon be over

Looking at that list, you've probably already thought of other ideas that will almost certainly be good ones as long as they are along one of those three lines. The point I want to bring out here most of all is not so much the "strategies" as how we get there and why they work. The reason for this is that there are thousands of potential trigger situations, and millions of traumatised children, all of whom are different. Trauma-informed practice is just the action element of a way of thinking and relating, and that is where it needs to start.

Positive Relationships Ground Strategies

It's also much more (and in some ways radically different) than "behaviour management". The main reason for this is that absolutely none of those strategies, nor any others we can think of, would have the slightest effect unless Lucas regards the intervening adults as sources of safety. An obvious way to show this would be to suppose that the adult we choose to sit next to him and hold his hand is a stranger he has never met before - how well is that going to work?

So let's look closely at what is happening in terms of mind-mindedness and co-regulation.

Mind-Mindedness

It would be easy to describe what is happening using "frisbee" type concepts and language (see Chapter 8 for what this means!). So Lucas could be seen as a boy who "can't sit still for a story", or "doesn't comply with requests". Both of these are of course in some ways true. But mind-mindedness is not prepared to stop there. We understand children, and what they do, in terms of thoughts and feelings. Using our knowledge of trauma, we recognise an element of flight in the behaviour, and so a good first hypothesis is that Lucas for some reason finds the story situation scary or unpleasant.

Co-Regulation

We also get from this a picture of what is going on in Lucas's brain. His young stress system is sounding the alarm. His regulating systems are confirming this. Both due to the level of stress and Lucas being only 5, they are not able to soothe the stress system, or to prevent a flight response, though they do turn it down from running away screaming to wandering off unobtrusively. And his action systems only know one thing to do about all this, which is to get away.

As adults we can help Lucas's brain out here. This is what co-regulation is. So we can reduce the stress response using our calmness, assist the regulation systems to soothe and manage actions, and find better solutions for the action systems to try - and help them do them. Here are the same strategies set out as co-regulation:

Stress system *(making it less bad)*	*Regulating systems* *(managing the bad)*	*Actions systems* *(doing what we need)*
Leaving out the song and using a different transitional cue Doing some quiet singing with Lucas at other times so he gets used to it Chatting gently to Lucas about how the song will soon be over	Having an adult sit close to Lucas Offering a hand hold, or a hug on the lap Asking Lucas to choose the song Letting Lucas choose how close or far away to sit Giving Lucas the storybook to look at to reduce attention on the song	Keeping Lucas busy and bringing him in after the song is over Using a song with some actions that Lucas can join in

We will see quite why this is so important in the next chapter. This is unlikely to be the only trigger in Lucas's life, and over the years ahead he will face many more. It will be a smaller life if he has to avoid music, concerts, elevators, you name it. But he doesn't, because as educators there is so much we can do to grow his capabilities to manage triggers, and even to help him process away some of the steam pressure in the original memory. Co-regulation is a key part of that as we will see soon.

Before we leave Lucas and his friends, though, I want to bring out how it is the elements of positive relationships, not the actual strategies, that are doing the real work here. For example, it is quite possible that the staff could have made the mind-minded judgement that Lucas was bored rather than scared. They might have then tried to make the event more interesting – perhaps including a livelier song and providing instruments for the children. It's a good strategy if Lucas were indeed bored, but is actually likely to deepen the stress and make flight even more urgent. By being *attuned*, they were able to read him correctly and come up with a response. Having got this far, they might have tried a strategy such as having an adult give Lucas a hug, only to find that he wriggled away. They might have concluded that this psychologist was talking nonsense and he was not scared at all, as comfort did not work. Alternatively, they could have stayed *interactive*, realising that Lucas's response to the hug is telling us that he found it confining, not comforting. As a result, they put their efforts into being *available* to Lucas, so that he could set how close was too close for comfort. They resisted the natural tendency to find the whole thing trying, and an instance of poor behaviour that needed to be controlled. As a result, they stayed *approachable* to Lucas, making clear they were there for him, trying to understand and help. Lastly, they wrapped whatever they did in *meaningfulness* using gentle words, explaining what was happening, naming how he might be feeling, and what they were trying to do.

So we have three frameworks for thinking how to support children with trigger experiences. We can use the trauma triad to consider how to make an experience less difficult, how to increase a child's sense of control, or make it easier for them to feel helped. Or we can reflect on what is happening in terms of a highly responsive stress system that we can soothe, overwhelmed regulating systems that we can assist, or a lack of suitable actions that we can suggest and support. Finally, we can consider how we can stay attuned, interactive, available, approachable, and meaningful to the children. Each of the three is trauma-informed and each of them can lead us to solutions worth trying when we encounter behaviours with elements of fight, flight, freeze, or flop, whether those are driven by traumatic memories or not. You might find one of them more useful than the others, which is fine. Or one might be better in your setting for some situations and not for others.

Managing Avoidances

> Minh seems happy enough in the setting, engaging with all kinds of different activities and playing well with the other children. He has made some good friends. But he tends to avoid the adults. If one comes over to what he is doing, Minh somehow disappears. If forced to interact, he looks away, talking very softly and wriggles off as soon as he can.
>
> Elspet is the life and soul of the setting, always up for playing with other children, and taking an enthusiastic part in group activities. But she won't go outside! If taken out,

> either individually or in a group, she finds an opportunity to nip back in again. If staff keep the door closed, then she hangs back close to it and refuses to engage in anything.
>
> Aled does not seem unhappy, but he is not that happy either. It is like he goes through the motions of play. He's perfectly cooperative, doing anything he is asked to. But there seems to be no enjoyment, in fact no feeling at all. Staff describe him as lacking empathy since he shows little reaction to other children's feelings either.

The first two are obvious avoidances. Minh is avoiding adults, and Elspet is avoiding the outdoors. They are also avoidances that are not really adaptive. We need to do something to address them as they might start to cause real problems for the children themselves and for those working with them. Aled might be more of a puzzle until we recall from Chapter 2 that dissociation can be a way of coping with traumatic memories. Instead of physically avoiding triggers, people can "shut down" their emotions so as to avoid the strong feelings that triggers bring.

Thinking about the trauma triad for each child can help us to think of ways to help. Ideally, one day we want the children to be able to regulate the feelings for themselves so that they can feel safe enough to do what they need or want to. But we are still at the stage of helping them establish a sense of safety so we have to do more of the work. The triangle has three elements that sustain it - a difficult experience (the thing they are avoiding), a feeling of low control over what is happening, and a lack of accessible help.

Increasing Subjective Control

This is sometimes a difficult one to explain. After all, children who are avoiding experiences or people are already exercising quite a lot of control! We might sometimes hear them described as "ruling the roost" or being "in charge". It is an understandable reaction from worried or exasperated adults. But the trauma-informed step is to look from within the child, to see the situation through their eyes. For both Minh and Elspet there is pressure to do something, either because they are picking this up from us or because they are noticing what other children are doing and realising they are expected to do the same. But this is not the main loss of control that matters, even if reducing this pressure would be helpful. The principle lack of control here is over what happens when they meet the trigger - a flooding of terror and/or rage, plus sometimes horrible memories, that they cannot stop.

We can help them with this by finding ways for them to have some control over how much they expose themselves to the trigger they are avoiding. So for Minh, we might come closer to him, but still outside the distance that is his limit. Then leave it up to him to approach us. He might not immediately or for some time. But what might happen at the same time is he gradually will let us closer. It is important not to take this too quickly as we might end up back where we started if Minh feels forced. For Elspet, we can leave the door open so she can follow us out if she feels she can. Or we could give her some choice over what we are going to do when we are outside, or where we are going to do it. She might love to sit and have a story, for example, nice and close to the door back inside. Or she might, once she's got there, love to climb the tree; so being able to choose in advance that this is what she is going to do will reduce the uncertainties and uncontrollables. For Aled, we might stop trying to elicit or expect emotional expression, but instead offer some low key and mildly enjoyable things to do, gently labelling the experiences as we are sharing them. Look out for the small smile, or just the inclination of the body that shows he is enjoying it too, and don't make a big deal out of this (while high fiving yourself in your head).

Making It Less Difficult

This again can be difficult ground for the practitioner. How can it be that being with me can be a trigger for Minh when I do my best to be kind and caring? We've created this lovely outdoor area - how can Elspet not like it? And we are great at understanding and managing children's emotions - why can't Aled trust us? The answer is that Minh knows we are kind, Elspet loves what's out there, and Aled does trust us. But the traumatic fear is greater than all of those, and it overshadows them.

Successful strategies all involve making the trigger less of a trigger. Perhaps Minh will come closer to an adult if the practitioner is doing something he is particularly drawn to. It might be anything from drawing a picture to counting beans in a tin. The interest and positive emotion balances the fear down sufficiently that he can manage it. But keep the control with him - let him come as close as he feels he can manage. It might be best not even to notice. But with many different such experiences over time, we might find he joins us, and has forgotten it was ever a problem. For Elspet, that tree did not just give her control, it made the outdoors less scary. Alternatively, there might be a particular friend she would like to go out with. Or making the experience shorter (and guaranteed to be shorter) might make it feel more manageable. For Aled, maybe he's ok just hanging in there without us adding an additional expectation onto him.

Increasing Support

The question here is not whether there is support. Of course there is. The issue is whether the child can feel it and access it. With Minh this looks difficult as he is avoiding the main tool we have for supporting children - co-regulation with an adult. But there are other supports, such as his peers. Maybe he can manage being with an adult if he is in a group, or a pair. Nobody is doing anything, it is just the support of other people around. Elspet might need an adult's help just to get as far as the tree, or to set the timer, and then she is fine. Aled might appreciate us labelling the emotions he is probably feeling deep down, of enjoyment and interest.

Support becomes more essential when the thing being avoided is something we really do need to do. Minh might need to sit with the nurse for a checkup; Elspet has to go out to the minibus. Children will often go along with these things but suffer inside, which will only reinforce the avoidance. If, however, they can manage to do the feared thing, with help, then this will build their coping skills. More on this in Chapters 12 and 13.

Beyond Coping

In this chapter we have explored the detailed ingredients for positive relationships and interactions. The more we can stay attuned, interactive, available, approachable, and meaningful, the more children will feel safe, seen, understood, and supported. This can help them to manage triggers and avoidances, but also sets the essential backdrop to anything else we want to do to help them grow and develop. But it is about much more than simply coping in the moment, or managing a difficult behavioural response. We are also changing children's worlds and, as a result, changing their futures. This is the topic of the next chapter, and why it matters so much for children who have experienced developmental trauma.

Chapter summary:

- Children need to feel that we are attuned, interactive, available, approachable, and meaningful
- Putting these into practice may vary by child and situation, and we can use their responses to guide us
- Positive relationships provide the means for children to cope with intrusions and avoidances

Practice points:

- Reflect in the moment and in planning on the quality of relationships that are being provided
- Take your lead from how children respond to what you do
- Use the elements to help children cope with intrusions and avoidances

10

Positive Relationships 3 - Changing Children's Worlds

This chapter will provide:

- Information on how positive relationships start to change the impact of developmental trauma
- A template for planning experiences and interactions to achieve this
- Practice examples to illustrate the large effects of small actions

The paramount need for children who have experienced trauma of any kind is to provide them with a sense of physical and psychological safety. Nothing can help without this, and if it can be established it can change the course of a lifetime. In Chapter 9 we saw that young children derive most of their safety from the adults around them, both in terms of ensuring their world actually is safe, and in helping them cope with any pressures that arise. In Chapters 8 and 9 we have looked at the building blocks of positive relationships that bring this about. The fundamental concepts of mind-mindedness and co-regulation are about becoming aware of, and responding to, children's inner experiences of situations that challenge them. The practical ingredients of positive relationships, such as being attuned and available, show us how to co-regulate with children. We then applied these tools to some examples of traumatic triggers and avoidances to see how we can help children manage these more adaptively.

But this is not enough. Firstly, we have an opportunity as early educators, when children's brains are still undergoing rapid and radical development, to make more of a difference. We can help children learn and practise how to manage for themselves, and to develop the capabilities that will provide resilience against future troubles. Often this is not much more than ordinary play experiences, with sometimes an added element of co-regulation. Chapter 8 showed the wide range of development that we can nurture, from self-regulation to curiosity, creativity, and joyfulness. Some practical ideas for all of these are in the next chapter. And because these are skills all children will need, whatever their experiences to date, it makes sense for the whole setting to be trauma-informed, and we will see what this means in Chapter 13.

DOI: 10.4324/9781003563808-14

The second reason providing management of difficult moments is not enough is that for many children trauma goes deeper than a small number of traumatic memories. In Chapter 6 we saw how if traumatic experiences occur early enough and often enough, then children's brains and bodies start to make long-term changes in how they develop. To recap, I presented a stark contrast between two otherwise similar children growing up in very different contexts - one is a difficult and dangerous one, and the other is mostly safe and manageable. The table shows how development might differ for the two boys:

	Diego	*Daniel*
What kind of world?	Difficult & dangerous	Mostly safe & stable
Language & communication	Act rather than talk Reduced language	Express needs & negotiate More language
Cognitive development	Rapid assessments Concepts for action Coping with randomness In the moment	Deepened thinking Complex concepts Cause & effect Reasoning about future
Executive function	Scanning environment Changing focus often Low impulse control	Controlled focus and attention Higher impulse control
Stress regulation	Vigilant, reactive	Calm, self-soothing
Social and self	Negative expectations Self-reliance Reduced help seeking	Positive expectations Confidence Help seeking

It is important to remember, as we saw, that there is nothing "wrong" with Diego. His brain and body are doing their best to adapt to the world he is growing up in. It is the fact that this is a very different world to the ordered, calm, and loving one of our settings that makes him seem disordered. And it is Daniel's developing profile that best fits the needs of the modern world and workplace, so he is meeting all his milestones on the way towards that. Diego is growing up towards something else, with his brain and body prioritising short-term survival.

It is also important to remember that this is not learning in the same way that I can learn the best route to drive from New York to San Francisco, or that the capital of Myanmar is Nay-pyidaw. These processes are not about storing information in the brain, but about changing the way the brain itself develops at the most basic level of the networks between brain cells. Daniel and Diego have different looking brains, if we could see at that level of detail.

How to Change the World

In Chapter 4 we met Jessica, who was having a difficult time with a muddy puddle. We left her waiting for help while we gathered the tools but are now ready to see what she needs and how we can provide it.

> Jessica goes outside with her group after a few days of rain. One corner of the yard which used to be a nice square of grass has become a swamp. Jessica hangs back and watches as another child recklessly jumps into the middle of the muddy puddle and

creates a wild spray of yucky, cold water. Some gets on her face, and some on her coat. She shrieks and runs back inside.

Without knowing much more about Jessica right now, let's think about what might help her. I'm going to phrase that in what might seem a slightly curious way, but which will turn out to be a helpful approach with children who have experienced developmental trauma:

What do we want Jessica to discover:

- About the world?
- About us?
- About herself?

When I do this as an activity with early educators, we tend to come up with ideas like this. You will probably think of several more too.

About the world?	This is an interesting place Surprises can be good as well as bad Clothes and people clean up, no harm done If I say what's wrong, people are pleased and help me
About us?	Adults help children Nobody gets cross when children are playing We know what to do We notice when children need things and do it
About herself?	I can have fun I can manage new surprises I am worth caring for I don't have to be in trouble

So far, Jessica's story is not that different to many children. I still remember an encounter of my own, aged 4, when I fell into a deep pool of mud! For nearly all children a one-off experience of getting cleaned up, and a bit of encouragement, will see them splashing around in the freezing puddle again like there never was a problem.

But we notice that Jessica remains avoidant of the puddle, and indeed of any kind of messy play or risk of spills, drops, and accidents generally. We notice that any sudden surprising change, even a good one, can be difficult for her, that she is reluctant to seek our help even when she obviously needs it, and shies away when we approach her. Jessica stays within tightly defined bounds, only doing what she knows. These are important observations. The trauma-informed step is to ask ourselves the following question:

What does it seem Jessica has discovered so far:

- About the world?
- About adults?
- About herself?

It is clear that, at least in outline, it is the opposite of what we want her to discover following the puddle experience. To sum this in one table, we have:

	Jessica has discovered	*We want her to discover instead*
About the world?	There are lots of threats A surprise is probably a bad thing Getting messy is a very bad disaster There is no way to get help It is bad to need help	This is an interesting place Surprises can be good as well as bad Clothes and people clean up, no harm done If I say what's wrong, people are pleased and help me
About us?	Adults make things worse They get angry when I play wrong It's up to me to sort things out	Adults help children Nobody gets cross when children are playing We know what to do We notice when children need things and do it
About herself?	Having fun is risky I can't manage anything new I'm not worth caring for I deserve to be in trouble	I can have fun I can manage new surprises I am worth caring for I don't have to be in trouble

We can then take this one step deeper and consider how Jessica's brain might have developed so far in order to cope with the world she has been living in. Her stress system will be based on the default assumption that anything unexpected is likely a threat. Regulating systems are designing themselves to inhibit any exploration to avoid threats, and to rely on her own resources, limited as they are, if threats appear. Her working model for relationships is that they are risky, and likely to go badly for her. There is therefore no point developing social scripts, apart from doing her best to please everyone. But this is not because she is a good person, but in order to survive. It is a little different to Diego above, because Jessica lives in a different world to Diego. But just as with Daniel and Diego, Jessica's brain is making long-term changes to how it develops. It is not difficult to look ahead and imagine how Jessica might be as an adult and how life might be for her.

Unless . . . What if Jessica has some encounters that give her developing brain cause to change course. What if she has experiences and interactions that show her something different? That is where we come in, because an early education setting is just the place where this can happen. Let's look at what we want the developmental messages to be again, but consider in how many ways we can provide these without actually doing anything particularly difficult or expensive - and certainly nothing outside our core roles. For example, Jessica's stress system has a strong association between getting messy and high levels of fear. The answer here is not to provide her with lots of messy play so she gets used to it! That is simply confirming her brain's view that the world is full of threats. What is worse, it is removing any control from her as to what she does, making it even more difficult being stuck doing these terrifying things.

What we can and need to do also goes beyond managing one incident. The point here is not the mess, the running away, or getting Jessica to love puddles. We want to change her whole worldview so that her brain will decide it is safe and ok to take a different developmental pathway. So whatever we do needs to be consistent across all areas of her life. There are limits on what we can do here, as Jessica also has a life away from our setting. But there is much that we can do. Here are some basic ideas – if you can think of others that convey the same messages, then that is great.

What we want to show Jessica's brain	*Ways we could do it*
This is an interesting place	Offer a range of low key and gently interesting things to do Letting Jessica make the choices whether and how much to engage
Surprises can be good as well as bad	Keep things as routine and regular as we can Introduce very small variations (e.g., a new book to read together if she likes reading; or a new colour for the paint) Tell Jessica about these in advance and explain what and why Support her through the change
Clothes and people clean up, no harm done	Model clearing up some small spills etc. that Jessica has not been involved in Ask her if she'd like to help and praise her when she does Let Jessica see other children getting messy and then cleaning up
If I say what's wrong, people are pleased and help me	Model this out loud with other children and adults ("can you help me carry . . .") Ask Jessica to help you with things (that she can manage)
Adults help children, notice when they need this and know what to do! I am worth caring for	Notice when she has a need herself, and talk through how you notice it, interpret it, and meet it
Nobody gets cross when children are playing I can have fun I don't have to be in trouble	Share joy and laughter gently in the course of play When "things" happen, stay approachable, label them as accidents, and talk about how you are solving them Notice and label the good things that Jessica does, especially when she learns something new or overcomes an obstacle (start with literal ones, such as moving a chair or climbing a step)
We know what to do	All of the above

The main thing to take from this list of ideas is absolutely not "these are the strategies to use with children who have experienced developmental trauma"! These might be great things to do for Jessica, and some of them will overlap for other children. But every child is different, and their brain will have acquired different models of the world that they are adapting to. What the list does illustrate is that the ways we can change those messages about what kind of world this is are often quite simple and easy to do. When they are consistently part of the world that we provide for a child, then their course of development will begin to change in ways that have impact for decades and into the next generation.

A Simple Map for Helping

Can we make all this even simpler? If the actions are simple, this is quite an effortful process of describing a whole world model and thinking out how to change it. It's also a process where a certain amount of confidence is needed (but also not too much). The answer is that yes we can, and in a way that gives us a useful template for planning provision and interventions.

So far in this chapter and Chapter 4, I've been showing how children adapt their long-term development to do as well as they can in the world where they find themselves. It's time to show *how* they find that out. There are basically four "channels" of information. Remember that this is not information in the sense of looking up a bus timetable, or being told the key events of the French Revolution. It is the brain scanning the world through what happens to the child, and how the people in it respond to what the child does.

Imagine you are on holiday and are looking for a restaurant for lunch. Most people make quite a quick judgement as to whether to go in, and whether to stay. We glance at the menu and, if what is on it appeals to us, we walk in - and either walk straight out again or decide to stay. Let's suppose the latter. What kinds of information have influenced our decision? Well, the menu might have contained things we liked and knew. Perhaps there is also something fresh and new to consider, but not too outlandish. We are intrigued. We open the door and lovely cooking smells reach us. Yum. It's a cool room away from the hot sun, too. The staff acknowledge, welcome, and smile at us. We feel comfortable and sit down. Here are the four channels of information we used:

- Nice smelling food! Pleasantly cool room
- Welcoming staff
- New things, but not too new
- We understood the menu!

In much the same way, children's brains assess what the world is like using the same channels. The first is about the physical environment and care - this can for children literally be about whether there is food they need. The second is about the kinds of relationships that are offered. The third is about the kinds of stressors that are available. Like the interesting menu, it is about having some "spice" but not too much. For children, this means moderate and resolved stress as we will see below. And the fourth is about whether the things to do satisfy what the developing child needs, whether it combines being do-able with also containing manageable challenge.

Here, then, is our map for intervention. We can influence children's adaptation by providing messages about what the world is like by using four channels. Here they are, expressed more formally.

- Physical environment and care
- Positive relationships
- Moderate and resolved stress
- Developmentally appropriate stimulation

We covered positive relationships in the previous two chapters, and the next chapter is all about developmentally appropriate stimulation. So here we will look at the other two, making links between what we might observe and what we can do.

Physical Environment and Care

In Chapter 8 we met some children on an expedition to the beach, including one who was doing something rather concerning:

> Martha squats down and starts eating the sand

More observations can reduce the mystery. Staff have noticed that Martha tends to grab food as soon as she sees it, and this can extend even to items that are not food but could be. There are a lot of problems at snack time, as Martha struggles with waiting and sharing, and can become very distressed if staff try to support her to do so.

We can use the approach of this chapter so far, by asking the question:

What does this suggest Martha has learned so far about:

- The world?
- The adults in it?
- Herself?

The most natural answer to these questions might be that Martha has picked up that food supply is not to be relied on, so it is best to grab it while one can. As a result, her brain has developed less inhibition and reduced the resources directed to learning social skills such as sharing. She's not going to be able to learn those skills until we have convinced her brain that it is ok to do so. And that is only going to happen if there is a regular and reliable source of food, as often as Martha's brain feels it is needed.

The other answer we can consider from our observation is that Martha has experienced a world where adult help is also unreliable. Her "self-service" approach to food suggests not selfishness but excessive self-reliance. Her development is proceeding to prioritise looking after oneself, rather than relying on others. Again developmental resources go into this kind of problem solving, rather than into the language and social cognition that underpins negotiating, cooperation, and expressing needs. So it is not just about providing food as it were on trays for her to pick up. We need to make this relational, to establish patterns for her where adults notice her needs and fulfil them. In this way, on the beach, one of the practitioners gently touches her arm and says, "I think you are hungry, Martha?" And offers her a small (and healthy) snack, sitting with her while she eats it. This starts to push back at what Martha might have learned about herself, which is that she is not worth helping. But she is worth helping, of course - and this is what we are showing her.

This example is about physical care in terms of food, which is an obviously basic need that can be disrupted by different kinds of adversity and trauma, including neglect, but also family poverty or chaos. There are other aspects of the physical environment that provide the developing brain with information about what the world is like and how to adapt to it. For example, a young brain that experiences consistently safe and adequate shelter to live in will adapt differently to one that is growing up with constant moves or unsafe housing. Warmth, cold, and protection from the sun are all basic physical care needs, as is adequate sleep. So we can summarise what this channel might contain as follows:

Is there enough food?
Is there safe shelter/spaces?
Do these stay constant day to day?
Am I looked after when too hot, cold, or ill?
Is there time and safety for rest and recuperation?
Is the world generally stable?

There are many ways in which our education settings can provide positive answers to those questions for all children, but particularly for those who have been building alternative models of the world with less positive answers. Here are some ideas:

Is there enough food?	A regular and expectable supply of healthy food Noticing and responding to children's levels of hunger and energy between these Keeping up hydration
Is there safe shelter/spaces?	At least parts of the setting that are "soft" with comfortable and comforting contents (cushions, rugs, etc.) Some actual shelters such as a tent or a booth Making sure children know of these and how to use them; with easy access as wanted General good repair about the setting - an environment that conveys value to the children
Do these stay constant day to day?	Introducing changes slowly and gradually Involving the children in planning changes Providing narrative to explain any changes
Am I looked after when too hot, cold, or ill?	Noticing needs as soon as they arise and taking action Talking children through what is happening so they can build a narrative and connection
Is there time and safety for rest and recuperation?	Balance of interesting activity and rest times Some children may need naps at a later age than usual Some quiet spaces where children can just chill
Is the world generally stable?	A similar routine and rhythm to each session Advance cues for internal transitions, with support to manage as needed (see Chapter 12)

As a last point, some readers might be wondering why these items are in a chapter on positive relationships? There are two reasons. Firstly, from a child's point of view, a relationship is not so much about how people feel as what happens. How we provide sensitive and responsive physical care for them conveys a lot of information about the kind of relationship we have. Secondly, this is the more the case for the younger the child, and many children who have experienced trauma, especially developmental trauma, are effectively operating with "younger" brain systems. We will see more about this in the following chapter, but what it means here is that these forms of care will speak particularly clearly to them.

Moderate and Resolved Stress

It might seem strange in a book about trauma-informed practice where the *emphasis* throughout is on ensuring children are safe and feel safe, that there is a section on providing them with stress. It is important to be very clear about what is meant here (Gunnar et al., 2009). Let's start with a very early example - peekaboo!

Peekaboo is a wonderful game in all kinds of ways. The usual version is that a parent or carer having engaged the baby's attention then hides their face with their hands. After a second or two, they open their hands, opening their eyes wide and going "here I am!" or "boo!" Babies love this game and seem willing to do this for hours. It's fun, for sure, but not that much fun - so what's the attraction? The game is providing something critical for development, and we are designed to seek out these experiences when we are small. For a baby, peekaboo contains a rollercoaster of stress. All is well, and then the beloved caregiver vanishes! The baby is all alone in a wild and difficult world, how will she cope? And then they are back - what joy and relief!

Of course most babies have got the idea quite early and have learned the narrative of the game (ok - not ok - ok again). So their experience of it is not so much actual danger as the kind of thrill that adults get from watching crime investigation box sets. We know the bad guy will be caught, but there is still a thrill in following the story. That's the point. These early experiences build a core concept, or schema, for how the world works:

> ok - not ok - ok again

Again I have to stress this is not an idea or information in the same way that I can learn how to make a pancake. It is about how the brain systems become structured - it becomes "wired in". If I show you a garden fork, even if you have never seen one before you can work out roughly what it does from the shape and materials. If I show you a feather duster you can do the same. They look totally different, so they do different jobs. If I show you a child's regulating systems built around the schema [ok - not ok - ok again] you could similarly tell me: "oh, that's for dealing with small setbacks that pass". If I show you a different child's regulating system that is built around a different schema [ok - not ok - stays not ok], you'd be able to tell me that this is for dealing with bad things that go on and on without relief.

In fact I am showing you inside the brains of Diego and Daniel. Daniel has had lots of experiences of manageable stress that gets resolved. It started with peekaboo and continued via getting used to broccoli to having his toddler tantrums sensitively managed, and then his scraped knee cared for. His brain therefore built a model of the world where the schema [ok - not ok - ok again] really works well. So that is his script for reacting to stressors. Hopefully you can see that this is an optimistic and resilient approach. Diego has been growing up in a different context where bad things often go on and on. Sometimes things get better, but often they don't - for example an ongoing major stressor such as violence in the home or community or neglect, or a simple lack of resources. So his brain needs to get ready for a world in which this is the general rule, in which case the schema [ok - not ok - ok again] is the one to major on. This is a less optimistic and, in our context, less resilient regulating system.

Two more points are important. Firstly, the growth of the [ok - not ok - ok again] schema depends on the "not ok" experiences being manageable. If the stressor is overwhelming, then the stress system will just go straight to high alert and fight/flight/freeze/flop responses with no other processes going on. In which case all that grows is the schema:

> [ok - REALLY bad - stays bad till it stops]

Instead of Diego's pessimistic sense that life sucks and is likely to continue to do so, we have a regulating system built on the assumption that everything that goes wrong is a catastrophic threat - and that anything that happens is more likely than not to go wrong. Let's meet one of these children:

> Sonny is a gentle child who is no trouble at all, indeed very anxious to please. He tends to "play it safe", avoiding any new experiences. But when even a small thing goes wrong, like being told he can't have another banana slice, or if his tower of blocks falls over, he becomes a different child - a major tantrum with streams of tears and flying fists

We can understand these moments as triggers and won't go far wrong. But it also seems to be a more general pattern of avoiding any small thing going wrong, and then not coping when it does. Sonny is also much more focused than most on keeping things even with the adults, going out of his way to be "good". It is tempting to think, "well, a basically easy child who will grow out of the tantrums". Maybe. But if he does not, life is going to be very difficult. Even learning to read involves experiences of challenge, as does making new friends - and both of these are harder if any setback sets off a catastrophising response.

Changing the Course of Development

We can look one step deeper with Sonny by asking our key question, and reflecting on possible answers. Here are my thoughts:

What does this suggest Sonny has learned so far about:	
The world?	It is full of things that can go wrong When things go wrong, this is a major threat
The adults in it?	I've got to please them at all costs . . .
Himself?	I can't solve anything (Perhaps also - I'm a bad out-of-control person)

Sonny, like all the children in this book, is based on a real person, but I am not going to give you the full story as we often do not know this. But we can see from this brief reflection what he might need from us. We can provide different messages with different answers to those questions:

What do we want to show Sonny about:	
The world?	There are lots of low risk things to do (and enjoy!) Most times things go wrong, it doesn't matter that much and we can solve it
The adults in it?	There are adults who love you whatever Ups and downs are part of any relationship - it's the solving problems that matters, not the going wrong
Himself?	You can solve lots of things, especially if adults help you You're a great kid - learning to live and be you just like everyone else

Reading that list you are probably already thinking of ways you would do that. A good start would be to go along with Sonny's immediate need of the safe and familiar for a time, and then start to gently introduce some novelty. Maybe leave the door open and see if he goes outside? Or introduce a new item into the loose parts, modelling what to do with it and telling him what it is. We might build his tolerance to "things happening" by introducing occasional nice experiences, and so on. And notice and label for him the times that he is already solving problems - even if it is tiny things such as pouring some water, putting on a coat, or moving some items out the way so he can get at what he wants. We might then think of some problems to offer him that we know he might be able to solve - maybe a new route for the tricycle, an obstacle course, or just making a slightly higher tower of blocks.

What is going on at the brain level is extremely important so at the risk of too much oversimplification, let's look at it briefly. Firstly, a parallel example to show how it works. Imagine I have a drawer containing nine pairs of socks, all of them grey. Here's a very rough picture of my drawer:

Grey socks	Grey socks	Grey socks
Grey socks	Grey socks	Grey socks
Grey socks	Grey socks	Grey socks

I am not that with-it in the mornings, so it is basically a matter of picking random socks without really looking. What are my chances of picking out some blue socks? Zero. There aren't any. Now suppose my partner, knowing how things are, replaces one of the grey pairs with a blue pair, what are my chances now? We can see from a picture of my re-arranged drawer:

BLUE SOCKS	Grey socks	Grey socks
Grey socks	Grey socks	Grey socks
Grey socks	Grey socks	Grey socks

Hopefully it's easy to see it is 1 chance in 9. Suppose instead that all of the socks are replaced before tomorrow with blue pairs. I am now certain to pick out the colour I wanted!

Now for the neuroscience version (Ryan et al., 2017). Imagine a really simplified version of Sonny's regulation system that instead of socks has nine connections to the action systems. What Sonny does depends on which of these connections is activated (used). Here's a rough brain scan of the pathways in Sonny's brain:

[ok - REALLY bad - stays bad till it stops]	[ok - REALLY bad - stays bad till it stops]	[ok - REALLY bad - stays bad till it stops]
[ok - REALLY bad - stays bad till it stops]	[ok - REALLY bad - stays bad till it stops]	[ok - REALLY bad - stays bad till it stops]
[ok - REALLY bad - stays bad till it stops]	[ok - REALLY bad - stays bad till it stops]	[ok - REALLY bad - stays bad till it stops]

Sonny's brain has built these nine pathways in order to adapt to the world as he has experienced it so far. We see the results in our setting. But we are providing lots of experiences that don't fit, including some of the ideas above, but many more too. If there are enough of these, and they happen consistently enough, then Sonny's brain will start to assess that sometimes the alternative [ok - not ok - ok again] is worth a try. So one of the pathways changes:

[ok - not ok - ok again]	[ok - REALLY bad - stays bad till it stops]	[ok - REALLY bad - stays bad till it stops]
[ok - REALLY bad - stays bad till it stops]	[ok - REALLY bad - stays bad till it stops]	[ok - REALLY bad - stays bad till it stops]
[ok - REALLY bad - stays bad till it stops]	[ok - REALLY bad - stays bad till it stops]	[ok - REALLY bad - stays bad till it stops]

Just as with my socks, there is now a chance that Sonny's brain might pick the non-catastrophic pathway. It is not yet a very big chance. We might not notice much change yet. But if we persist, then over a long time and a lot of experiences, gradually more pathways will flip to the resilient version rather than the catastrophic one. We may even get to something like:

[ok - not ok - ok again]	*[ok - not ok - ok again]*	*[ok - not ok - ok again]*
[ok - not ok - ok again]	*[ok - not ok - ok again]*	*[ok - not ok - ok again]*
[ok - not ok - ok again]	*[ok - not ok - ok again]*	[ok - REALLY bad - stays bad till it stops]

We've rebuilt a young child's regulatory systems by changing their world. And this is done simply by providing moderate stressors that Sonny can manage. And by tailoring very carefully what we mean by "moderate". What another child might not even notice is to Sonny a massive challenge that might set off the stress system.

Again, you might be wondering why there is such a long section on moderate and resolved stress in a chapter on positive relationships. I have left out a key element of the resilient schema for simplicity, but it is the most important part. The peekaboo game is not about whether the adult is back. It is the fact that they "came back". What's the difference? It's the difference between the frustrating but common experience for all babies of a toy temporarily vanishing, and a key person disappearing. In other words, the manageable stress in peekaboo is *relational*. And what makes it bearable is the *relationship* - the fact that the baby can trust the adult to come back. So the full schema is more like:

[ok - not ok - manageable with help - ok]

Growing up with ordinary sensitive care, we experience thousands (millions?) of experiences that embody this script (Wu, 2021). Maybe there is a short delay in feeding, maybe we are tired a little before anyone notices. We fall over and bump our head and someone makes it better. We do something we shouldn't (touch the TV!), but people forgive us. Over and over the pattern of stress-help-ok, stress-help-ok gets built into our brains. If this happens often enough, we end up with two linked schemas:

> [ok - not ok - manageable with help - ok]
> [ok - not ok - I can manage this - ok]

How does the developing brain come to know which of those to use though? We don't want children to try driving a car nor do we expect them (I hope not) to just comfort themselves if in pain. On the other hand, we'd be delighted if they could wait just a second for us to pay attention, or pick up things they drop for themselves. This is a form of risk assessment, and we look at how children develop an ability to tell what they can manage and what they can't in Chapter 12.

Towards Resilience

We have seen how the relational environment is an essential foundation for supporting children who have experienced any kind of trauma to learn and develop as well as they can. The next three chapters look at how this development can happen and the different experiences we can provide to help this.

Chapter summary:

- Developmental trauma has a deep impact, but so do our positive relationships with young children
- By providing good physical care and moderate and resolved stress within a positive relationship we can impact on brain development
- This can be done in the usual course of play and exploration

Practice points:

- Reflect on what children's actions and emotions tell you about what they have learned about the world, the people in it, and themselves
- Plan experiences and interventions on the basis of what answers you would like them to have about these
- Provide consistent and reliable physical care and positive relationships, so that children can experiment with minor stressors and exploration

11

Resilience 1 – What We Are Doing

This chapter will provide:

- A comprehensive ecological model for resilience
- Understanding of what elements of resilience matter for different types of trauma
- A map for planning what experiences and strategies to prioritise for children

What Is Resilience?

This chapter is about how we can help young children develop resilience. It is important for every child, and essential for those who have experienced trauma. "Resilience" is a concept that is now familiar, but still often misunderstood, so we will start by getting clear just what it is we are trying to develop. Here is an example of resilience in the face of stress:

> I am starting to feel hungry. I remind myself that this is my normal reaction to any task, and it is not long until lunch. A few minutes later, I decide the hunger is distracting me too much to concentrate on writing, so I get an apple from the bowl in the kitchen and can get back to work.

You might think that's not much, a trivial task that most of us can manage without effort anytime. For most adults, it is, but that ease masks what a triumph of resilience it is. Remember that picture of me as a baby back in Chapter 3? That's what mild hunger looked like then. If I could voice the infant me, it might go like this:

> I am starting to feel hungry. This is a threat to my life. Emergency! Cry and scream!

The difference between these two scenarios shows just how much goes into creating adult resilience. It also clarifies what the concept is because I have not given you the whole story of what happened while my father was taking that photo in order to embarrass me years later.

> Vi (my mother) hears me crying. She picks me up and jiggles me, shushing soothingly. Soon I am fed and all is well; now there is the new problem that I am ready for play!

Both of these are resilient outcomes. By this I mean that a stressor has been coped with, and a solution that works has been found. Resilience is simply when this tends to be the norm.

DOI: 10.4324/9781003563808-15

And we have learned that resilience is not just about "me" - my capacities, my "grit". For infant James, the resilient system involved both me (signalling need) and my mother (noticing and judging need, regulating stress, meeting need). So we have two different systems, each of which is resilient:

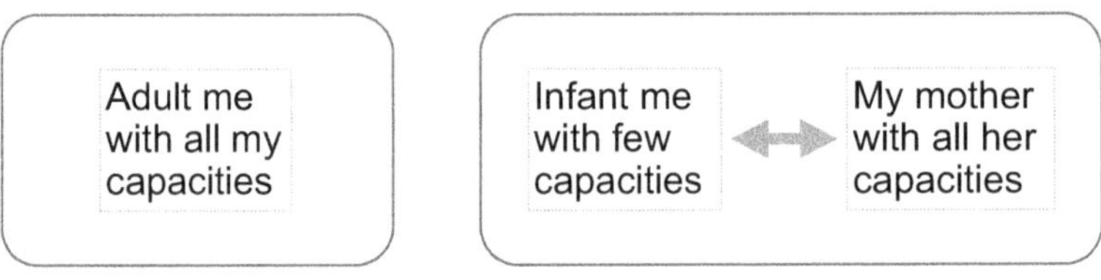

Figure 11.1

The difference between adult James and infant James is that the resilience is all built into my adult brain. The stress, regulation, and action systems work together in the way we saw in Chapter 1. When I was a hungry baby, my mother's brain was helping mine to create an overall resilient system - in this case a mother-baby dyad.

Here are two concepts we have seen before. Firstly, that resilience is established when we overcome challenges through co-regulation. Secondly, in the course of development, gradually more of that comes from within me than from others (Eisenberg et al., 2010; Feldman, 2020; Pauen, 2016). It is the same developmental sequence as in Chapter 10:

You do it   You do it with me   I do it with you   I do it

Chapters 8-10 have been all about the first three of these, as positive relationships gradually help children along the developmental sequence. This chapter is about the last stage, how we help children from co-regulation to self-regulation. A lot of this will involve learning skills, and a lot of that will be through planned activities and play. But make no mistake, this never becomes about just building the child's own capacity to the point that they become independently "resilient" (Ungar, 2015). And, as we will see in the next section, children can only learn these self-regulation skills if there is, for some, a lot of prior work in establishing the basic brain hardware to do so.

There is no such thing as individual resilience. Many adults think there is because most of us cope with most things most of the time. Hence a stereotype of resilience as some kind of square-jawed, gritty, tough guy. One example shows this is an illusion:

> The adult and square-jawed James arrives late at night at his Geneva hotel only to find they have no record of the booking. Suddenly homeless in a strange city! The hotel staff ring through and book him into a hotel in the same chain (though more expensive!) and call a taxi to take him there.

I can have all the grit I like but raise the challenge far enough and it turns out that I need co-regulation just as much as when I was a helpless infant.

One more feature of resilience is important for developing skills with children. There is another component of all these resilient systems, which is best described as "stuff". Too often we talk about resilience as a psychological concept, but the material world is part of the system. In the first example, I have apples in the house. In the second, my mother had time and leisure to respond to me. In Geneva I had the money (just!) for the other hotel and the taxi. And there were taxis available even that late at night. Our resilience is an interaction between the people who help us, and the things that are around to support it. All these elements work together and, to an extent, compensate for each other. The technical word for these things used in the child development literature is "affordances". Here's an example:

> James, 18 months, is starting to grizzle as he is getting hungry. His mother has to finish some work and needs another ten minutes. Fortunately James is easily distracted with the car keys, and the interest generated keeps him going until food can be offered.

The car keys are not just a distraction. Being given them is an assurance of care, and that my mother will come back. Instead of being jiggled by my mother, I jiggle the keys. The material object has taken on the task of soothing, and I can use it myself. That's what an affordance is, and we will see many more in this chapter.

Reflective Activity

Think of a time when you helped a friend or a colleague with a small setback. What personal qualities did they have that got them through it? AND how did you help them?

Resilience and Trauma

It's hopefully clear by now that building resilience for many children is not going to be a simple matter of playing a few games of Heads, Shoulders, Knees, and Toes, or a weekly yoga session. We will get to some ideas for activities in the next chapter. But to help us choose what to offer, we need to get clear what we are trying to do. In fact, we will see that almost any feature of a high-quality early learning environment can be involved.

In Chapter 7, we saw different aspects of development that can be disrupted (or, better, diverted) for children who have experienced trauma. These were:

Developing safety	*Developing a self*

Coping with sensory input
Tolerating affect
Calibrating stress (getting the right level of response)
Creating a sense of safety
Emotional regulation
Assessing and managing risk
	Core self
	Cause and effect - a coherent world
	A capable self
	  Motor coordination
	  Language development
	  Executive function
	  Social schemas
	An effective self
	A worthwhile and wanted self
	A self in relationships

Curiosity and Joyfulness	

Taking my adult triumph over hunger in slow motion will show us how these are related to developing resilience. Thinking how I got to this peak of performance will show us what children who have experienced trauma might need from us, and how we can decide.

> I am starting to feel hungry. I remind myself that this is my normal reaction to any task, and it is not long until lunch. A few minutes later, I decide the hunger is distracting me too much to concentrate on writing, so I get an apple from the bowl in the kitchen and can get back to work.

In contrast to baby James, for whom hunger is a signal of threat to life, for adult James it is nothing that difficult. In fact, it is almost a pleasant sensation as I anticipate what's for lunch (sensory processing). It is a feeling I can put up with (affect tolerance), and I can distract myself by typing the next sentence (emotional regulation and soothing), secure in the conviction this is at most an irritant rather than a threat (judging and managing risks). All that is made easier by knowing I can solve it if necessary, drawing on a range of skills from asking my partner to bring me an apple (language and social schemas), to getting one myself (coordinated movement, executive function, "how to").

There's a bit more going on too. I am assured by a general sense that I can solve problems (self-efficacy), that usually good things happen to me (positive self-image), that I can call on help if I need (developing relationships). And behind all that is a sense of coherence, that the succession of moments is smooth and reliable, and that I am the same now as I was a second ago, will still be ok in a few minutes.

And all of this is easier because I can, if needed, express what I want (language), move to fulfil needs in a planned way (coordination), balance the hunger with the need to get on with writing (executive function), know how to get help if I need it (social schemas) and many options for how to solve the problem ("how to").

Without labouring the point, you can hopefully see that all those same attributes were there for baby James, too. The difference was that they belonged to my mother and she shared them with me through mind-minded co-regulation. By the time I get to being able to jiggle the keys to distract myself, some of that is now within me too, even if it still needs the help of objects and a sensitive adult to prompt their use.

We saw all these different elements, and how simple and developmental trauma can disrupt them in different ways, in Chapter 7. The focus here is what is needed to build them up. Let's look at typical development first. How did I get from baby James who is dysregulated by mild hunger, to adult James for whom it is at best a distraction from composing the following table:

	Resilience component	*How it develops*
Sense of safety	Sensory processing	Experiencing and exploring lots of different sensations
	Affect tolerance	Experiences of mild excitement within what I can cope with
	Stress calibration	Experiences of many different kinds - happy, sad, etc.; and at different levels (boring, funny, hilarious)
	Emotional regulation	Meeting challenges I can cope with, and being helped with ones that I can't
	Judging & managing risks	Chances to try things out; experiences that feel risky to me but are actually safe

(Continued)

(Continued)

	Resilience component	*How it develops*
Coherent sense of self	Core self	A stable, routine, reliable world
	Developing relationships	More skilled others to learn from; and others to try it out with
	Positive self image	Doing things I value, and others value - and knowing this
	Self-efficacy	Making changes, getting things done, making my mark
Developmental skills	Language	Many rich two-way conversations
	Coordinated movement	Multiple opportunities to explore increasingly complex action sequences
	Executive function	Interesting things to do, support to focus, chances to make choices
	Social schemas	Modelling, teaching, chances to try out and get it wrong

If you look at those promoting elements in the third column, you might well think, "but aren't these part of any high-quality early learning environment?" And you'd be right. They are. All children benefit from all of these. What makes it trauma-informed is using mind-minded positive relationships to see which children need more of what. And prioritising that alongside any other program, policy, or plan (see Chapter 15).

Be in no doubt. For some children this is a simple matter of learning new skills - using a soothing toy as a distractor, for example. But for many, this is about first helping their brains develop the necessary structures and connections to even start learning new skills. The next section explores this difference.

Simple Trauma

Children who have experienced simple trauma are often secure in all these elements just like their peers. But when they encounter a trigger, they can seem to lose all this development as the fight, flight, freeze, flop responses come forward and they are flooded with strong feelings. Or we may see the system under strain as they anticipate triggers and develop avoidances. We cannot necessarily expect them to draw on their internal resilience when they meet a trigger.

> Jack is a happy 4-year-old who loves playing and learning in the setting. Except at drop-off! As soon as he comes into the room, he walks up to the nearest child and hits them. A minute or two later and it is as if nothing has happened.

We see what looks like it could be a "fight" response, and there are some candidates for a trigger. It could be the separation from family, or the sudden busyness of the setting, or just the change from one environment to another. So we also have some ideas to help, using the trauma triad (see Chapter 2).

> Tess, a practitioner, decided to meet Jack outside for a few days. He enjoyed climbing, so they would have a go on the frame and on some wooden steps. After a few minutes, she asked "ready to go inside?" And in they went without problems.

Tess has used all three parts of the trauma triad here. She's made the experience different (and nicer), has offered an attuned relationship, and given Jack some control over the trigger. I'm looking at this in detail so we can be clear what is happening. If we could look inside Jack's head at the moment of trigger, we would see:

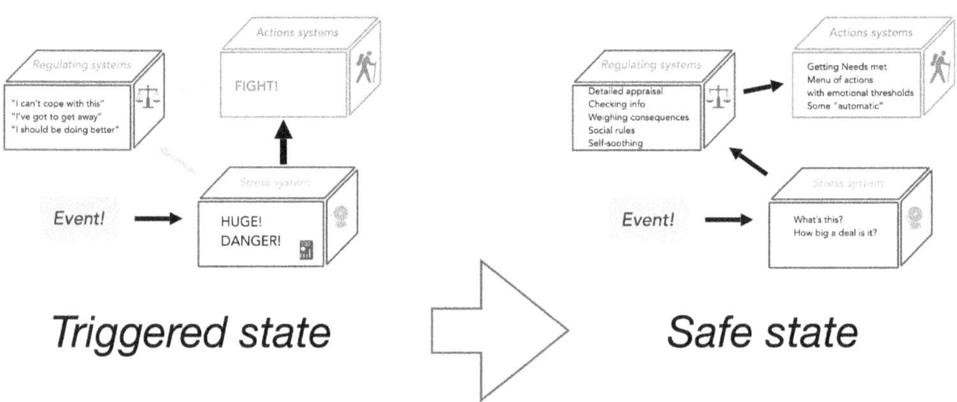

Figure 11.2 Safety as the foundation for self-regulation

Tess's idea has worked because it has helped Jack's brain move from the triggered state of fear and fight to the usual, everyday, balanced state where he can function fine (as long as there is no trigger). The same would be the case if instead of hitting another child, Jack had shown a freeze response such as hiding behind a pot plant.

Tess did most of the work here, and we want Jack to come to the point that he can do this himself. There are some ways to do this below. Before we get there, it is important to understand why they might not work for children who have experienced developmental trauma, or at least not as well.

Developmental Trauma

Developmental trauma, as we have seen, disrupts any or all of the elements as children adapt to function as well as they can in a difficult or dangerous world. This means that the default "every day" mode does not look the same as it does for Jack. We saw these differences in detail in Chapter 4, and here is a reminder of them, comparing two children. Jack, we have already met; Jake has been developing in the context of early trauma and adversity:

	Jake	*Jack*
What kind of world?	Difficult & dangerous	Mostly safe & stable
Language & communication	Act rather than talk Reduced language	Express needs & negotiate More language
Cognitive development	Rapid assessments Concepts for action Coping with randomness In the moment	Deepened thinking Complex concepts Cause & effect Reasoning about future
Executive function	Scanning environment Changing focus often Low impulse control	Controlled focus and attention Higher impulse control
Stress regulation	Vigilant, reactive	Calm, self-soothing
Social and self	Negative expectations Self-reliance Reduced help seeking	Positive expectations Confidence Help seeking

The effect of this is that Jake does not have the "safe state" to return to that Jack has. Nor, and this can be difficult for practitioners, are adults necessarily experienced as a source of safety either (Perry, 2009). We can help him deal with a trigger, but where this takes him is not back to smoothly functioning self-regulation, but to the default state in the table. So he may remain highly vigilant and reactive, with low impulse control, and so on.

This means two things in practice. Firstly, with Jack what we want to do is help him find ways to move himself from trigger state to safe state. We might, for example, help him become aware of when he is getting overwhelmed and to learn some new actions instead of hitting - coming to ask for help, maybe, or having a run-around outside. This won't work so well with Jake, because he does not have a safe state to move back to. Hence the second practice point. Jake is going to need us to help him build that safe state. The good news is that this can be done, at least partly, through the sorts of things we might have and do anyway in early education. The implication is that traditional behaviour management (tell him to "be kind" and reinforce "good" behaviour) won't work. Our settings need a pedagogy and an approach to behaviour that allows us to understand children's experiences and respond in a mind-minded way. More on that in Chapter 15.

Finally, and I hope this is clear by now without being stated, but just in case - children cannot learn new skills and strategies when the stress system is "hot". Remember me and the Loch Ness Monster. All my brain wants to do is to get safe and it powers down any aspects of me that are not to do with that. It is not a great moment for me to learn some Spanish irregular verbs, nor to ride on a unicycle. If we want children to learn and take on board new ways of interpreting their inner experience and new actions to respond to it, this has to be when they are calm and connected to us. For children who have just a few (simple) traumatic memories, this means when they are not being triggered or are not transfixed by hypervigilance or worry about avoidances. For children who have experienced developmental trauma, it is a matter of helping them build that internal sense of safety and coherence from the bottom of the brain upwards. That might need years of work before they can learn to "take a slow breath" or "use your words".

How Do We Tell What Children Need?

I've drawn a contrast here for convenience to make clear the differences between simple and developmental trauma and how we may need to respond differently. There are two ways that this might be misleading so I want to clear those up now before we go on to practices and strategies. We do not need to, nor can we, embark on a diagnostic process. There is no need to work out what child has experienced simple trauma and needs *this*; and what child has experienced developmental trauma and needs *that*. This is because the differences in practice may not be as sharp as I have drawn to make the concepts clear. Children, even with one simple trauma, for example, can sometimes be generally fearful and need to do a lot of work to recover their sense of safety. They have the safe state available in their brains, but a general sense of threat pulls them out of it frequently. Other children, who have experienced early trauma and adversity, might have perfectly functional emotional regulation, but get into difficulties because of gaps in their language development that means they can't say what they need or understand our attempts to guide them.

Also, although I have broken down the processes of resilience in some detail so that we can understand exactly what we are doing, in practice the same experiences and activities tend to do more than one thing. So we don't necessarily need to work out which child needs to develop more affect tolerance and which needs to recalibrate their stress response, as the ideas in Chapter 12 under "Sense of Safety" mostly cover both.

> Divya is trying out finger-painting for the first time, accompanied by Alo, an adult she has come to trust. She has some edible paint and a large sheet. She dabs a finger cautiously in the paint, and quickly pulls it back. Alo smiles and dips his own finger, makes a couple of dots on the paper and says "ooo!" Divya copies him. Then she splats her whole hand into the paint and sticks it in her mouth. "Yuk!" says Alo. Divya giggles and makes a splashy hand print.

Note the importance of co-regulation here. None of the ideas in the next chapter have a chance of working without that. That given, how much is going on here? Let's see the ways:

	Resilience component	*Divya's experience*
Sense of safety	Sensory processing	Trying a new sensation; Alo shows it is ok to explore, even by mouth
	Affect tolerance	Alo co-regulates this through his actions and words
	Stress calibration	Together they find this is not just ok, but fun!
	Emotional regulation	Alo's mind-minded actions and labelling of feelings soothe Divya's initial surprise
	Judging and managing risks	Alo thinks it's ok, so it is (she trusts him)
Coherent sense of self	Core self	Linking different sensations and movements
	Developing relationships	Having fun together; co-regulating
	Positive self image	Learning a new thing!
	Self-efficacy	Making a mark

(*Continued*)

(Continued)

	Resilience component	*Divya's experience*
Developmental skills	Language	Labelling of experiences from Alo
	Coordinated movement	Comparing the splodge with what she intended
	Executive function	Something really interesting to focus on; and someone to make it even more interesting
	Social schemas	Basic turn taking, and help seeking
	"How to . . ."	Paint on paper is more fun than in the mouth

It should be no surprise by now that the way we can tell what each child needs comes from mind-minded observation and reflection as they encounter different aspects of our setting - both things and people. There was no need to do complicated assessments for Divya, for example, since a sufficiently interesting experience, within a positive relationship, seems to be covering what she needs. Some of this might be general observation. This is what Tess did above, reflecting on how Jack might be experiencing the transition into the setting and thinking how the trauma triad could help with ideas. Some observations are from how children respond to how we try to help. Maisie loves a hug when she's upset. Molly feels trapped by a hug and needs us to sit nearby till she's ready for contact. For example, suppose Tess tried the same strategies with Jake that worked with Jack. She might then observe that, while he enjoys the climbing, it doesn't really help reduce the hitting behaviours - Jake needs something more as well.

We can separate out two different sets of decisions. Firstly, which of the elements do we need to work with, and secondly what might help each child to develop that element. With respect to the first question, there is a basic order of function, as we have seen throughout the book:

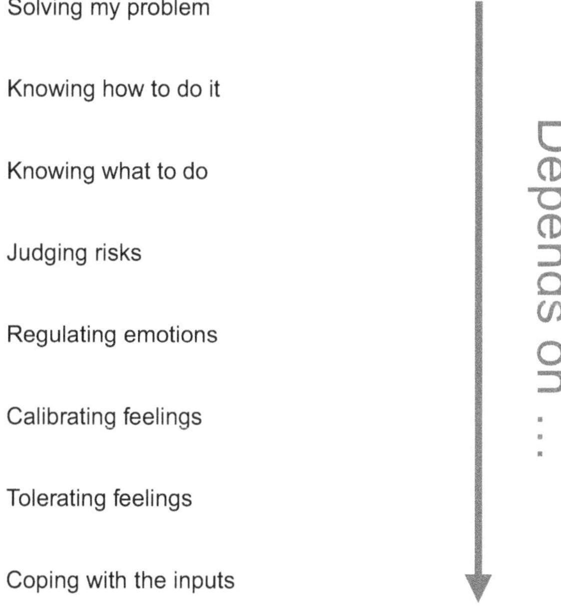

Figure 11.3 A heuristic for deciding where to start

This is a "heuristic", a way of giving shape to complexity and not in any way a diagnostic process or an assessment tool. But in general, if our observations show us that a child has trouble with any of these, it tells us that we need to do some work to build the lower level, and probably the ones below as well (e.g., Feldman, 2020; Lloyd, 2020; Matson et al., 2024; Perry, 2009). We saw this with Jack and Jake, above. With sensitive co-regulation and a chance to practice, Jack was able to learn a way to manage his trigger experience. The same approach did not work with Jake, as he did not have some of the lower levels to draw on. This tells us we need to do more to build his sense of safety, his sense of being a coherent self, and his developmental skills.

What will do that for Jake? There are so many ways, and the next chapter lists some of them. Exactly what to try can only be learned from knowing Jake, from seeing what he is drawn to and trying out different things. Whatever we do, though, it is important to remember that this is not about behaviour management. It is not primarily about solving the hitting at the start of the day. Trauma-informed thinking moves from the issues that trouble us to the realisation that Jake has a much more fundamental agenda for learning and development. Trauma-informed practice uses the relationships, spaces, and experiences of our setting to help Jake along that journey. We may not get all the way in his time with us, but we will make the essential start on which others can build.

If in doubt, we can be sure that if we offer children things to do that interest them, in a climate of positive relationships where we are mind-minded and sensitive in responding to their needs and planning for their learning and development, then we will be doing a lot of what they need from us.

Chapter summary:

- Resilience is an interaction of individual factors with the supports available to them
- Simple and developmental trauma impact on children's resilience in ways that differ and can be different for individuals
- Effective intervention has an order of implementation and rarely starts with teaching new behaviours

Practice points:

- Plan all interventions and strategies in the context of co-regulation
- Expect some children to need a lot of work before they can take on self-regulation without support
- Plan through observation of what experiences children are drawn to and enjoy

12
Resilience 2 - Developing Safety

This chapter will provide:

- Strategies and experiences that help develop children's sense of safety
- Playful ways for children to gradually acquire skills of self-regulation
- Guidance and cautions on using soothing and grounding approaches including mindfulness and yoga

Although for clarity in the previous chapter I made a separation between a sense of safety and a coherent sense of self, when it comes to practice, the two often go together. I am more likely to feel safe if my moment-to-moment experience feels coherent and consistent. And my experience of myself as the same from moment-to-moment in part rests on the smooth rhythms of stress-regulation-action that happen many times a minute. That can be disrupted by frequent overwhelms or triggers.

When it comes to offering experiences, the same kinds of things develop both the core self and the basic rhythms of stress-ok, stress-ok, stress-ok that also develop the stress system's ability to handle sensory input and tolerate the resulting feelings. So we will look at ways to support these together, as a foundation for later work when they are more established. This and the next chapter should therefore be read in parallel - safety and core self develop together and interactively, rather than one after the other.

Two points to remember. Although for clarity, the material in this and the next chapter is set out under headings, in practice children's development does not fall into boxes. Any given experience will support more than one, or even all, of these aspects. As a result there is some overlap between the suggestions - what angles each towards the developmental area it is under tends to be the scaffolding that we provide around it, especially the mind-minded commentary and interactions. Secondly, the order in this chapter does not imply a strong hierarchy in the sense of "do this first, then this". But it does broadly move from foundations upwards. As explained in the previous chapter, if a child is not responding to, interested in, or taking benefit from any of the below, then it may help to move "back" towards earlier material.

DOI: 10.4324/9781003563808-16

A Core Self

Almost anything that has rhythm and repetition that children are interested in will do. Often one can get ideas by seeing what they are drawn to, and then build on those. It is important to be led by the children - we can offer a wide range of things to do, but it is their choice and control that will make the connections in their brains. Further, some children will only need a little of this - perhaps a short session every day - while others who are working on their fundamental systems of interoception and response will need much more or even nothing else for a while. Again, the best guide is the child themselves - if they lose interest, fine; if they become absorbed, go with that.

As with everything else in this chapter, the essential addition that links whatever is happening into the growth of a coherent sense of self and a well-connected self-regulation system is the adult relationship surrounding it. Just being company is effective, but most of all is wrapping what the children are doing in gentle, attuned, mind-minded commentary. Say what you see, with some language about feelings and mental states, and you will add value to whatever children do. Again, take their lead. Some children find it more intrusive than others, so be there, but not "too there". If a child turns away, or moves off a little, or disengages as soon as you get close or start to comment, it is fine to give them the space they are telling you they need.

It is possible to get too precise about what activities develop interoception, which develop coordinated movement, sensory processes, or vestibular function. In practice most things we offer do several things at once, and again the children can be a good guide. It is better that they do something they enjoy and find interesting than are pushed into doing whatever we think they need - this can then often provide a platform for introducing variations.

> Yasmine needed a lot of sensory experiences, but she really loved drumming! She would engage with the foam or the pine cones for a while but quickly lost interest. Qasim sat with her drumming one day, and started to experiment with different "drumsticks", such as a squidgy cushion and a soft brush. He made comments about the different sounds, laughing at the unexpected ones. Yasmine of course then wanted a go, and began to get very interested in how different textures and materials made different sounds. She began to tolerate the different feels and weights and began her journey of sensory exploration.

Having said that, it is useful to set out ideas by rough type, provided this is not used as an iron guide. And none of the lists in these chapters are definitive - they are to indicate the kind of thing - you, and even more the children, will have better ideas by far. I have not included here interventions that can be effective, when done with care, but which are best offered after or with specialist advice. These include providing deep pressure or using weighted blankets. Another important consideration is that almost anything we offer might turn out to be a trigger, and sensory activity is more likely to connect to difficult experiences with young children. So choose carefully based on what you know the child likes or can manage, always offer choice, and keep a careful eye.

Sensory Exploration

Loose parts. Have an interesting array of different weights and textures. Natural materials are great, but so are some interesting made ones such as materials, coins, bells, etc. Give children time to explore and gently offer ones they have not noticed.

Squidging. This can be bought or made materials such as doughs, or found opportunities such as mud. Look out too for squidging that is built into other activities such as cooking together, or tidying up cardboard boxes!

Water. Still and gently flowing, opportunities to splash, "paint", pour, immerse parts of self or object (feeling the water push back). Some children may enjoy exploring different temperatures, which is a great chance to add some feelings concepts such as "ooo, cold!", or "this one feels nicer!" Liquids with different consistencies can also be interesting and a source of conceptual exploration - "yuk, sticky!"

Painting with fingers. Includes an encounter with liquid, but also the feel of different mediums - paper, walls, etc. Make sure it is edible paint, as some children might use the opportunity for oral exploration. Children may enjoy making repetitive patterns of swirls, circles, dots, lines.

Feely bags, jars, or pots. Put various materials in a container (soft bags are good) and encourage exploration; add language and model emotions to encourage. Some children may enjoy guessing games too.

Snacks. Foods come in all kinds of textures, so let children explore if they need to (rather than eating "properly"). Squish a banana, feel slippery pasta, and so on.

Décor. Have a variety of surfaces - e.g., squares of material, bubble wrap, foam, plants, etc. - around the setting for children to explore opportunistically (everyone will enjoy this!). Some children may enjoy a structured sensory walk, or even a treasure hunt - find something smooth, something wet . . .

Pongs. Make some smell jars (with pleasant odours!). Could be ground coffee, orange peel, mild spices, cut grass, anything. Explore with the children, labelling the different smells and how they feel.

Outdoors. The natural and built environment is one big sensory playground to explore. Encourage this with modelling, commentary, structured "walks" and treasure hunts. Don't forget the feel of the weather, be this a cold wind or warming sunshine.

Sounds. See below for music, but for example fill shakers with different materials that have different weights and sounds when shaken or tapped.

Proprioception

Trampolines. Fun and repetitive so soothing, but also provides feedback through the bouncing muscles. Space hoppers if child has sufficient coordination; wobbling on an exercise ball or bean bag.

Heavy things. Pushing, carrying around, putting in a bag and carrying, pulling carts and so on.

Using materials. Kneading, threading, building, tearing, squashing; anything with an element of resistance.

Animal moves. Games where everyone has to move like an animal - a bee, a frog, a worm, an elephant. Some children may need this modelled.

Work outs. Gentle exercises such as push ups, wheelbarrows, lifting, running on the spot then walking, and rolling can be great for giving whole-body feedback.

Oral proprioception. Blowing up balloons, drinking different texture liquids (especially through straws), blowing a trumpet, chewing different foods (or safe chew toys), blowing bubbles, playing blow football.

Vestibular and Balance

Tummy action. This needn't be baby-level tummy time, although some children may enjoy it. Opportunities to wriggle or crawl around on different surfaces - can be extended using obstacle courses or movement challenges.

Slopes and inclines. These can be those found outdoors, or indoor versions. Let children set the level of challenge involved, and support if they are wanting to explore beyond their capability.

Playground items. Swings, roundabouts, spinners, springers, slides, bars to swing on, seesaws, balancing beams, hammocks. If there are some safe grass slopes then rolling down is often enjoyable, but build this up by starting close to the bottom at first.

Indoor equivalents. Rocking chairs or horses, spinning chairs, wobble boards, lines to walk, stepping stones (you can add an element of gentle emotion regulation by pretending there is water, or even for braver children, sharks, but if so model that it is fun). Can include just gentle rocking with a trusted adult in a hug or on lap.

Movement games. Spinning, dancing, statues, skipping, jumping. Also more controlled movement such as slowly crouching or bending, or getting up and down.

Simple **yoga** sequences to give a sense of flow and to feel the changes.

Internal Rhythms - Experiencing Oneself

Musical. Tapping, shakers or drumming, clapping to a song, dancing to a beat, repetitive or predictable songs (especially with call and response or fun choruses), enjoying listening to music or natural sounds with patterns (rain drops on the window, waves of the sea, bird song).

All the ideas above that have **rhythm** and **repetition**!

Affect Tolerance

The aim is to help children feel safe while feeling an emotion. For some, even positive emotions might be difficult if their stress systems treat any feeling as a sign of threat. So we want to start with gentle experiences of very mild positive emotions, providing co-regulation as needed. Over time, and if children are tolerating those, we can move to exploring and holding more negative but still very minor experiences. It is best not to create these as that might be unsafe or even re-traumatising - the "found" ones that happen in the daily course of play and learning are usually easier and more effective.

Some ways to develop affect tolerance in play include:

Pretend play. Children can try out different scenarios and emotions using puppets, etc., or by dressing up. Provide some narrative, "the fireman is worried about the cat, so he's rushing to get there!"

Turn-taking games. Ranging from simple passing back and forth to more complex games. Add in emotional labelling language. "You caught it! I'm so happy". More complex games can include co-regulated experiences of waiting or losing, or something going wrong, "You've got a snake! That's hard! Back up a ladder soon!". "You really want a turn - it's you next"

Use it when you see it. When children experience small triumphs or setbacks, notice and label this and provide a narrative. "That's sad, they've fallen down. What a big tower you are building - maybe next time it'll work!"

Art and crafts. Label activity with feeling words. "That looks a happy colour!" "The girl in the picture looks sad".

Jokes and pranks. Without using too big surprises, create moments of gentle humour with jokes, or deliberate mistakes. Drop an acorn and pretend not to be able to find it, be an elephant at snack time. Have a daily simple verbal joke to tell children and for them to share.

Model the ups and downs of feelings. "I'm all hot and fizzy. Help me take some breaths to calm down?" "That makes me so happy, my heart is fluttering, thank you!"

Have **regulators** to hand. Offer safe ways for children to express rising feelings as this will help them feel manageable. Could be going outside to throw balls, scrunching a cushion, drawing what you feel, using a quiet space, anything.

Vary **controlled movement** games such as animal walks by introducing feeling challenges. Can you be a happy frog? A tired elephant? Laugh kindly and label what you see as great - it pairs the experiment with feelings with social support and enjoyment.

Stories. Tell (as often as the children are interested) stories involving emotions. These might be specific books on emotions, such as the Colour Monster, but just as effective are any with a plot of difficulty and overcoming with a happy ending. Chat with the children about what the characters are feeling and how it is resolved. Support re-enacting the story with props (some children will need modelling to use them). Some children may enjoy making a simple story map - drawings can represent key incidents (home, off to see grandma, scared of wolf, triumph, everyone happy).

Creativity. Some children may be able to, and interested in, painting, drawing or sculpting different feelings. We can engage them in feelings-based chat. "Show me your colour for sad", "is there something angry in the picture?" For others, just scribbling (or even other apparently destructive acts of creation) can be a way to express and put feelings outside to look at; again emotional labelling can be helpful. "I think you are tearing that to show me you are really sad right now".

Music and dance. Play tracks with different feels (quick, slow, bouncy, smooth, happy, sad, etc.) and all move about as you want with them. Keep an eye so that children don't overexpress and start to escalate themselves.

Stress Calibration

Once children can tolerate feeling feelings at all, they start to develop abilities to tell the difference between feelings and how strong they are. Initially this is a black and white contrast – ok or not-ok. Gradually, through many experiences of different feelings being resolved, they come to a wider scale and can tell the difference between something that is mild and ignorable, something that is not huge but needs attention, and something they can't manage themselves.

Often the best times to develop stress calibration are in the natural ups and downs of playing and learning where children face both challenges and triumphs. Through careful planning and co-regulation, we can keep these within what we know they can cope with, and provide gentle support to take this further. Apart from this, there are lots of ways to help children develop stress calibration, including the following.

Sensory explorations. Have a selection available of contrasting things (e.g., loud and quiet instruments, hard and soft natural items, hot and cold liquids) for children to explore. Label and chat about the differences and link this to feelings "are you feeling loud right now?" Offer some challenges if children are interested – "can you play the drum quiet, now loud, now in-between?"

Balloons or feathers. A variant of "keeping up" games. Invite children to hit the balloon or blow the feather with different intensities. Comment on the effects and on what it feels like (model your own feelings as well as commenting on the children).

Controlled movement games, such as mirrors or animal walks. Introduce variations such as high energy animals (frogs, etc.) and slower ones like tortoises. Children might manage and enjoy contrasts and contradictions – a fast tortoise or a slow lion.

Back and forth games. Rolling objects, kicking or throwing balls; offer different ways to do this. Big throw, slow roll, high kick, and so on, varying them. Model what you mean. And see if children can spot your "mistakes".

Stories. Take the feelings narratives a stage on by chatting about "how sad" the character feels. Simple concrete language at first "big sad or just little sad?" Chat through the "arc" of the story (initial concern, then resolution, etc.). Possibly extend if the children are interested into chatting about what makes you or them big sad or little sad, and what helps.

Charades. Only for children who do not easily dysregulate, but it can be fun to act out different levels of emotions. They could start by copying you, and then guessing your feelings, before trying themselves. "Little happy", "middle happy", "big happy", and if that goes ok try some negative feelings (but with care if you know about particular triggers). "Little sad", "a bit more sad", "really sad"! Make it exaggerated and funny if that helps.

Parachute games. Include fast and slow contrasts - the children working together will learn from each other and calibrate each other.

Music and dancing. Speed up and slow down, introduce "stop" moments; chat about how they feel.

Sense of Safety: Turning Down the Stress System

Eventually we want children to be able to turn down their stress reactions using internal resources. We will get to the point where their own regulating systems become more effective and more automatic in regulating emotion moment to moment. To get there, it can be useful to offer, teach, and practice deliberate and conscious ways to regulate. That is what the ideas in this section are about.

None of them work if we first or mainly use them when the child is under stress. Until established, the children's ability to learn and use these strategies will be limited. We need to learn and practice them during calm and happy times - they are nearly all fun anyway and contain other aspects of learning such as attention or movement.

When children dysregulate, treat this as a question - can you contain me? Remember the order, to regulate and connect before trying any solution. As they regain control, prompt them to try one of the ideas below that they have *previously* learned and practised.

Mindfulness

Firstly a note on using breathing and mindfulness with young children, especially those who have experienced trauma. The purpose of these is to help children be in the present by using sensory anchors, such as the breath or any kind of experience including body sensations or sights and sounds. There are two ways of doing them. One is to create a focus on internal experience - this is the classic mindfulness of the meditation of the breath or the body scan. This can be quite uncomfortable for people with traumatic memories, since the whole point of a lot of what they do and how they are is to avoid a potentially overwhelming awareness of their internal experience. Without care it is possible for them to flood with unmanageable feelings or even be re-traumatised. This is even more the case for children, who are more easily overwhelmed anyway, and for children with complex trauma who may not yet have the internal safe space for developing mindful awareness.

As a result, it is often safer to try the other route, which is to focus on external awareness. There are some ideas for this under "grounding" below. Also, mindfulness can use outside awareness or movement as an anchor. This could involve offering activities such as:

Blowing bubbles. Blow hard, blow soft, watch them float away; feel them pop and splash if you touch them.

Blowing pinwheels, feathers, balloons.

Gentle **stretches** - or animal movements; how does it feel when you do that?

Sensory walks. Wander around outside, prompting to notice the feel of the air, any sounds there are, the temperature, what you can see.

Moving gently to music, sometimes fast, sometimes slow; stopping when the music stops. Whatever we offer in terms of mindfulness it is essential to bear in mind these caveats:

- Always make it a matter of choice to do, and offer choices within it, continuously. For example, "if you want to, stretch your arms up to the sky; hold them up if you can, or put them down"
- Keep it short and safe
- Only offer these activities from an adult with whom the child or children have a positive relationship and is a source of safety for them
- Monitor carefully how children are experiencing what you are doing
- Only offer to children who have a basic internal sense of safety to draw on

The same cautions apply to a common recommendation to offer glitter bottles. These are jars or bottles with a mix of liquid and glitter. When shaken they create an engaging display, and some people find it soothing to watch the glitter gradually settle. But not everyone. For some children, it is an external representation of their internal chaos and so can bring forward feelings of loss of control, dissociation, or overload. Adults too - so practitioners may also be affected. Glitter bottles can be useful, but bear in mind the same caveats as for mindfulness.

Soothing

A calm and cozy corner to go to. Involve the children in creating this with whatever they find soothing. This might include things adults would think of like soft cushions, pillows, stuffed animals; but children may think of other things like favourite toys, books, sensory objects, anything they find soothing. Let children have free access to this and never question whether they need it. If children use it a lot or seem to be avoiding certain experiences or spaces, then consider how to adapt these (see sections on triggers and avoidances in Chapter 8). Lastly, never ever use this corner as a sanction, consequence, thinking time, anything of that sort.

Hugs are great for children who like them. We can teach them to hug themselves, for example the butterfly, where you wrap yourself in your arms from shoulder to shoulder. Some people recommend slow shoulder "butterfly taps". Be careful with these, and best only with specialist advice as we need to be sure the children are using the taps to reinforce internal safety (rather than a triggered memory).

Squeezing! Sponges and squeezy balls or springs are great for this. Just squeezing or clenching hands and fists might trigger towards fight responses, but for some children it'll be fine. One way to use the body is a whole scrunchy curl up - you can put scripts around this, like the snail in its shell or the hedgehog curling up. But the point whatever we do is squeeze *and* release. This is actually another rhythm of stress-then-relief, but under the child's own close control.

Big breaths. Breathe in and blow out. Any of the oral blowing ideas above can be good. Use your hands as a balloon and blow them up, too.

Gentle **rocking** or **swinging**. **Tapping** a foot or a finger.

Enrol stuffed animals, or treasure objects, including photographs, as companions to spend time with and provide comfort. Children often enjoy choosing their helpers. Sometimes what can work is to set up a story where a stuffed animal is feeling worried, scared, or angry, and ask if the child can maybe help them when they feel bad. Children are not deceived for a moment but are often pleased to help anyway.

Drawing and mark-making. Having a good scribble can release tension, and this can gradually turn into more controlled expression. Have opportunities easily to hand, with crayons, or outdoors with brushes.

Have a regular **song** that the child finds calming. Sing it with them at first, and then support them to try it themselves.

Recognise and offer **alternatives** to children's behaviours that appear to be self-soothing, such as tearing things up, throwing, bumping head, hiding in corners.

Strong positive memories. Young children may struggle to create a clear and detailed verbal account of a happy and safe memory, but if they can, this can be helpful as a "happy place" they can think about when feeling stressed. Alternatively, children may like to draw a happy place or a happy memory and keep it with them (or ask you to look after it for them). The same for a prized photo.

Positive self-talk. More verbal children may, with prompting, be able to use or join in with positive talk, such as "I'm ok", "I can do this", "Soon be over", etc. Don't expect children in our age group to make much of this, though, as the verbal centres are not well enough connected - but the effort involved can work as a controlled distraction!

Grounding

Body grounding. Children may enjoy standing and pretending to press their feet into the ground - can they push into it, and feel the floor pushing back to support them?

Body control. Similar to the animal moves above. Lift up your arms high, can you reach the sky - and now drop. Lift up your shoulders, can you touch your ears, hold and drop. A variant, as above, is to squeeze balls, springs, etc. Or pretend to do a big yawn (people usually do then yawn!).

Grounding objects. Children might choose an item - anything will do as long as it feels good to them, doesn't go "off" and can be kept close by easily. Stones, squidgy dough, a cloth, a fidget. Teach them to hold it, and think about what it feels like - smooth, heavy, rough, comforting, squashy, whatever.

Controlled movement. Gentle drumming, playing statues, slow movements copying a leader.

Toes and fingers. Wiggle your toes, or wiggle your fingers. Can you wiggle all of them without falling over? Children can be shown how to do this so others cannot see - for example under a table, or inside their shoes.

Senses check. Can you name something you can see? Something you can hear? Something you can smell? Something you can touch? A taste you like?

Spot the. Can you point to a chair? To a cup? To a door? To your nose? To a bird? Anything around will do. Children often love challenging you back - be prepared for some difficult challenges, and to develop some joy. If children know colour words, this can be extended to "find something blue, something red, etc.".

Quiet grounding. Some children may like to draw, scribble or make marks, or paint. Or to have a story, or listen to some music. Others may like to trail their hands in some water or sand while sitting quietly. Chat about how it feels if they wish.

Emotional Regulation

Once children can manage to soothe their stress system using some of the ways above, they may be able to take on board and try out some of the strategies for regulating their feelings deliberately. There are many ways to do this, and an online search will quickly show a large selection of specific tools and resources. None of them will work if we try and teach them in "hot" situations. Children need to be calm and feeling very safe (see Chapters 8-10 for how to co-regulate this with them). And they need chances to practice in easy situations, which includes being able to get it wrong many times before they manage by themselves. The step from "I do with you" to "I do it myself" can be long and difficult. It might involve developing the following ingredients in this order:

Window of Tolerance. Draw one with the child, using a suitable metaphor (fizzy, hot, growly, anything meaningful to the child). It can be something like the window, or a temperature gauge like a thermometer, or how full of ants their tummy is - anything! Help them work out and draw what it feels like at the edges; and what they can do to come to the middle. Support them to practice their ideas.

Growing a self-regulation **vocabulary**. Develop with children a way of describing what they are feeling in difficult moments, linked to the chosen metaphor. Use their words for the experience (if they say "sad" when it looks more like anger, go with that as it means something to them). If children understand concepts of size or strength, add this ("big sad or little sad?" and so on).

Linking their experience into a whole. Help children identify emotions in their bodies. Again and not to overstate this, only do this when teaching when they are calm. It can help to start talking about yourself so they see what you mean - "when I am sad, my body feels heavy, my mouth feels droopy" etc. Some children will need to have a non-personal focus for this - "when children are scared, what does their body feel like? Can you point to where on me that is?" Others are fine talking about themselves. Using a cutout paper body can be helpful to draw on; if each child wants their own, so much the better as everyone feels things differently.

Linking their experiences to solutions. Helping children identify what works for them when they feel that way. Again it might be easiest for them to start with you modelling. "When I feel sad, I stand up straight and think of something that makes me happy, and then go and do it. If that doesn't work I go and talk to a friend". Give them a menu of possible solutions for strong emotions including using any of the soothing and grounding ideas above, or going to ask an adult for help, or sitting quietly, or counting to ten, or . . . Children can choose what they think works for them and try it out.

Supporting the learning. It can help to use visuals with a simple "I feel . . . I try" structure. Never use these as performance targets, but instead as prompts for you and for the child. An example might be "I feel angry . . . I squeeze my cushion . . . then I go and tell X". Better with pictures too, especially if the child can draw them. If the script does not work, then it is a helpful learning in itself for the child to critique it with you and think how to improve it. Perhaps squeezing the cushion just makes them more angry! In which case maybe just go tell X about it, or try a mindful stretch.

Managing Risk

Judging and Managing Risk

Although it might be where we want to start, since reluctance to explore can be as much of a problem in early education as children taking too many risks, we can't accept or manage risk until we can tolerate affect, calibrate our response to it, and to an extent regulate the feelings. Otherwise it is hard to tell what is a big risk or a small risk, and to process and come to decisions about whether the level is manageable or needs to adjust (more for interest or less for safety). Where children struggle a lot with risk taking, either way, it is worth including the earlier ideas in their daily diet of experiences as well as any of the ideas below. We might, through observation and experience, decide to go back several stages and leave judging and managing risks for the future. Until then we can help children through co-regulation as in Chapters 8-10.

If children are interested, able to engage with, and respond to them, then the following can be great ways to develop understanding and acceptance of risk. Just be aware of some basic guidelines in this area of work:

- Always be on hand with co-regulation as needed. Supported risk taking will gradually become independent risk management - overwhelm will not.
- Remember the trauma triad. Make sure the experiences are manageable, supported, and within the control of the child.
- Children's control is key. Offer experiences where they can adjust the risk, or more relevant how risky it feels to *them*. Help them do this: "Is that high enough for today?" "Do you want to try again?"
- Use failures and setbacks as ways to learn. Talk children through how they made a big effort but maybe it's too hard for them today. Point out the progress they have made. "You had a good look at the slide and decided it was a bit scary for now. Well done having a look and making a choice. Shall we come back another time and look again?"
- Same with emotions of frustration, annoyance, despair, etc. This is how it feels for anyone, so model and label and offer solutions.
- Model all of this yourself. Talk aloud about how you feel about trying something, what it is like to succeed at it or fail, or nearly get there.
- Don't be concerned with stops and starts and setbacks. Judging risks is a rhythm of trying out, leaving for a while to reassess, loss of nerve, gain of (too much) courage and

readjustment. It is the process that matters and that we can record as an achievement. "James is exploring new risks and learning how it feels".

With those reflections in place, here are some interesting things to do:

Choosing. Building choice into any experience can make it more interesting and engaging, but it also lets children experience uncertainty and have their choices affirmed (so uncertainty turns out to be ok, and even fun!). Some children may need help to learn to choose (see Executive Function in Chapter 13) so offer simple binary choices such as "shall we go up or down?", "this log or that one?"

Obstacle courses. Can be indoor or outdoor. Include choices between elements of climbing, jumping, walking slow or fast, balancing, crawling, under and over, etc. Allow children to make their own routes.

Make mistakes. Drop things, lose things, draw a picture without any nose, call something the wrong name or colour (it can be funny), knock your own tower over by mistake. Model recovery, or let the children call it out and correct you; thank them for it.

Treasure hunts. Indoor or out, looking for things creates small uncertainties that are resolved when we find them. Gradually increase how hidden the things are. Let the children set you challenges too.

Nature walks. Explore a new place, or a familiar place doing different things - e.g., climb a log, draw chalk stepping stones on a path, balance on a (small) rock - whatever the children want to try. Introduce sharks, etc. if children can manage imaginary danger.

Beach. Play with dodging (small) waves. Who can stay longest before they move back? Model that it is ok, and even fun, when you get wet feet.

Silly dancing. When this is done on purpose - who can be silliest - it makes it feel safer to children to experiment and to perform too.

Spinners or dice. Set up a spinner with some things the children already know and one or two that are new or have not been done for a while. Make them easy to do (e.g., touch your nose, bring me a book) - the point is in the uncertainty and the new action. Include some emotion expression if the children enjoy it (Smile! Fold your arms! Shrug!).

Pretend and role play. Children may be drawn to acting out risky or brave roles such as explorers or firefighters. If they want to be soldiers, that's ok. Wrap language around this about being brave and careful.

Puzzles. Choose ones the children can do but haven't tried yet, or that are just about on the edge of what they can do. Help them keep trying if needed, and comment on the effort, trying, and good ideas.

Build, build, build! How high a pile of boxes can we make before it falls over? Same with towers of blocks (be careful about actual safety with any building).

Novelty. Have something new available for children to explore or have a go at. It can be an object, or a tool (different colour paint, or something intriguing like a magnifying glass or some transparent colour sheets to look through). Let them choose whether to engage (having shown them what to do if they are uncertain). Accept different ways of playing with an item and celebrate the creativity.

Stories with mild suspense or risk. Almost any story has these, but they can be brought out in chatting about the story, how the characters feel and manage, or acting them out. Let the children be the troll under the bridge as you try to cross.

Risk Taking

Once children have a tolerance of risk, they can cope better with the levels of risky play that can grow that tolerance. Some children will need more risky play in general so that they can gradually move from their model of a difficult and dangerous world to one where the risks are manageable. Risky play can be a helpful way for them to examine, process, and re-evaluate feelings of fear or loss of control. Some ideas for risky play that often appeal include the following. As always, let children control the degree of perceived risk while making sure it is always actually safe. I have categorised some of these for convenience around fight, flight, and freeze responses. Children who tend towards these responses can try these activities as adaptive replacements, but the main determinant is what they enjoy, find interesting, and are drawn to repeat or prolong. Note that sometimes the risk can be emotional, as in the exposure or self-expression involved in dancing, rather than physical. For example in hide-and-seek they "know" they are not really lost, but experience the thrill of it anyway.

"Fight"

- Gentle rough and tumble
- Chasing and tag
- Dancing and bouncing around
- Throwing things about, preferably in a controlled way such as a contest with a target or similar
- Ball games
- Tearing up and squashing things

"Flight"

- Being pulled around, e.g., in a cart. Pulling others puts it more under their control, as long as the others do not mind!
- Swings
- Pedalling or scooting around. Can be made more controlled by setting out a course, or obstacles
- Chasing games - some children find being chased difficult so need to be chasers, others it is the opposite. Similarly be careful with "I'm coming to get you" games, though if children can manage them they are great risky thrills
- Slides, whether playground-type, mud, or snow
- Obstacle courses

"Freeze"

- Dens, tents, hidey-holes
- Exploring - can be as simple as a walk in the park, or even round the setting garden noticing the snails, or counting the birds
- Hide and seek (child regulated in case they end up feeling lost and abandoned)
- Camouflaging
- Parachute games

Heights

- Have a range of different heights to climb, and different difficulties
- Balancing beams, stepping stones, low walls
- Seesaws, swings, and slides
- Small ramps with varying steepnesses
- "Build your own" challenges with available crates and planks (do the safety assessment before they are used!)
- Ropes and handrails

Tools

- Pretend play with pretend tools
- Helping with food preparation (using suitable implements)
- Gradual move to real(er) tools and implements such as blunted knives, mashing spoons
- Real tools are advisable only if staff are familiar with how to use these with children and suitable risk assessments have been done, and some children may need very close supervision

Sensory risks

- Puddles and taps
- Hot and cold buckets of water
- Hose pipes, squeezy bottles with water
- Carrying buckets of water about
- Watering plants
- Mud
- Blowing out candles

Less and More Than It Looks

There are a lot of ideas in this chapter, and they can easily feel overwhelming. If we do feel this, then we can be assured that we are at least in part reflecting the feelings of the children as they recover from trauma and build a new relationship with a new self and a new world.

By way of balance, you might also feel looking through the lists "we do a lot of that already!" I am sure you do. There is not much in this or the next chapter that is not part of any high-quality early education setting (see Chapter 15 for more on this). It is not the strategies that make our work trauma-informed, but the children's experiences of them. Are we mind-mindedly tuning in to their needs and responding sensitively to them, reflecting all the while on what it feels like to them? Are we understanding what we see in terms of developmental needs for safety? If so, it does not matter that much whether you take up any or all of the ideas in this chapter, or add your own. You will be providing trauma-informed early education, and making a lifetime's difference for all the children you encounter.

13

Resilience 3 - Developing the Self

This chapter will provide:

- Strategies and experiences that help develop children's sense of a coherent self
- Playful ways for children to gradually acquire skills of self-regulation
- Strategies for addressing gaps in development in key curricular areas including language and executive function

Core Self

How do you know that you are *you*? How do you know that your hand is *your* hand? You might wriggle the fingers, or touch something, or tell me that you just know! Our sense of who we are at the most basic level is based on millions of brain cells and hundreds of brain systems mapping our bodies and responding to what happens when we do things with them. This gradually builds up into our sense of consciousness, of being here, and of being "me", who I am and how I fit in.

As we saw in Chapter 7, this can be disrupted by trauma. With simple trauma, trigger moments can temporarily put children into a smaller self, consisting of basic emotions and FFFF actions. Developmental trauma, by contrast, leads to an adaptation to a chaotic and inconsistent world. The self that develops will itself be chaotic and inconsistent to match that world.

Building a coherent and stable sense of self therefore requires coherent and stable experiences of the world, and of our internal experiences of it. What can help children are the same opportunities as are outlined at the start of Chapter 12, under Core Self. Almost anything that has interesting sensations with rhythm and repetition will do. All the better if we are there too, to wrap it around in meaning and encouragement.

Cause and Effect - A Coherent World

Cause and effect is built into the world all around us to the extent that it is impossible to avoid. But it is very easy not to notice it. And children who have experienced life in chaotic

DOI: 10.4324/9781003563808-17

or inconsistent contexts may not have the internal templates to map on to, or make sense of, the way one thing such as a consequence can regularly follow another such as a cause. What we can do is firstly to help develop those templates, and then to help children to notice cause and effect when it happens. One consequence (!) of this is that forms of behaviour management based on consequences, even just on positive ones, will lack effect for many children. We need different approaches, as discussed in Chapters 8–10 and promoted as a whole setting policy in Chapter 15.

The following ideas meet both of these needs, because children can engage with them at different levels. It can be a very fundamental (though hardly simple) engagement through senses and body experiences, or it can over time become a deep engagement with the laws of nature through adult scaffolding and commentary. As with everything else in these two chapters, the more we wrap the play in attuned commentary, the deeper will be the learning and development. Sometimes the best activities are the "found ones" where we happen (on purpose) to have a rich chat about what is going on - why does it rain? Where has the mouse gone? What happened to the last biscuit?

Here are some ways that cause and effect can be most easily experienced, noticed, and eventually thought about:

Physical

- Rolling things around. Can be made more interesting with ramps or obstacles
- Pushing and pulling - doors, carts, trolleys
- Setting up and knocking over - skittles, dominos, block towers
- Blowing up balloons and letting go
- Musical instruments
- Squeeze or stretch toys or other items
- Water ripples and splashes
- Water funnels, containers, pipes. An outdoor plumbing system on a fence or wall with different colour water and routes has hours of exploration
- Mixing colours. As a free activity, but also guided to explore interesting mixes (e.g., blue and yellow to get green)

Procedural

- Cooking
- Setting a table
- The routines and rhythms of the day, getting involved in creating and running these (ring the tidy up bell!)
- Tidying up (so that we can then use the floor for dancing, for example)

More Abstract

- Stories and narratives. All stories contain chains of events. More concretely, cause-and-effect picture books for exploration

- Pop up and flap books
- Sorting games by different characteristics - colour, shape, size; change them over
- Noticing patterns in nature (e.g., rains, get wet; sun, dry and warm; wind, trees move, hat blows off)
- Imitation and follow the leader games - e.g., dance slow, dance fast, and notice how it feels
- Modelling, narrating, or recalling social causes. "You gave me your picture and it made me happy". If children don't grasp this, or the even more abstract "you took the toy and it made James cry - what else could you have done?" they need much more experience of physical cause and effect and/or verbal scaffolding
- Games with consequences, such as snakes and ladders

A Capable Self

Trauma can disrupt the usual course of child development in multiple ways. As we have seen, this is a process of adaptation to promote survival, but it leads to difficulties in other contexts that present as delays and disorders. The overall effect is that children are less capable to deal with challenges, and to put in place the actions they need in order to resolve them. As a result they fall back on "younger" strategies (behave your need rather than speak it, for example). Or they have trouble putting into practice better ones, even if they have been taught them. This section provides ways to develop four key areas - motor coordination, language, executive function, and social schemas or skills.

Motor Coordination

Passing games. These can be as simple as handing something back and forth, moving on to short throws of a soft item such as a small beanbag. Rolling back and forth across a table or the floor can be fun. Once children have enough coordination to kick a ball, this can be a simple kickabout or turn into an obstacle course (let children help set it up and decide how difficult it should be)

Transporting games. Children are often drawn to carrying things about, so we can make it more interesting by providing objects with different shapes, weights, and textures. Again simple obstacle courses can be made indoors or outdoors. Some children love being given missions or errands, where the challenge can gradually increase - for example a gradually higher pile of soft blocks over increasingly wide stepping stones.

Spatial awareness. Any games involving using behind/in front, up/down, in/out, and so on. Again obstacle courses are great, along with sorting challenges. Also labelling when these occur in other situations, from cooking to getting ready to go out.

Joining it up. Design with the children some simple movement sequences. Could be "crouch, jump, clap", or for some just a two element sequence to start with. Make a visual script of them, and call them out. Once they've got it a few times, create some more with variations (crouch, jump, hop). Enjoy the confusion; the children may want to challenge you too.

See also **animal moves** and **obstacle courses** above.

Loose parts. Children will enjoy exploring, fiddling, poking, etc., all the while developing fine motor coordination. Similarly for bead threading and similar, but make sure this is playful not a production line. Add some clothes pegs, tongs, etc.

Keepy-uppy. Great with balloons, feathers, etc. Vary the challenge with different sizes or with more than one!

Art. Large art outside can help develop motor concepts that children can later deploy in smaller art indoors. Have a big wall, some large brushes, sponges, and so on. Also filling squeezy bottles with diluted washable paint can be fun on wall or floor.

Squeezing and squashing. Can be dedicated toys, but also anything squishy. Have items that need two hands working together (a big cushion) and some that need fingers only. Also great for emotional regulation.

Dancing about. As above, and consider adding ribbons to wave about - this can help with making movements smooth.

Action songs. There are so many, so pick ones the children enjoy. Heads Shoulders Knees and Toes might be too cognitively demanding for some, but they might enjoy following on.

Dough. Poking, prodding, shaping, squishing are all sensory fun and learning (see above) but also develop fine motor control and finger independence. So does having finger lights to point at the ceiling or a wall.

Fairground games. Child-friendly variants of hoopla, rings, skittles. For variations fill a bucket with water and see not only who can get the ball in (vary the distance) but who can make a splash!

Language

Promoting language development for young children is a huge topic that we cannot cover with any justice here. What I can do is indicate some of the main areas to consider and outline ways to support their development. Language is a key part of developing resilience for some of the reasons in the following table:

Aspect of language	*Supports resilience by*
Vocabulary	Expressing needs Reducing stress through understanding what is going on Supporting self-regulation through self-talk, internalising strategies Supports action, such as making requests or learning a script for what to do
Sequence and narrative	Providing meaning and understanding that reduces the stress of whatever is happening Helping to order and pattern response sequences (deep breath, then . . .) Putting any difficulty in a context - yesterday was better so tomorrow might be A vehicle for acquiring complex concepts, e.g., through stories
Pragmatics	Enabling some "how to" scripts and social schemas such as how to express a need or an emotion, or to ask for help

As a result, if children are struggling with any of the things in the right hand column, the other interventions in these chapters will be boosted if we also work on their language development. There are some packages and programs that can help this. They have the disadvantage that they may focus on only one aspect (e.g., boosting vocabulary) and also need money and training.

Much effective work can be done just day-to-day by ensuring:

- Lots of meaningful two-way conversations between children and adults
- Building on children's turns in conversations and adding to them ("A dog? Yes, a big, friendly dog!")
- Modelling vocabulary and using language to get things done
- Telling stories, especially with props for some of the main items
- Providing mind-minded commentary on their play, saying what you see and reducing questions
- Introducing new items and topics of interest and telling children what they are called, using some of the related words.

Executive Function

This is all about focusing attention, choosing some actions and inhibiting others, breaking off from one task to begin another, and processing complex information. Most young children are still in the early stages of developing adult-level skills in these areas. We can accommodate this and support their growth by providing a careful balance of stimulation - enough to engage, but not so much as to overwhelm. We can ensure experiences are long enough to capture interest, but not so long as to exhaust it. And, as with everything else in these chapters, the best way to support the development of executive functions is through rich experiences alongside a sensitive and reflective adult.

There are also specific approaches we can plan and experiment with, to see which ones attract the children and sustain their attention. As always, we can be guided by their responses.

Learning to choose. Some children struggle with this either because it does not feel safe (what if they choose wrong?) or because they do not have much experience choosing. Start with modelling choosing and talking out loud. "Do I feel like some apple or some banana today? I choose apple!" Offer children binary choices between two alternatives, each of which are fine - "do you want apple or banana?" Gradually extend to more open choices as they can manage - "what would you like for snack?"

Small and tolerable delays. This can be just in the course of the session as children are supported to wait. Or it can be a "wait for it" game. Perhaps the children are lined up for a race and waiting for a signal. Or as a game we wait one-two-three-four-five before going down the slide.

Simon says. Make the instructions easy to do; and make it fun and funny when people are caught out. Let them set the challenges too; they love it when you make a mistake.

Backwards Simon. This is quite challenging for children so it is all about the fun rather than the performance (don't do the "you're out" for this unless the children really can cope). They just have to do the opposite of whatever you say. So "sit" means "stand" and so on.

Silly sorting. Level one is just to sort things by a property, such as all the red ones, blue ones, etc. Level two is to sort the same things now by a different property - perhaps size or shape.

Mirror movements. The children have to copy a leader who makes various simple movements. Focuses attention and purposeful control.

Cognitively rich movement games. For some children just remembering who is "it" in tag is enough. Can extend - e.g., can only tag if walking, or if you say "fish".

Aerobic activity. This is fun in itself, as well as a way of expressing FFFF responses in an adaptive way. But also is good for developing attention and calm focus.

Statues. Freezing when the music stops, or when the leader says a particular word.

Storytelling. Make a story of the day with the children. What can they remember doing? Support this with some visuals of different possibilities they can choose from. Do similar things re-telling a story the children like and know well - what happened next? And next?

Animal moves. Include some larger switches. Instead of from cat to frog, go from bouncy cat to sleepy frog, now sleepy cat, now bouncy frog. Chaos may result.

Tidy up. Make tidying up more fun and interesting by doing it by category. For example, big things first, or red things first, or floor then table, and so on.

Timers to support waiting or inhibition. Sand timers are better than electronic as they are easy to understand and it is fun to watch the grains. Children often start spontaneously using them for self-help.

Simple guessing games. What hand is the coin in? What's missing from the picture, or the snack table? Similar to treasure hunt but less active, I Spy games based on descriptions the children can manage. Could be traditional "beginning with p", or more easily "I spy something big", or "blue" or "that I'm wearing". The point is the directed attention and search.

Social Schemas

Children can relate well and happily with their peers but not necessarily have the social scripts that can deal with difficulties or extend and deepen interactions. These scripts or schemas include asking for help, joining in play, sharing or declining to share (if you really need this stick) and so on. Some ways to support children to develop and test these include the following.

Model it yourself. Talk out loud each step. "I don't have enough glue! What can I do? Please can I have some of yours? Thank you". Or the alternative ending "oh, you need it all? That's ok. Now where else can I find some?" And so on.

Scaffold the same for children. "You've run out of glue? Oh dear, you need some more. What we can do is ask James if he can share some. Shall I help you? Ok, James, please can we have some of your glue?" And so on.

Puppets. These have all kinds of social dilemmas and difficulties that the children can give them advice on. The poor dinosaur wants to play but the monkey hasn't noticed, what could they do? Act out different "solutions" and their consequences, with the children as consultants. The dino steals the ball - then what? Ok, next time what could he do? Let's try that.

Make a simple **visual script** (and display where it is easy to see - all children will benefit from this). For example, can't reach something; please help! Or, hungry; ask for snack.

Practice these scripts with the children. Model it first - state the issue, go to the board with the script, and follow it. Prompt them to use the scripts too. This can be great in pretend play, which is lower stakes than a real social dilemma. Notice and praise (if children like praise, otherwise just notice) when children use the scripts.

Songs. Make songs with scripts in them. These are easy to remember, and the rhythm and repetition will connect them to soothing the stress system too. Many examples can be found online to inspire you (I'm not very good at making them up!).

Stories. As above, stories contain many social obstacles that you can chat to the children about.

Coaching. When a child needs to wait for a turn, or to use a scarce resource, talk them through it using mind-minded language. "It's hard to wait, it'll be your turn soon". "There isn't room yet at the mud kitchen, let's do this while you wait. We can check later".

An Effective Self - Self-Efficacy

Self-efficacy is about much more than self-esteem. As well as feeling good about themselves, resilient people also have a belief that they can make a difference to what happens to them, and to the world around them. Sometimes young children have an overabundance of self-efficacy! They might overestimate how high they can climb, or how big an object they can lift. Working all of these out by trying out challenges is an important part of development. Children who have experienced trauma might feel very powerful as a defence against a deeper sense of helplessness. Or they may simply feel ineffective and without control. All of the following might help either of these to develop a sense of their power and their limits so they can be both hopeful and realistic.

Shared event storytelling. Chat about what happened, what the child did, and what the effects were. Can be supported by audio or video recordings of children singing, telling a story, painting, playing, anything - they might enjoy watching it with you, as you narrate it or support them to.

Play with shadows. Making simple moves and shapes with the shadow projected onto the wall. Model some ideas for them. For more confident or able children, can add some scripts and stories, or else challenges.

Control and mastery experiences. Any play or learning that is just a little beyond them but they can do with help, and then gradually come to do without help. Best if it is a goal that they value, even if it is as simple as getting to the top of a ladder. Add narrative as it happens to provide meaning and encouragement, pointing out the child's effective actions and trying. Even better if the child is setting the goal - create challenges together (how many blocks can I carry? How fast can I run to the tree?).

Involve children. when you are doing something and talk out loud about the challenges involved, and how you are overcoming them. Invite their suggestions and try them out. Ask them for help, and thank them for it, pointing out what they helped do.

Model and talk aloud about goal setting, planning, and agency whenever you do it or see it happening around you.

Use **setbacks and failures** as chances to talk about the efforts made and to support the children to plan what to try next time. Make sure to notice and narrate their future successful efforts.

A Worthwhile and Wanted Self

It is possible to be very capable, and also very lonely - even to be alienated from oneself. Children get their sense that they are worthwhile and wanted (or not) from every encounter and interaction they have with us and with others. So the foundations are to be built from the material in Chapters 8, 9, and 10. Note, this is a bit different from helping children feel "I am a good person". "Good" is too loaded with expectations that many children will not manage yet. But they can be worthwhile and wanted along the way to that.

We saw in Chapters 2 and 3 that often people will take negative assumptions about themselves from traumatic experiences. Young children in particular seem to assume that the bad event was their fault, so their core view of self might include:

- I am a bad person
- I should be punished
- Bad things happen because of me
- I shouldn't exist

These heartbreaking views of self are not necessarily verbal, especially if they are formed very young. Cognitions can be coded into motor systems and the basic stress system (see Chapter 1 for how this happens). But we will see children behaving as though they are true - for example that their world only makes sense if they are being punished. It is a way of making the outside world match their inner experience. We can be powerful in changing that inner experience if we treat what they do as a *question*:

- Am I a bad person?
- Must I be punished?
- Can I do good things?
- Is anyone pleased I am here?

Reflect what answers you want your responses to children to convey, and everything else will follow. Some specific examples of other experiences we can provide include the following, with the proviso that none of them will work unless we are providing these messages in every encounter.

Positive Experiences of Self

Small acts of caring, be it for a space (such as a bit of garden, or keeping a part of the setting tidy, or watering a plant). Also set up chances to be caring for others; model this and show what to do. This can be as simple as passing the fruit round, or more complex such as offering comfort.

Creativity. Decorating a small space, drawing a picture, making (what they think is) sweet music with some drums, planning a garden, re-arranging the books - anything they enjoy that has a delightful product or process.

Cooking. The small acts of mastery in creating even a simple mini-pizza and enjoying the result. If also making for others, it helps with the next part too.

Superhero play. A chance to act out roles where one has useful powers and can solve problems for oneself or others.

Being Experienced as Positive

Any successful play or learning with others (success being defined by shared enjoyment).

All of the previous section, with positive reactions from adults and other children. Say what you like, what you like about what the child did, and what this means about them. "What a tasty cookie! You made it so well. You are a great chef!"

Positive communications to family and others. Being aware of how we frame our communications, making sure there is good news. Follow the same pattern. What did they do, what do you like about it, and what does this say about them? "James built a huge tower today. I was amazed how long he worked on it. He's getting much better at concentrating!" More on family engagement in Chapter 16.

Show off. Make displays of children's achievements. Even better, support the children to make them. Ensure these are easily visible to the children and refer to them often. Both your comments and the contexts of the displays can involve the same elements - what they did, what you like about it, what it says, positively, about them. "James pulled some weeds up. Our garden is much nicer. He is good at caring for it". Do not underestimate the degree to which this will be news to James.

A Self in Relationships

We can have all the social skills but still feel left out. This section is about how we can change that for children, especially those for whom relationships have not always been consistently and reliably positive.

There are also lots of ways that children can try out, develop, and deepen relationships with adults and other children through shared play. Almost anything that they enjoy and value will do. We need to bear in mind that children may have very different histories of play experiences and some will not know what to do (see Chapter 4). If a child is happier and feels safer hanging back and watching, or playing by themselves in parallel, trauma-informed thinking tells us that is fine, we can and should let them set the distance.

Here are just a few of many possible ideas:

Building site. Adult or children set a goal for what to build - a spaceship out of boxes, a "zoo" out of stones, a den out of sticks. Anything will do that people have to work together to create. Allow children to regulate their own level of participation - working alongside is also taking part. Co-regulate tensions over what to put where; "let's try it and see".

Social hub. Children who can't quite play or work easily with each other, but can with a supportive adult, can play with a key adult individually in the same time and space. Gradually this can be used to create a child-child dyad, then other children might join.

Mirror games where the children copy a leader. Start with an adult to show what to do, and let the children have a go at leading; they will enjoy setting you a challenge too, so if a child struggles in a group, be their mirror till they get the idea.

Turn-taking games. Some children won't cope with turn-based activity with (to them) long waits such as board games with more than one other. Start with very small and quick turn taking (e.g., alternate throwing a hoop, or building a tower). Natural turn-taking such as passing or throwing a ball or frisbee back and forth may be enough for some. Imitation games such as follow the leader or mirrors are also a good start as they build a basic me/you pattern.

Small world play or pretend play. This can often involve social roles (and some negotiation about them) in the normal flow. The characters or objects might relate to each other in more complex ways than the children can directly manage if they were not pretending (e.g., two chefs work together). See next point . . .

Learning to pretend. Children, especially if they have not done much before, or if inhabiting a different world through dissociation is a habitual way of being, may not know how to do pretend play. We can help them through

- modelling (make it amusing to catch their attention)
- using routines and themes they may already know such as cooking or shopping
- giving them open-ended prompts (a hat, a box) and talk out loud as you try different ideas (look, I'm an astronaut!)
- Add story-like commentary to their play: "I can see the teddies are all in a heap – perhaps they are feeling cold and want to snuggle up"; follow the lead of the child's response
- Become part of their imaginary play to enrich it (but try not to take over or "make it happen"); be an incompetent chef or a timid firefighter.

Choosing games. Can be a random chooser such as a spinner with a turn for each child (remember to regulate the wait times). Or starting with adult-child dyad and then extending to child-adult-child and eventually to groups of children – everyone takes a turn to choose what to do (jumping, crawling, clapping, for example). The same for games with a leader – like follow-me or Simon Says.

Stories nearly always involve some kind of social dilemma. Chat about this as you read; provide props for the children to act it out in different ways. Are there ways they would have handled the situation better than the dragon?

Moments of service. Use times like snack or getting ready to give children helping roles (that they can manage); e.g., each child fetches the coat for another, or serving the banana. Make sure nobody is accidentally left out, and help children to do their task; scaffold thanking each other.

Parachute games. There are so many of these, most of which involve joyful cooperation and working in synchronisation.

Singing together. This builds shared community and joy, especially if it involves rousing choruses or call-and-response. Don't get tired of hearing about the wheels on the bus . . .

An Expansive Self

It is not enough to recover from traumatic experiences, or to be able to live without them intruding. We also want children to live well, find joy in life, and be curious about the world around them. There are many ways to cultivate both joy and curiosity. First and foremost are in the interactions we have just in the course of learning and play. For example, we can:

Show what we are feeling - show and talk about your enjoyment of what is happening, how it makes you feel and where in your body you feel it. Link this to being with the children and what you are seeing and doing together.

Curiosity

Some people are naturally more curious than others. But while there is an element of temperament, a lot depends on context too. In her book on the development of curiosity, Susan Engel describes one of her studies where young children in different settings were given a curiosity box to explore. In some settings they explored more than others, and with more depth. What made the difference was the amount of times the adult smiled as they were exploring. So there's a simple, low-cost intervention to promote curiosity and creativity - smile and encourage! There are children, though, who need much more. They might have been growing up in worlds where curiosity is risky or seen as bothersome behaviour. If your brain is adapting to a dangerous world, too, then it pays not to be curious as what is round the corner may be a bad thing.

Fortunately there are lots of ways we can encourage the emergence of curiosity. Often we have to model this, and bring it out through the way we interact and co-regulate. There are many opportunities to do this such as:

Time and space. Make sure children have unstructured time just to explore, and provide a range of enticing objects, including some novel ones. Natural materials are great as they are open-ended, but any curious manufactured thing can be great as well. No need for complicated and expensive toys - the box is more curious than the toy.

Explorations. Similarly, time and scope (within adult sight!) to explore a space outdoors and encounter the things there freely. Just to look, touch, and listen.

Sensory play. For children who are drawn to it, sensory play is creative and exploratory. See Chapter 12 on developing Core Self for more on this.

Lend your brain. Model being curious yourself. Say "I wonder what/why/how/who . . ." rather than using a question as this invites thinking rather than providing an answer. Beyond this, display wonder yourself: "I've not read this story before, I wonder what will happen!" "What a huge muddy puddle, I'd love to see how deep it is!"

Be careful with questions. They are great for helping children to structure a train of thought. The best are open-ended ones like what and why. Be aware of children's levels of understanding of questions (tools such as Blank's hierarchy are very useful for this).

Be careful with answers. Sometimes it is best to answer a question so a child can get on with whatever they were doing ("how do I open this jar?"). But often if instead of giving the answer we say "Great question. I wonder how we can find out?" then we can support some rich exploration and the development of curiosity.

Have open discussions. If a child wonders why the sky is blue and grass is green invite theories from the children; then guide to how we can find out. Or set up testable ideas (do toy cars roll faster down a slope than toy trucks?).

Celebrate and **display** children's enquiries. It could be a wall or display board where accounts of finding out about different things can be posted, and referred back to.

Develop long form **projects** around children's interests, honouring whatever they want to investigate. If it is the entrancing subject of what happens to our poo after the toilet, then it is still science and exploration! By all means do dinosaurs and space (the usual topics!) but look out for the more left-field or minority interests that others can become interested in.

Guest stars. Children mostly love having visitors so invite in from the community or the families people who have had interesting lives, done interesting things, or have different jobs. Support the children to ask questions - and to follow up after if a new interest is inspired in Amazon exploration or working in a call centre.

Joyfulness

You may have noticed that this chapter on building resilience has included some bad jokes or silly examples. This is deliberate. We are getting to the point and purpose of trauma-informed work. This is, yes, that children can recover and find resilience and learning. But above all it is so that they can find JOY. And for joyfulness to become the routine and expectable tone of their lives going forward. So a last section on this, our most important and lasting gift to them.

As with curiosity, joy emerges naturally from almost anything we might do in early education. But not all children may notice it, and the feeling of joy may be unfamiliar. Some ways to change this:

Little victories. Notice and celebrate even the smallest steps of progress a child has made. Use emotion language "I am so happy you've tried some carrot - did you enjoy it?" "Your picture is really beautiful, I am proud of you for spending so long on it".

Positive problem solving. Instead of "stop that", "let's do this instead".

Fun. We can't expect children to manage 12 more years of deferred gratification in education unless they have fun at the start. Have lots of moments of music, dancing, jokes, silly time, and generally moving about.

Creating together. Music together, group dancing, making a mural outside.

Laughter. Read funny stories as many times as the children find them funny. Have a joke of the day (there are dreadful books of them), tell the children funny stories of things that have happened.

Chances to care. It may be as simple as helping to water the plants (and the floor), or a class pet, or looking after a space. Promoting chances for the children to care for each other, from helping to put coats on to modelling how to praise and compliment.

Enjoy the world. The outdoors is good for our mood, as is exploring it, splashing puddles, making the world's biggest collection of interesting twigs or small stones. If funds allow, try some new places like a beach or a park.

Story of the day or session. Find some time to take the children through the events, and what they liked and why. Model this for them: "I loved it when we went out and saw the pigeon".

Share the good news. Make sure to tell families about some of the above, so they can chat to their children about it too.

If In Doubt

Show the children you love them. They will remember it for the rest of their lives. And some of them will live on it, literally.

14
Trauma and Neurodevelopmental Differences

This chapter will provide:

- Information on common developmental disorders and how they relate to trauma
- A transdiagnostic approach to helping that does not depend on diagnoses
- Observations of how trauma-informed thinking can help any child

"What Is It?"

Trauma-informed practice provides us with an approach that can help us work out what to try in complex situations. One of its main principles is that different people may experience the same situation very differently. Let's take as an example a fairly routine transition within the day of a typical early education setting. The children are going to stop whatever they are doing, and gather to sit for a story and some singing. Here are four children who react to this very differently:

> Alfie ignores the signal and carries on doing what he was doing
> Bethany ignores the signal and carries on doing what she was doing
> Cassie ignores the signal and carries on doing what she was doing
> Diarmid ignores the signal and carries on doing what he was doing

That repetition isn't a mistake. Yes, it looks like four children all having the same reaction. But if we look more closely, with a trauma-informed view, what we see is four children all doing the same thing (or rather, not doing it!), but their actual experience of the moment might be quite different. A second key principle of trauma-informed practice is that we can understand unexpected or unwelcome behavioural responses if we think about exactly *how* the people reacting that way are experiencing the situation. So let's take a first guess at what is in these children's heads.

> Alfie heard the signal but didn't realise it was for him
> Bethany is so absorbed in what she is doing, she didn't hear
> Cassie finds any change and uncertainty frightening
> Diarmid wants to avoid being with the other children as it usually goes wrong

DOI: 10.4324/9781003563808-18

This is just the mind-minded step we looked at in Chapter 8. Of course we can only really do this once we know the children and have observed how they respond to different events – I am shortcutting all of that here.

But now we have a first guess, we also have some ideas for what might help them. Alfie and Bethany might both benefit from advance notice of a change or a more personalised signal, perhaps even a visual. Cassie might respond to those but may also need some adult co-regulation, and to grow her concepts of now/next. Diarmid needs some positive experiences with peers, and meanwhile perhaps some adult scaffolding to help him manage – or perhaps he can even just listen from a comfortable distance.

There are many more ways we could help the children, and one or more of them are likely to be successful eventually. You have probably thought of more ideas as you were reading. But there is something I have not told you about the children, so here is some more information:

Alfie has recently been diagnosed with autism
Bethany is a typically developing girl with no known issues
Cassie experienced a major trauma a year ago
Diarmid was both preterm and spent some time on oxygen in a neonatal unit

Does knowing that about the children add anything? Of course it does. We have more background on the "why", as well as a common platform for discussing with families and with other professionals if needed. But also, we were able to come up with some good ideas for helping even without the diagnostic information. And all the ideas are the same as the ones that are recommended for children with those diagnoses. So we have more information, but we are not necessarily changing what we try.

This chapter is not about the debates concerning diagnoses and labelling. The point here is that trauma-informed practice works in early education as what might be called in the jargon a "transdiagnostic" approach (Astle et al., 2022). This is a relatively new way to look at developmental issues that considers individual profiles and needs for support. These can overlap across different diagnostic categories – and also one child with language development issues may have different needs to another with the same diagnosis. Being mind-minded in our observations and planning is an effective way to consider individual needs whatever the underlying causes.

There are also two good reasons to take a trauma-informed approach with developmental differences. Firstly, it is a horrible fact that these children are much more likely to have experienced trauma than others (Jones et al., 2012; Kerns et al., 2015), including maltreatment (McDonnell et al., 2019), peer bullying (McQuade et al., 2018), or sexual abuse (Helton et al., 2017). Secondly, as we will see below, the challenges that living with neurodevelopmental difficulties raise for young children can themselves make an early education setting difficult to cope with. There may be many triggers of overwhelm and bumps that make managing harder that are not necessarily traumatic in themselves, but which a trauma-informed approach can help with.

In the rest of this chapter I will provide some outline descriptions of some common neurodevelopmental issues. These are necessarily sketchy and are certainly not guides to diagnosis or support. The aim is to point out the aspects of the different diagnoses that have issues in common with children who have experienced trauma. And to show how developmental differences can make life more difficult, even to the point of being traumatic for young children. In doing so, we come up against difficult questions of language. In the diagnostic manuals, and many healthcare settings, what a growing neurodiversity movement suggests we should see as developmental differences are still described as "disorders". These are quite complex issues, that bear on trauma-informed practice as we want to be both culturally sensitive (Norbury & Sparks, 2013) and respectful of individuals and their experiences (see Dwyer et al., 2024 for a nuanced discussion). With due regard to both of these, and asking pardon for it, I refer in this chapter to differences and diversity, except when discussing described diagnoses where I retain the official terminology to reduce confusion.

Sketches of Developmental Differences

Autism

Autism spectrum disorders are also sometimes called social communication disorders, which describes well what they are essentially about. Sometimes the signs of autism are clear, and sometimes they are more subtle. And the range can differ from person to person, and in different settings - this is why they are "spectrum" disorders. But there is a common core that is often seen with young children. These cluster around two sets of differences (APA, 2013). The first is to do with interactive communication. Autistic children may not follow social cues or pick up social information. For example, they might not respond if you speak or smile at them, or spontaneously share how they are feeling. Talking may be developing later or more slowly, or children may not speak at all. The second cluster is patterns of behaviour such as preoccupations. This can include lining up toys or items, or paying intense attention to details such as the spinning of a toy car wheel. Verbal children may have strong interests in particular topics, especially those involving complex categories such as dinosaur species or car makes. Part of the same cluster is a frequent difficulty with changes or transitions, whether this is stopping doing something and starting another activity, or a new food item on the menu. Finally, some children may be highly sensitive to different kinds of sensory experience, be this sounds, textures, or smells - a few are the opposite and are undersensitive to the point of not seeming to notice pain.

Even in this very sketchy description we can see some common behaviours with children who have experienced trauma. A child who is very shut down emotionally or dissociated may not respond to communication. Children who have experienced trauma are often aversive to change, and may try and create pattern in their environment, even insisting on toys being in a particular order. And they may have sensory triggers for particular traumatic memories.

There are some common pathways here. One reason autistic children try to impose pattern on the world around them is to make it easier to understand and more predictable. This reduces the cognitive burden as well as anxiety levels. Children who have experienced trauma might do similar things for a similar reason - to avoid the preoccupation of triggers, or make the world feel more predictable so they can stay within their zone of tolerance.

ADHD

ADHD is a complex range of difficulties that tend to be seen in two clusters (APA, 2013). Issues with attention are at the core of diagnostic criteria. These might include being easily distracted, flickering from one thing to another, not "locking on" to a focus, as well as some of the effects of unreliable attention such as losing things, resisting complex tasks, or getting side tracked easily. The second cluster is about being hyperactive and/or impulsive. This might look like being "on the go" much of the time. If sitting in one place, children might jiggle and fidget, tapping fingers or ending up poking others. Staying in a seat for a length of time can be hard, and children may need to run about a lot. There may be "timing errors" when a child erupts into the play of others in an uncoordinated way, or interrupts conversations, or else just keeps talking energetically.

The causes of ADHD are complex and seem to involve a number of brain systems (Mehta et al., 2019). We know one well already, that handles inhibition and conscious control of actions - the ability to stop ourselves doing something or switching from one thing to another, or to carry out a complex action in an organised way (Wodka et al., 2007). This has various secondary effects as these children can easily be seen and labelled as disruptive or badly behaved. Parents, carers, and educators may find themselves exhausted keeping up with the hyperactivity or the chatter, and there may be relationship impacts with other children due to the problems with play and interaction. Children may feel themselves to be out of control, and frightened by this, which is likely to increase their levels of arousal and therefore escalate impulsive responses.

Developmental Language Disorder

This affects up to 1 in 12 children and covers a range of difficulties that can be different in range and depth for every child (Bishop et al., 2017). Children may have trouble learning new words and using or understanding them. But it is not just about vocabulary as there may be difficulties with grammar and putting thoughts together. In terms of understanding, instructions of any complexity might be difficult to follow as well as stories. The impacts on social interaction, so much of which is based on language and communication, are obvious. If I cannot easily express a need I am more likely to have to behave it. Much play involves communications and interactions that coordinate actions and feelings in real time, and slowness or disorder in language processes can put children out of sync with each other. This can easily look and feel like disruption to adults and other children. Slowness or difficulty responding might lead to reduced or less rich conversations as others naturally shorten them, avoid them, or oversimplify them. Having difficulty expressing what we need, or with smooth interactions with others, can be very frustrating. Not understanding others, what is going on, or why it is difficult can also be frightening - as anyone who has been lost in a foreign city where they don't speak the language can testify. This, along with the other obstacles, can raise stress levels further so that children are described as having difficulties with emotions and behaviour (Burnley et al., 2024).

Developmental Coordination Disorder

Also called dyspraxia, developmental coordination disorder is not diagnosed before the age of 5 in some countries, but the signs can be seen much earlier (Zwicker & Lee, 2021). Often children are slower to develop physical milestones such as crawling or walking. In later years they can be described as "clumsy", fumbling fine motor tasks such as scissors, running in an awkward way or seeming to lack control over movements. Judging the space around them, and the people and things in it, can also be difficult, and they may get into trouble with others for bumping into them.

There are some secondary effects of these coordination difficulties. Children may become reluctant to do certain things or to try new physical challenges. This may be a sensible assessment on their part of their capabilities or else an understandable effort to avoid feelings of difficulty, failure, or frustration. A lack of coordination and skill may mean they give up tasks more easily, which can look the same to adults as inattention or distractibility. Finally, being in a situation when you never know if the next challenge is likely to be impossible, humiliating, or a disaster - even when that challenge is as apparently simple as getting across the room - can lead to a steady state of anxiety and vigilance (Cairney et al., 2013; Missiuna & Campbell, 2014). One way to reduce this anxiety is to keep things the same and predictable, so children with coordination difficulties may prefer simpler social situations or struggle with unexpected changes to routines, spaces, or people.

Conduct Disorder

Along with the associated term "oppositional defiant disorder", conduct disorders involve violent or aggressive behaviour, along with high levels of anger that are easily provoked. The behaviours might be directed at objects, property, or people. In young children, what we might see most often are difficulties in complying with simple requests or instructions, tantrums or outbreaks of anger out of proportion to provocations, or trying to provoke these in others.

There is a debate about the status of this disorder in young children that we will not enter into here. For our purposes, the point to note is that a lot of these signs are very similar to fight and flight responses that we have learned are common effects of traumatic memories. For a diagnosis of conduct disorder, the criteria specifically rule out a history of maltreatment (World Health Organization, 2019). While that sounds reasonable, it is not that helpful to educators on the floor who do not have access to the child's history. Also, there are as we have seen many forms of trauma that are not maltreatment. Ruling out trauma as a cause of the difficulties requires a total knowledge of the child's experiences, and we have seen that this is difficult to gain as trauma is often hidden, unknown to adults, or forgotten by them.

Premature or Difficult Birth

With advances in medical care, many babies born early or with complications now fortunately survive and do well who might not have done in the past. Many of them have few long-term problems, but for those who do, these can be subtle and in a range of apparently unconnected areas (for a review see e.g., Chung et al., 2020; McBryde et al., 2020). Often when these present in early education, people do not make the connection between what they see and a child's very early experiences, and this can lead to misunderstandings and mislabelling.

While developmental issues are more likely the earlier children were born, a difficult or complicated birth can be a stressful experience for both baby and parents. We know enough about trauma to understand how effects of this can persist long after everyone is safe and well at home. In particular, babies who need intensive care after birth often experience high levels of pain, and often have to manage this on their own. Infants in special care units or similar often have less skin contact, less interaction and soothing, and hear their parents' voices less often or consistently - all due to necessary medical care. In Chapter 4 we saw how the developing brain learns from the environment what kind of world to start to get ready for. It is therefore no surprise that children with complex or premature birth histories may have difficulty managing emotions and coping with stressors. There is a traumatic element to their early lives.

This is compounded by some of the other known developmental impacts. These are complex and vary between individuals in complex ways but tend to involve difficulties in one or more of the following areas.

Visual	Following movement, e.g., of a ball or person Slower reactions Difficulty seeing verticals (steps, etc.)
Cognitive	Short attention span or distractable Short- or long-term memory issues Impulse control Managing complex information or situations Inconsistent learning - can do today but not tomorrow Specific issues with maths and number
Movement and coordination	Balancing Putting sequences of movements together Catching, kicking, throwing, etc.
Language	Remembering words and using them Difficulty speaking in sentences

Perhaps related to all of these, social difficulties are also common. Joining in a game is harder when a child has difficulty expressing themselves, or following the motion of an object such as a ball. If the child tries to join in and does so clumsily they may end up with poorer peer relations and even experience bullying. Lack of social opportunity can then impact further on their development of social skills and scripts, so we might see what looks like unsocial or anti-social behaviour.

Another element of premature or complex birth is the impact on parents. They will have been through a period of intense anxiety about their child, as well as of often feeling utterly helpless. For parents of a new baby this can be traumatic. Long-term effects can therefore understandably include a higher level of anxiety about their child. In essence, any difficulty or issue, however minor, can serve as a trigger for memories of the early experience. Alternatively, parents may strongly wish their child to have a "normal" life, and to feel that the past is behind them. This may present to the educator as either avoidances of conversations about difficulties, or else a heightened pressure on the child, or themselves, to make sure everything is going well.

Attachment Disorders

Attachment has been one of the most important and influential concepts in child development for decades. While it is often described in early education in terms of four or more "attachment styles", more recent research suggests a more nuanced picture (Del Giudice & Belsky, 2010). This is discussed in Chapter 4 with respect to overlaps with developmental trauma. Here, we are concerned with some labelled disorders of attachment that might be applied to children in our settings. The links are easier to make with these since they are all thought to be caused by significant trauma. So for practical purposes, if educators are working with children with attachment disorders, everything in this book about developmental trauma will probably apply.

There are different ways to characterise attachment disorders, but one of the most prevalent is reactive attachment disorder (Minnis et al., 2006). There are two variations for this (APA, 2013). In one, the inhibited subtype, children have difficulty forming relationships with key adults, especially in trusting them. The children might be very watchful for danger and self-reliant in trying to deal with it. On the other side, they might not accept comfort, or share experiences of joy. With the opposite, disinhibited, version, children are often described as "over-friendly". They might treat strangers the same as people they know well, making close contact, chatting freely, holding hands, or climbing into their lap. In some ways, there is a superficial easiness in caring for the children as they are often smiling and compliant - even over-compliant. Some children might be prepared to do anything for positive attention from an adult.

The vulnerability of both groups is clear. Not drawing on or seeking adult support is as risky as trusting anyone and being willing to do anything for them. We can also see the reflections of what we learned about developmental trauma. In response to a difficult and dangerous world it makes sense for the brain to adopt one of two strategies. It might prioritise developing self-reliance since this is an "everyone for themselves" world lacking in help and relief. Or alternatively, and especially when the sources of the danger are powerful adults or even caregivers, then getting really good at keeping them happy and staying close to them may be the best path for survival.

A Child's Eye View

The essence of trauma-informed practice is to look at a situation from the point of view of the person experiencing it, and to notice ways in which it may be feeling unsafe to them. For young children this might be because it is actually terrifying to them, or because they lack the capacities to manage the feeling or to respond effectively with actions. We have seen even in the short sketches above that all three of these may hold for children with neurodevelopmental disorders. Because of problems understanding what is happening, things may be more scary. Because life is so complex to manage anyway, or because of the nature of their difficulties - and also because of a history of not coping - their ability to regulate this feeling may be less. And they may struggle with controlled and coordinated action, and have to fall back on more basic fight, flight, freeze, and flop responses.

But we are there too, with our capacities to co-regulate, to adjust difficult situations, to calm and soothe, and to support effective action. By seeing the child as an individual who is doing the best they can right now, and by seeing what is happening through their eyes, we are likely to be able to help – whatever the cause.

Chapter summary:

- Disentangling different diagnoses and comorbidities is complex and difficult
- Trauma-informed practice provides a way to respond and help even without knowing a specific diagnosis
- Children with developmental differences can experience the world and themselves in ways that have traumatic aspects

Practice points:

- Whatever else is known about the child can help a mind-minded reflection on how they are experiencing a situation
- An emphasis on what is needed can help individualise support

Section 3

The Whole System

15
The Wider System

This chapter will provide:

- A more general context for trauma-informed practice beyond the individual child
- A map to help reflections on what parts of the wider system we can change
- Specific guidance on the elements of a trauma-informed whole setting

A Useful Model

So far in this book we have considered trauma, and how we might help, in terms of the children and their immediate relationships with key adults. However, this occurs within a larger, interconnected system. A practitioner's ability, for example, to provide a calm response to a frightened child depends on the time and emotional space that they have available. This relates to the staffing levels in the setting, and also whether the setting policies prioritise the development of positive relationships. Early education settings can only do that if they exist in a policy context that supports it, and are sufficiently resourced to do so.

This is an ecological model (McLeroy et al., 1988). It is sometimes called an "onion" model because of the way it shows complex situations are made out of layers. Different versions have different numbers of layers, but we can manage with three:

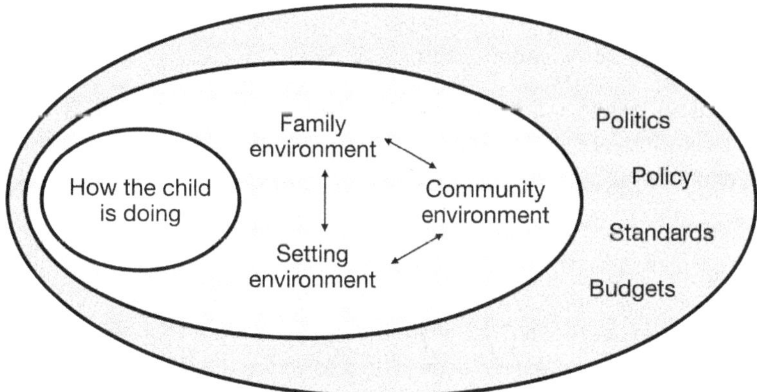

Figure 15.1 An ecological model for wellbeing

DOI: 10.4324/9781003563808-20

Thinking ecologically means realising that what we see from the children is only part of the picture. The setting environment, family environment, and community all have an impact. And these three interact. For example, a supportive community where people drop off unwanted cardboard boxes for the children to use in play provides a setting with more scope for offering open-ended activities at low cost. A family who has got involved for the first time in the setting by contributing some boxes and experiencing being welcomed and thanked is now a more willing partner in supporting their child. The setting was encouraged to start this scheme because family engagement is a priority in local quality standards, supported by training for staff.

This is a "virtuous circle". In trauma-informed work we are often dealing with less positive interactions. What we have learned to see, rightly, as a child struggling with developmental trauma, or occasionally overwhelmed by triggers, is part of a complex, interconnected web. Of course early educators have more influence on some parts of this system than others. A practitioner on the floor might feel they have limited scope to influence central government decisions about funding, for example. But they do have some scope, and there are other aspects where they have much more. In this chapter we will explore the different levels of the system and how a trauma-informed setting can work to influence them.

Working Systemically

Talking about working systemically can sound abstract and theoretical, but it is about making real changes. It is also about realising how some quite small interventions can turn out to have ripples across the whole system and therefore beneficial effects out of proportion to what we did. Here is an example:

> Bart (4 years old) comes willingly to the setting and greets his keyworker gladly each morning. But then he hangs back during the day, keeping away from the other children. When he does interact briefly, he can become hostile, sometimes even pushing them away if they try to play with him.

So far, we might consider Bart to be a typically developing child with some difficulties with social skills. He can manage adults, but does not have the skills to play with peers. The setting manager books a conversation with Bart's parents, and learns some more:

> Bart comes from a family of Romani travellers. Their small community has no other children his age, but he is much-loved, in part because of the caring way he plays with and even seems to mentor younger children.

We have learned something important about the system around Bart here. What looked like a lack of skills seems to be related to context. In the home environment he is even so skilled at interactions and play that he can look after younger friends. Why such a different child in the setting?

> The setting manager reflects that it took some effort to get Bart's parents to agree to come in for an appointment, so it occurs to her to ask them about their general experiences in the neighbourhood. They share that they are often shunned, have names called after them, and there have even been instances where the family have been threatened in the shopping mall. They have been careful to teach their children to be wary of others.

We can hardly blame Bart's parents for encouraging wariness of people outside their community, given what they are experiencing. We can even recognise this for what it is - an attempt to stay safe even when this involves other costs. With our trauma-informed thinking, we can now understand Bart's hanging back, and also his tendency to push other children away, as defensive strategies.

But we also want to be clear what is driving this. We have moved a long way from suspecting poor social skills. In fact, we can now do the step from Chapter 4, and ask "in what kind of world does Bart's behaviour make sense?" The answer is now obvious - a world in which he is exposed to danger because he belongs to a particular group. We can go on to ask the second question - "what kind of world do we want this to be for Bart?" And there are two areas where we can influence this. I hope this extended example has made it obvious that one of these areas is not to put Bart on a social skills course. This is not an intra-child issue, as our "onion" thinking has shown. Instead two other factors are key:

1. Bart and his family are stigmatised and are objectively not safe in the neighbourhood
2. Bart's brain is assuming that the same is the case in the setting

The setting manager decided to address the second of these first as it seemed easier to make changes quickly. As part of the curriculum, they had a week celebrating the different family backgrounds of the children. Every family was encouraged to bring in items that reflected their cultural heritage, and to offer traditional stories and songs. The manager made sure that Bart's family felt included in this, and kept some of their contributions on permanent display, while encouraging Bart to learn more about his community using the setting's Wi-Fi and to tell the others about it. She also made a point for several weeks of making sure Bart saw her warmly greeting his parents at drop-off and pick-up, and waved to them when she saw them in the street. Bart started to see that the setting was a place where his family was not stigmatised and were not in danger, and started to relax and play. He no longer needed to defend himself there.

Problem solved? No. There was still the issue in the neighbourhood, and the setting manager decided she wanted to do something about that too. At the next families event, where parents and children spent a few hours in the setting playing and socialising, she introduced Bart's parents to some other families that she knew would welcome them. She encouraged them to bring some traditional foods for the pot-luck lunch and made sure to try them herself, while also passing round the plate. Not all the other families played ball but most of them did, and some new friends were made. Bart and his family now began to see there were places and people where they were welcome and safe.

Over the next few months, the manager noticed that other "hard to engage" families were spending more time in the setting, were less reluctant to chat with her, and were starting to bring in and offer ideas and activities from their own cultural traditions. Not only were more families now feeling welcomed and included, but the children's learning about the world and about how to rub along with different people had become exponentially richer. The manager dared to dream about how this might change the neighbourhood as these children became adults and community leaders.

We can see even in this fairly simple example just how much of the wider system the manager engaged with and influenced. In the next section we will look at the different parts of the "onion" and the trauma-informed role that settings can have for each.

A Trauma-Informed Setting

Pedagogy

This is a book about trauma-informed practice in early education. Learning is at the heart of what we do, and it is fundamentally what our settings are for. However, as we know, there are many different models for early education and many different approaches to pedagogy (how we think children learn and how we put that into practice). The purpose here is not to describe all of these and evaluate how trauma-informed these are - be it Froebelian or Montessori practice. All of them are strong in some trauma-informed aspects and less strong in others. The key (trauma-informed) thing is to be able and willing to adapt the theories and frameworks to respond to the needs that the children are presenting us with.

I have summarised some of the key features of a trauma-informed pedagogy in the table below. Practices connected to all of these can be found in Chapters 8–13, and they relate directly to the needs described in Chapter 7.

Mind-minded	Being aware of and responding to the ways children are experiencing what's happening, including feelings, thoughts, and interests.
Relational	Using positive relationships with adults to connect children to learning experiences and help them regulate the feeling and thinking that is needed. Providing rich, two-way, dyadic child–adult interactions to support development and learning.
Developmental	Awareness of the developmental status of each child and framing realistic (though still ambitious) expectations around that. Prioritising child development in itself and as underpinning curricular learning.
Holistic	Paying attention to every aspect of children's development and understanding how they interact - including motor, spatial, language, emotional, social, executive function, etc.
Agentic	Providing children with opportunities to influence what happens both in specific experiences and in the wider setting environment and planning. Supporting children's choice making and helping them learn how to choose if needed.
Safe	Settings are objectively safe. They also prioritise psychological safety for children, staff, and families; with an understanding that everyone can experience the same situation differently

The Environment

Trauma-informed thinking requires us to look at the setting environment in a particular way, which we explored on the beach in Chapter 8. Some traditional approaches to early learning have focused on the environment in terms of things, with a constructionist view that the learning is done by the children interacting with those things. However, as we saw on the beach, different children can have entirely different experiences with the same thing. For one child, the waves were a way to learn to be more aware of danger, while for another they were the opposite, providing a chance to try something new and edgy. And both of these are affected - often decisively - by how the adults interact with the children. The relationships we provide are often the bridge into learning that open up possibilities the child would not have dreamt of themselves.

The national practice guidance in Scotland, *Realising the Ambition*, puts it like this:

> We often talk about the environment in terms of physical spaces, but the key part of the environment for children is the human, social environment of positive nurturing interactions. (Education Scotland, 2020, p. 15)

In keeping with that approach, we will look at a trauma-informed environment in terms of primarily of the interactions and experiences on offer and how we can plan for them, as well as the spaces and things.

Interactions

We have covered the essential features of interactions and positive relationships in some detail in Chapters 8–10. If we look around a trauma-informed setting, we will see interactions that have the following features:

- Safe
- Attuned
- Interactive
- Available
- Approachable
- Meaningful
- Co-regulating

Again we can take our guide from the children and how they respond within interactions. That can tell us if we are too distant, or too close. Or if our assumption that they were interested in the shape of a leaf was premature, and it turns out they are exploring its fragility.

Experiences

A key element of children's experiences is how the session is organised. Many children have so far experienced worlds which are either chaotic and unstable, or else unresponsive to their needs and state of mind. Others have experienced one or two particular traumas that have disrupted their sense of the world as smooth and safe. Routines can help both of these. And in fact the conditions I am about to describe are the best ones for most people to learn most things, so taking a trauma-informed approach to routines can help everyone.

Different localities use the word "routines" to mean different things or else use other terms entirely. I am talking loosely about the different levels of activity in the setting that can have a predictable rhythm. As we saw in Chapter 7, all children benefit from experiences that are rhythmic, repeated, responsive, and meaningful to them.

This can be so at the level of the whole day or session; or even the whole week. Maybe Tuesdays are always the day for a walk in the park. And maybe the walk in the park is always followed by a rest and a story. But it can also be at the very small level of anything that happens regularly or needs to be done. Where do I sit at the table? Where are the things I like to play with? Is it socks or shoes first?

Children will use this regularity to feel safe since they are not having to worry or think about what's coming next (remember that children who have experienced trauma may have the working assumption that if they don't know what is next, then it is probably a bad thing). Further, as we saw in Chapter 7, they can use any regularity and rhythm to start to recalibrate their stress and self-regulation systems.

That happens only if the rhythmic and regular is also responsive. Responsiveness means adapting and changing to be in tune with the children's thoughts and feelings. So any routine we establish also needs to have some flexibility. If we decide that at 10am everyone stops what they are doing for a song then we create two risks. Firstly, children who were on the cusp of important learning, being highly engaged in whatever they are doing, will lose this for the lack of five more minutes to finish the drawing, the tower, get to the top of the tree or whatever. Secondly, some children, especially those who have experienced unstable or frightening worlds, may need more time to bridge across the change smoothly. So we need to have elastic and responsive boundaries in our routines.

And there is no point doing all of this if the children are unaware of it, or are unable to use that knowledge. The routines and rhythms need to be meaningful to them. This can take the form of visual timetables for the larger routines, or visual scripts for smaller routines (e.g., coat - shoes - play outside). For some children, a verbal commentary may be enough, and it is always useful to accompany whatever is happening with narrative especially if this uses mind-minded language referencing children's feelings and thoughts. Another way to make routines and rhythms meaningful is to involve children in creating them. The simple question "It's time to stop this soon; what shall we do next?" can be a helpful bridge into uncertainty for a child.

With all of this in place, transitions can become easier. This includes big transitions, like being dropped off. It also includes small transitions, such as going outside or stopping to have a snack. A trauma-informed approach to transition is based around how the children might be feeling and thinking about stopping or letting go of whatever it is before, how they experience the transition change, and their feelings and thoughts about whatever it is after. This includes allowing time for them to process whatever it is we are trying to convey to them, and being prepared to repeat this gently. Some children may need us to do more of this work for them, especially if their sense of cause and effect and of now and next is not well developed (see Chapter 7).

Some trauma-informed aspects of transitions are in the table below.

Why might a transition be difficult?	*Ways to support*
General hyperarousal	Have predictable routines Background of positive relationships Emotional co-regulation (soothing voice, touch, etc.) Interact positively for a while leading up to the transition Playful transitions (walk like a dinosaur, etc.)

(*Continued*)

(Continued)

Why might a transition be difficult?	*Ways to support*
Change or uncertainty as a trigger	Use a comforting object (stuffed animal, etc.) to stay with the child Provide before/after information Put this on a simple visual strip
Fear or reluctance about the next thing	Practise transitions from nice thing to nice thing; gradually introduce the feared thing Name and validate feelings Consider using a social story
"Glued" into the current thing	Advance warnings of change Gradual countdowns (10 minutes, 5 . . .) Sand timers Transition cues such as music Offer simple choices (do you want to bring X with you?)
Lacking now-next concepts	Provide narration of what is happening Talk aloud during your own transitions Use very simple first/then visuals for everyday activities (coat, then out) Work on these concepts using ideas from Chapter 13

Mind-Minded Planning

Children's actions, especially when they are inconvenient or difficult, often give us important information about their developmental needs. I mentioned in Chapter 8 the 2-year-olds who ignored the amazing "developmentally appropriate" equipment we had spent a fortune on, and just moved around for a couple of days. It was a strong clue to us that their brains were desperate to work on muscle growth and coordination. Another child I worked with had a tendency to put any loose object in his mouth. Of course we managed the choking risks, and also worked out that he had perhaps missed out on some early experiences of oral exploration (remember how babies will stick any new object in their mouths to investigate). So we provided some more age matched experiences with safer objects and after a few weeks the behaviours diminished.

Throughout the day, children give us many cues to their needs. For children who have experienced trauma, these can be heavily disguised. It is not possible to give a whole list, but some examples might show how we can "read" children's actions and work out what experiences to plan for them. The general idea is quite simple:

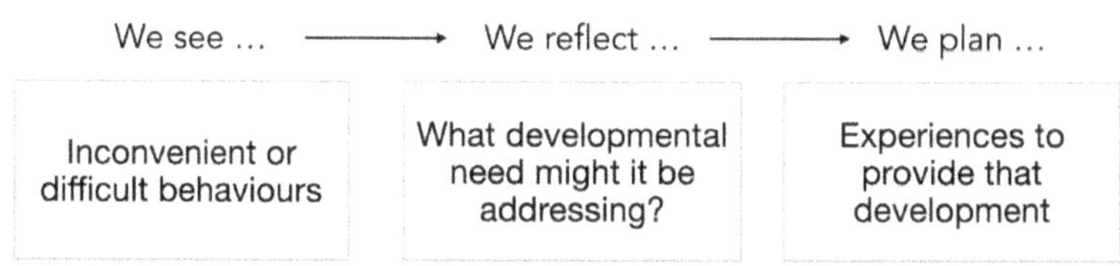

Figure 15.2

What we see	*What the brain might be looking for*
Throwing things around	Vigorous activity Exploring trajectories Hand eye coordination Exploring force and pressure
Not sitting still	Muscle development Motor coordination Short and interesting things to develop attention Dyadic interactions
Tearing book pages	Exploring concepts of print Exploring textures Irreversible changes Properties of different materials Having an impact on the world
Tantrum when told "no"	Understanding how to choose Limits of choice How to have a will of your own Different people want different things Exploring differences between wants (to fly) and can'ts
Fighting	Making contact with others Joining in Rough and tumble Experiences of risk How to play Developing strength How to compete Where do I fit?

One of the great things about the complexity of child development is that we do not have to be absolutely right in what we reflect and plan. Most experiences provide development along multiple different lines, and the worst that can happen is that we learn from how a child responds to what we plan for them, and use this to tune in more to their feelings, thoughts, and needs. If children are experiencing a lot of difficulties, for example, we might start by considering the balances that we are offering between structured and unstructured experiences. The trends away from single group work towards child-led learning through play can help with this (Yang et al., 2025) as long as we plan based on what the children need rather than on pre-existing assumptions about what we should provide.

Finally, on planning, a useful rule of thumb I learned from an insightful early years practitioner. We were struggling for ideas about how to support, or even contain within the setting, a 5-year-old who had experienced high levels of neglect and multiple foster placements. The practitioner was reflecting on what kinds of experiences the boy tended to create for himself and said, "I think basically he just wants to be babied". As we've seen throughout this book, children who have experienced trauma often have "stuck points" in their development, or else have wide-ranging gaps. The rule of thumb is this – to plan experiences that match the age and stage they seem to be. And to do this in ways that match the age they are. This 5-year-old had a baby-level need for physical comfort, but was far too "grown up" to ask for it. But he often accepted a hug and a sit on the lap when it was offered - and eventually learned first to ask for it, and secondly to start to comfort himself with a wrap-around blanket and stuffed tiger.

Spaces and Things

The physical environment of the setting is still important. We want spaces where children feel safe, comfortable, and welcome, with interesting things to do that match their needs for development. None of this needs to be expensive. A skilled practitioner and a cardboard box can create a whole world of learning and fun for a child.

A key aspect of a trauma-informed environment is that the children have a sense of control and ownership over it. This can be about the design and layout. We can involve children in decisions as to where to put the book case, how to arrange the books on it, or what we might plant in the window box. Similarly, having enough choice of activity and equipment for children to feel agency over what happens is important; while not overloading with no choice. And there might be small choices within bigger things that cannot change. Perhaps we need the book case to be *here* because it doesn't fit anywhere else - but how will we decorate it? Perhaps we have to do a story now, but which one, and where will you sit?

The following are some of the key physical features of a trauma-informed setting. Reading this list you might think it is more or less the same as any high-quality setting, and you are right. All of these help every child to belong, to feel safe, and to learn.

Spaces:

- Calm areas where children can relax
- Some enclosed spaces where children can feel safe and contained; can be little corners and nooks, or a tent or den
- Easily accessible outdoor and natural spaces; frequent visits to these
- Sightlines that make key adults visible to the children (and vice versa!)
- Enough room so people are not crowded
- Soft lighting that can be adjusted
- Décor with warm and calm colours
- Art and other work visible around the rooms at child eye level
- As little clutter as possible, balanced with a sense of happy busyness
- Plants and interesting natural objects that children can care for
- Calm, welcoming, and dignified staff spaces

Equipment:

- Soft and comforting objects - cushions, bean bags
- Lots of stuffed animal friends and supporters
- A full range of sensory items as detailed in Chapter 12
- Materials that can reduce stimulation - soft blankets, etc.
- Visual schedules and timers
- Some open storage so children can see and choose what they need
- Natural textures rather than too much hard plastic

- Signs and notices, etc., in the languages of families
- Cheerful display boards for families with signposts to supports

Policies and Paperwork

Anyone who has worked in early education for more than a few minutes knows that it involves a lot of paperwork. From policies to planning formats, curriculum frameworks, procedures for medication or care, practitioners can sometimes end up spending a lot of time with paper or on screens. The point of it all is to run a safe and effective setting for the children, but many have had the experience of the paperwork starting to take over and drive decision making. This is relevant for trauma-informed practice in two ways. Firstly, the time and energy involved can take away from the even more consuming but vital tasks of providing positive relationships for the children. Secondly, there is often something "hard-edged" about paperwork - have they achieved the milestone, have we documented the learning, did we follow the plan?

Douglass and Gittell (2012) offer the useful idea of "relational bureaucracy" as a counter to this tendency. The idea is to craft our policies and processes so that they embody and enable positive relationships. I've adapted a table from their paper (p. 277) to show what this might mean in early education.

Components	*Examples of relational bureaucracy*
People	Staff roles prioritise forming positive relationships with children and each other Wellbeing for adults and children is a priority Policies and practices reflect the cultures of families served Policies support the staff role by allowing for breaks, reflection times, etc.
Power structures and processes	Everyone has roles in decision making in the setting Staff, children, and families are consulted on policies and other changes Staff are supported to make autonomous decisions, to try things out and reflect safely on any difficulties
Relationship structures and processes	Flexibility is built into routines and procedures to allow for adaptation to children's changing needs Staff are trained and supported to develop positive relationships with children, families, and each other When things go wrong, this is recognised in an emotionally safe way with an emphasis on what has been learned Developing psychological safety for all is a core part of the curriculum Everyone has someone who can give them time when they need it

There are two chapters (17 and 18) on staff wellbeing that can support some of these elements. Adopting trauma-informed practices can result in many benefits, including a greater tendency for practitioners to experience more recognition and validation (Bartlett & Smith, 2019).

Behaviour Policies

A particular area of policy to consider are the setting's approaches to children's behaviour (Loomis, 2018). We have seen enough in this book to show that difficult behaviour is often driven by feelings that overwhelm a child's developmental resources to cope with them. Trauma-informed thinking tells us that when in particular we observe behaviours with elements of fight, flight, freeze, and flop, these may well be ways to manage feeling unsafe.

Behaviour policies need to have this thinking at their heart. Rather than a tariff of offences and consequences, we need to work mind-mindedly, asking how the child might have been experiencing a given situation, how their internal resources might have been unable to deal with it more adaptively, and how we can co-regulate to support that in future as well as developing their coping skills (Kurki et al., 2016). As well, we need to remember that if a child feels unsafe or stressed, this limits their ability to express their needs in adaptive ways, and to take on board or use "strategies" we might teach them. So a core element of any behaviour policy has to be ensuring that the whole setting environment provides psychological safety and nurture, and that the first-line response to any difficulties is to consider this. And any rupture, even the smallest accident, requires repair. Children need to know it is ok, they are still loved and cared for - we need to embody this through any behaviour management process.

The Family Environment

While practitioners can ensure that children experience trauma-informed care and learning in the settings, the family environment remains important. Educators have limited scope for influencing this environment, but they do have some. The next chapter looks at questions of engagement, how we can use trauma-informed principles to build respectful and effective working relationships with families, and also how we can reflect on our own assumptions and practices as we do this. This chapter is more about the *what* - the aspects of family life that we might want to influence.

Safety

Firstly, and most difficult, we need to do our part to ensure that children are actually safe. Without this, it is difficult for them to move on from traumatic experiences, but also, from a safeguarding point of view, educators have a key role in child protection too. I will not cover this in detail here, beyond stating that everyone in the setting needs to be familiar with relevant local safeguarding policies and procedures and to follow them, with regular training and support provided to staff. In particular, we need to balance our particular role in a multidisciplinary collaboration, but also remember that we have a unique insight into children's day-to-day functioning and experiences, and that sometimes we might be the only people who can complete a picture of a child at risk. Sometimes safeguarding fails because people do not take action or only have a part of the picture, so coordination and collaboration are key.

Hassles

It can be a common assumption that if there are difficulties in the home environment the best intervention is to send parents on a parenting programme. Trauma-informed thinking suggests some caution over this, however.

> Mandy is a single parent with four children, who attend three different schools and early learning settings. They are often late, or show up hungry or in dirty clothes. There seem to be few boundaries in the home, with the older children caring for the younger as Mandy does not often play with them, or take them out.

Gill manages the early year setting that Mandy's youngest attends, and has spent some time building a relationship with her. There is a multi-agency meeting coming up to discuss concerns about the family and Mandy shares how anxious she is about this. Gill asks, "what do you want them to understand?" Mandy shares the following:

> It's just so hard. The kids are at schools in three different directions needing different buses. I know I'm not looking after them properly, but I'm working two jobs and it's all going on debt payment. They grow out of clothes faster than I can afford them, and mornings are a nightmare - only one ring on the cooker works so we just grab cereal from a box.

Sharing this at the meeting helps the professionals realise just how many hassles Mandy is dealing with every day. They offer interventions to address these. Schools offer a staggered start to take the pressure off, and manage to pair up the older child with another family so Mandy doesn't have so many journeys. The early years setting offers to keep the younger child for an extra half hour to reduce pressure. A local voluntary organisation helps fix the cooker; another advice organisation helps her with managing the debt and also some benefits she did not know about. The schools make her aware of clothing banks they run. After a few weeks, everyone realises that Mandy's parenting skills are fine - they had been blocked by lack of time, and overwhelmed by emotions and planning. And the simple physical lack of money and basic equipment.

Early years settings often have closer relationships with families than any other part of the system does. We are well placed to put into practice the basic trauma-informed principle of assuming that is it not necessarily something wrong with the person, but more that they are dealing with a complex or difficult situation. And we are often well connected in the community to be able to signpost families to sources of help. Often the most useful thing we can do is to make ourselves aware of that supporting infrastructure so we can connect families to it.

Many settings also help with the "stuff" aspects that poverty or marginalisation can make so difficult, such as:

- Having a rack of books to take away and share
- A clothing store that anyone can contribute to or "borrow" from
- Providing a good meal for children as part of the session
- Linking with local food banks, or having a take and share basket with staples
- A toy exchange where families can leave no longer wanted things that others can use
- Participating in schemes to provide essentials such as nappies

Often the impact comes not from the actual help. The odd tin of beans does not make a big difference in itself. What impacts is the sense that people are helping, that a parent or carer is worth helping, and that they can access these things without shame. It can change a family's world, and we've seen what that means in earlier chapters.

Parents' Own Trauma

While there is a lot we can do to support children's recovery from trauma, we have less scope with parents, even when we can see that their past experiences are causing them problems and impacting on their children. But the small things we can do are often impactful out of proportion to the effort involved. These include:

- Being a safe, kind and welcoming place; this is nurturing in itself, but also allows parents to see themselves as valuable, liked, and worthwhile
- Conversations that show how their child is progressing, and small compliments about what the parents do to support it
- Showing parents that whatever is going on for them, their child is safe with us and can make progress
- Supporting parents' relationships with children through offering family days, play moments
- Connecting parents to others through social events, or having a "family room" where people can drop by for a coffee and chat
- Signposting trauma-relevant services in ways that normalise this - e.g., posters on the notice board

Supporting Child Development

There are many books on family engagement to support children's learning and development, so this is just a short section to highlight what is most important to develop. In particular, it can be helpful to show parents and carers how these are often part of daily life anyway and they don't have to spend lots of time and money doing special things. Even a short two-way chat a few times a day can have huge impact, and can be done at the same time as meals, cooking, reading together, walking to the shops, or even chilling with a favourite TV program.

How we talk to parents and carers about their children can be very influential. If we discuss an incident in the setting in a mind-minded way, and make mention of how we are planning to adapt how we co-regulate in order to solve it, parents can start to see behaviour in different ways and to feel more confident to respond differently. It can be especially helpful to explain and show how easily young children feel unsafe, and how this is about being small and inexperienced, not about us doing something wrong. And how easily we can help them feel safer through simple and gentle actions and words, or adjusting the situation to make it less scary for them.

Finally, there are particular domains of development that families can be really powerful in promoting. Here they are with some examples of home-based actions.

Emotional regulation	Lots of experiences of playing together and chatting about what's going on Two-way games such as kickabouts or catch Using language to label what a child might be feeling when upset Helping children solve a problem (e.g., tidying up a mess!)
Language	Two way conversations, giving children time to respond and then building on what they say When out and about pointing out things and saying what they are Reading together and chatting about the content

(Continued)

(Continued)

Sense of safety	Thinking about whether the home is experienced as noisy or overwhelming in another way Playing safe games that feel risky - swings, climbing frames, etc. Spotting early if a child is not coping and helping them manage Reading stories with action and risk, and chatting about how the "hero(ine)" overcomes them
Joyfulness and curiosity	Little moments of shared fun Modelling how to enjoy something (laugh even if you don't find it funny - the child might!) Trying new things slowly and a bit at a time Wondering out loud "I wonder where the bird has gone?" Helping children find out answers to their questions

As well as these, many of the ideas that we can share and model are the same as those in Chapter 13. This is especially so when children would benefit from doing "younger" things, or from having a lot of rhythmic and repetitious things to do.

The Weight of History

There is not scope in this book to do justice to this topic but it is often worth being aware of intergenerational trauma. There is some evidence that trauma can be passed from generation to generation, through a number of different pathways. One, called epigenetics, is biologically complex and little understood. It is about the way the expression of the genes of children can be influenced by the life circumstances of their parents and even grandparents. In terms of the model of developmental trauma used in this book, we can see how this makes sense. It is a process of adaptation. Epigenetic processes provide advance information about the world a child will need to adapt to from even before they are conceived. They do this by turning up or down the influence of different genes. Any more on this risks misleading through oversimplification, but enough has been said to show what it means for practice. Within the model of this book, epigenetics simply gives the developing brain information about what kind of world this is. By providing trauma-informed environments we can provide different information, and so change the course of development. We may well be doing so not just for this child but for their children and grandchildren too.

Another pathway for intergenerational trauma is via the impact of parents' traumatic experiences on what they can provide for their children in terms of psychological safety, appropriate stimulation and positive relationships. Linked to this are the impacts on circumstances. There are intergenerational patterns of deprivation and adversity, with families trapped in poverty or in unsafe neighbourhoods. The practice point here is again not about identifying or stigmatising families, and certainly not speculating about their generational history, but about how the setting can be an alternative world for the family, as discussed above and in the next chapter - a world of both emotional and practical support.

Finally, there are ways that generational trauma is not so much carried by families as built into the structures of society. Alvidrez and Tabor (2021) provide a comprehensive definition:

> macro-level societal conditions that limit opportunities, resources, and well-being of less privileged groups on the basis of race/ethnicity and/or other statuses, including but not limited to, gender identity, sexual orientation, disability status, social class or socioeconomic status (SES), religion, geographic residence, national origin, immigration status, limited English proficiency, physical characteristics, or health conditions.
>
> (Alvidrez & Tabor, 2021, p. 283)

This can be most obvious in terms of race, where some groups are marginalised not just as individuals but structurally - for example where we see different rates of health issues, or access to care. We met Bart's parents earlier in the chapter, whose fears are based not just on their present experiences but on those of generations of Roma people. And the news has been full of instances where discrimination against Black people has had horrific consequences that affect the answer to "what kind of world is this" across generations.

There are two things that early education settings can do that are potentially very powerful in mitigating the impacts of structural adversity. Firstly, we can, as discussed throughout this book, provide a world for families and their children where they are welcome, not stigmatised or shamed. How we interact with families, how we bring valued aspects of their culture into our settings, and how we model that for other families can build not just one family's sense of safety and inclusion but also the coherence of an entire community. Secondly, we can be influential in how we speak about the family to others, such as multi-agency teams, highlighting the family context of disadvantage, how structural factors may be causing or maintaining difficulties of concern rather than it being about individual parents.

Family Engagement

At the risk of overstating the principle, a running theme of this book has been that people do not necessarily experience a situation in the ways we might assume, and that people who have experienced trauma often feel unsafe even in apparently safe situations. In practice this means that we may be offering world class trauma-informed support to families that remains inaccessible or ineffective because they cannot connect to it because of feeling unsafe, judged, or ashamed.

The next chapter is therefore all about how we can engage with families in ways that help them feel safe to engage with us.

Chapter summary:

- The wider world around children can have a big impact on how well they can recover and flourish
- Early education settings can be influential in communities and families, and even further afield
- There are key factors that make up a trauma-informed whole setting that need to be in place to support the wellbeing of children and staff

Practice points:

- It can be difficult for individual practitioners to be trauma-informed in a difficult wider context
- There is much that we can do to influence those contexts
- Managers and policy-makers need to implement the conditions that support trauma-informed practice, assured that this will benefit all children and staff

16

Working with Parents and Families

This chapter will provide:

- An account of key models and practices for effective family engagement
- Reflection on how practitioners and families might experience each other
- Practical guidance for having sensitive or difficult conversations with families

Family Engagement

Working collaboratively with children's families has become part of the everyday operations of most early education settings. It is now incorporated in service standards and guidelines (Australian Government Department of Education, 2022; Department for Education, 2025; Education Scotland, 2020; National Association for the Education of Young Children, 2020). Overall these practices can have significant effects on children's development and learning (Ma et al., 2016), sometimes adding up to five months to children's progress (Sutton Trust, 2023). There are also benefits for social development and wellbeing (Barger et al., 2019). These effects are not surprising if we consider that children are with their families for more of the week than they are with us, and families are an unchanging part of their lives (Dempsey & Keen, 2008). And they are most likely if we can establish relationships with families that involve respect, empathy, and commitment; as well as understanding their issues within a wider context of stressors and opportunities (Forry et al., 2011).

Engaging with families can also improve practitioners' experience of providing early education, for example in increasing their sense of being able to make a difference (Trivette et al., 2010). But it is not always easy to do. Both families and practitioners are busy and pushed for time. Drop-off and pick-up can be a fraught and hurried encounter, with important practical information to impart either way, and therefore not ideal for an in-depth conversation about how to promote language development. Some parents may feel that education is up to the professionals so want them to just get on with it. Some educators may feel the same, and find it difficult when a parent has a suggestion for what or how a child might learn. And reaching the families who do not normally come to events (the "stay and play" or information sessions) is an ongoing problem.

DOI: 10.4324/9781003563808-21

Trauma and adversity adds further layers of difficulty. Families are under increased pressure to deal with their circumstances and the impact of these on both child and caregivers. Practitioners may also be under pressure to show progress in learning, even when children face multiple difficulties that stand in the way. These and other issues can put a strain on relationships (Lewis et al., 2024). It is important to remember also, though, that trauma and adversity add further possibilities for early educators to have life-changing effects for children and their families. Families are the constant in a child's world (Dempsey & Keen, 2008), so anything we can do to help them support their children's learning and development is likely to have lasting influence. And sometimes, as we will see below, even small actions or conversations can have large impacts.

> Lee needed to talk to Orla's mother, Riley, about her recent biting behaviour. She was initially surprised and defensive, but Lee explained gently that biting was sometimes a normal response to unexpected stress. He asked Orla's mother for ideas how they could make the setting more predictable for her. She was able to share that things had been difficult at home recently after losing her job, and asked if there was any support available.

That is not an unusual conversation, nor is it much more complicated than just showing kindness and consideration on Lee's part. I have no doubt the two adults feel more on the same side now, and this will help when future troubles come. But there is much more happening. To find out what this is, we have as always to try and experience the situation from the child's point of view. What does Orla see?

> Orla loves Lee but knows he is telling her mother about the biting. She is worried about what her mother will say and do. And guilty. Her parents have been arguing a lot, and here is another thing to fight about. And resentful – she trusted Lee and now he is telling, bad things might happen. But wait, Lee and mother are talking calmly and laughing. Lee talks really kindly, and Orla's mother is asking for help. Here they are coming towards her with smiles, and mother is looking happy as she picks up Orla's latest drawing.

Three surprising things have happened. First, Orla was in a state of fear and things turned out ok, or even better, in the end. This might be a new script in her life as she sees that fearful things need not happen. Second, she's been used to standing digging her foot into the ground as Lee and her mother have tense exchanges, but here are two of the most important people in her life getting on with each other! How safe does that feel! Third, although she has not followed all of the conversation, she can tell there is both gentleness and give and take. Maybe this is how to deal with other conflicts, such as her constant feud with Micky over who goes first with the mud pies.

This is of course a shortened version of a real story. It should not mask that this kind of engagement can be very difficult to do, or hard to sustain. But nor should it obscure that often what families need from us can be as simple as listening and respect (Lewis et al., 2024). This chapter looks at these difficulties and solutions in some detail, with an emphasis on how trauma-informed practice can make family engagement not only easier and more effective but also more joyful. There are three sets of barriers to this that we will consider in turn. Firstly, how families might seem to the practitioner; secondly, how educators might seem to families in the context of trauma; and thirdly the ways trauma means that educator-family contacts are more often about difficult issues of learning or behaviour.

How Educators See Families

A Moment of Reflection

And let's do this in a trauma-informed way, without blame or shame. We all have thoughts and attitudes we might feel are not what they should be. But rarely have we chosen to have them. They are shaped by our experiences, and the people around us. As we will see in Chapter 15 they can also be the product of being overstretched and overstressed. But what we can do is become aware of patterns of thought or assumption and make choices about whether they help or hinder us in working with children and families. So we will reflect briefly on two different clusters – attitudes to families, and our underlying models for family engagement in difficult circumstances.

Ideal Family Models

Most people have, more or less consciously, models in their heads for what a family is, or how families should be. These might be about structure, for example that there ought to be two parents or that a mother should be the primary caregiver. When we encounter families with different structures or ways of doing things this can mean we have to make some effort in adjusting. It can also be at the level of practices, for example that a family should eat together around a table, or that children below a certain age shouldn't do chores. Again, when we meet families who do things differently, it can take adjustment.

One thing the human brain really does not like doing is adjusting its basic scripts and expectations. We rely on these to get through a complex world – without some patterns and expectations there would just be too much to process. Encountering people and things that don't fit the scripts therefore feels, even momentarily, unsettling, bewildering, or even threatening. And we know by now how normal human beings react to these kinds of feelings. We start to move towards fight-like, flight-like, or freeze-like behaviours. We might find ourselves criticising (fight), dismissing or avoiding (flight), refusing to make adjustments (freeze), or giving up (flop).

This can be compounded when we encounter children who have experienced trauma. The bare fact challenges scripts about how parents should keep their children safe. We might encounter families who are buckling under intolerable pressures, which unsettles an assumption that children should come first. Women who have a series of partners who subject them to violence, parents who struggle to provide essential care, others who have left their children, or who have become frightening to them or disengaged.

It is natural to feel this is not how things "ought" to be. But that feeling does not help us to provide what families most need from us in order to engage. They need us to be different from what they might have met so far, to provide them as we will see below with safety, trust, choice, collaboration, empowerment, and cultural consideration (Champine et al., 2019; SAMHSA, 2014). Being aware, without guilt or shame, of our reflex responses and assumptions, can clear our heads so we can make the choices needed to provide these.

Family Engagement Models

This section is not yet about techniques and strategies, but about getting clear what we think we are doing. Different ways of understanding this can have big differences in practice and in effectiveness, and in how engagement feels to us and to families. This is especially so when we are working with children and families affected by trauma. As with the ideal family models, the point in this chapter is not to engage with them in great depth, but to become aware of what kind of thinking is driving what we do, and reflecting on whether we are happy with it and how it comes across. Here are three very different ways of thinking that lead to different forms of practice.

Rescue

I remember, long ago working in a school for teenagers with behaviour issues, a support teacher whose common line to the youngsters was, "look if you sort yourself out you could end up like me one day!" While he was a great teacher, and being such is a great thing to aspire to, it was not the most appealing or relevant goal for our 15-year-olds. It is an example of education as a rescue mission. We can, by providing what we do, help children out of their difficult circumstances into a future of safety and prosperity. And at some level, this is true. But if that is all, then family engagement is harder. This model conveys unintended messages about how things are now, that children's lives, worlds, families are merely things they have to be extracted from, that the only valid future involves something very different. It is less easy to connect with families where they are and to empower them with this kind of thinking.

Compensate

A related model is about education as compensation. Ok, this family, for whatever reason, does not talk much with their children. But that's fine because we can do that! Another family is too stigmatised in their community to take their children to the play park. Never mind, we can make up for this by providing lots of gross motor stimulation. The root idea is of educators who can expertly identify needs and gaps and bountifully provide for them. Again there is a truth to this. We do lots of things that families can't and have skills and knowledge that most parents don't have. But it misses two things. Firstly, that the home environment provides, or could provide, many things that we cannot; and that parents or caregivers have skills and knowledge of their own.

With respect to children and families who have experienced trauma, the compensation model can be very attractive. For some situations, we may rightly judge that there are things a family is just not in a position or a state to provide. I've worked with families where the cost and complexities of travel meant children did not ever go to a beach only a few miles away. We can take children on outings to experience a wider world than their families can show them. But how we do this, and why, can make a lot of difference. We can, in short, be complementary rather than compensatory, which takes us to the last model.

Collaborate

A collaborative approach to family engagement holds a balance between accepting on the one hand that families cannot do everything, and that on the other hand nor can we. While we bring immense expertise, skill, resources, and experience to the tasks of early education, there are things we do not know, especially about particular children. What we can do only has most reach when families do things that extend and embed it, but only if it is in ways that fit their context and what they can do. An example might make the differences clear:

> Angie read about a setting that encouraged families to read a bedtime story each night to their children. She consulted with some parents about this, who thought it was a good idea. But then nothing happened. Children were asked to report each day whether they had had a story, and there was no change over time.
>
> Angie was disappointed about this and decided to stop the project. But reflecting, she realised she was starting to blame the parents for not making the necessary effort. So she asked them again what might work better.
>
> Some parents said they were uncomfortable, feeling "under surveillance". Others said they had difficulty reading and this made a bedtime story fraught for both adult and child. Others said their households were very busy and it was hard to put all the children to bed with a story.
>
> A parent said, "why don't we make it just having a cuddle time, you know, whatever people can do?" Angie agreed and offered some examples of bedtime routines for families to choose. A few weeks later she was reading a story with some children and one of them said "my mum makes it more funny than you do".

Angie knows the value of reading with children, and different ways of doing a bedtime routine. Because she shifted to collaborating with the families, they were able to connect with her knowledge and choose ways to put it into practice that worked.

Regardless of more general theory, trauma-informed family engagement is necessarily collaborative. And collaborative family engagement is also essentially trauma-informed. The basic principle that people experience the same situation differently is respected, as well as the basic idea that in order to change things we have to understand those differences. The trauma triad can help us here - how can we make what we need to do less overwhelming for families, or give them more control over it, or provide some support to manage? It can also help to consider the different ways that families might experience our efforts at engagement.

How Families Experience Educators

Part of being trauma-informed is understanding how people react to situations in terms of what has happened to them in the past. Often we do not know, or never will, what actually happened, but we do know that when we see fight, flight, freeze, or flop responses, these are likely to be driven by feeling unsafe, and that this could well relate to earlier experiences that have something in common with what is going on now.

Families come to our settings complete with their past. Many have happy memories of education, schools where they learned interesting things, made friends for life, and found support in times of trouble. For others, it is more negative – perhaps of struggling with work, or a lack of understanding of their situation. They may have memories of education professionals as demanding or unhelpful. They also might have experience of relating to others, such as social workers or police, where they have felt vulnerable and judged, and bring this expectation to their encounters with us.

Bearing this in mind when we meet a family for the first time, or in our ongoing interactions, is the essence of trauma-informed practice. We know we are kind, loving educators, who will do all we can to help families and their children. We are steeped in trauma-informed practice and will make sure they feel safe with us, and experience the levels of control and support that they need. But we know as well that the past can intrude into the present, especially at moments of higher stress. Also we know that what might be routine stressors to us – starting a new setting, a change to drop-off routine, a normal chat about diet or behaviour – might be huge stressors to families, even containing traumatic triggers. And finally, we know that all this is difficult to predict in advance, and that our assumptions about families can get in the way of our understanding and helping them.

We already have some tools to understand and respond to some of the things that parents and caregivers might do or say. When we meet responses that have elements of fight, flight, freeze, or flop, we know we need to think about how to help people feel safer with what is happening – either in the now as it is occurring, or else next time if it is going to happen again. Here are some common examples with some ideas that might help.

What we see	*What's happening*	*Make it feel safer?*
Parent blames setting for a child's problems	Fight	Put time into building a positive relationship Reflect on how to hold conversations (see section Difficult Conversations below) Reduce levels of guilt or shame by . . . (see below
Parent blames a child for learning or behaviour issues	Fight	Provide developmental information to normalise the problem Have problem solving conversations (see section below) to show issues can be resolved Be clear it is not the parent's fault
Caregiver does not turn up for meetings	Flight	Be patient and show you understand life can be busy Consider with caregiver how and when to have meetings; offer choices Choose low tariff agendas to build confidence over time Have many positive discussions about child and progress
Family agrees actions but does not do them	Flop	Build confidence and capacity with small steps Ensure they know it is safe to disagree and question ideas Consider whether other pressures are making it difficult

Finally for this section, we need to recall that if children have experienced trauma, it is quite possible that the family has too, if only in a secondary way through worry about their children. Reactions, and the impact on styles of caregiving, can be complex and different for every family, as well as changing over time. But there are three basic patterns that we might encounter that affect how we work with families (Dorahy et al., 2013; Lewis et al., 2024; Scheeringa & Zeanah, 2001). As with all trauma-informed practice, the key step is to reflect on our assumptions about these, and understand that they are defences, ways to cope - even if they then cause further problems or make things worse.

Withdrawn or Unavailable Pattern

In some circumstances, the child themselves can be a traumatic trigger for caregivers. Nearly all families want to keep their children safe, and it can be overwhelmingly upsetting if harm comes to them. Parents and others can be full of shame and feel they failed to protect their child when they were needed most. This is common after some of the big and obvious traumatic experiences such as abuse or a child going missing, but can be seen even after a small bump in the car. The result is that even everyday acts of caregiving or play can bring up very difficult feelings of terror and/or shame and guilt. The parent or carer may also have acquired the belief that they are bad for their child, and the less they have to do with them the better for the child. So we might see withdrawal, or disengagement, or a reluctance to take up and try ideas, or a constant avoidance of discussions, events, or other ways of joining in. Alternatively, if a parent or carer is dissociating to avoid the strong feelings, then they may come across as cold or uninterested, or else mindlessly doing all we say - anything to avoid interaction.

It's important to realise that although it might look like not caring, these patterns of behaviour arise from caring a lot about the child and what happens to them. But it is too much to bear, and so the parent withdraws. It can be difficult for educators to work with, however. We might see the child's need for interactions not being met, or encounters that seem cold or otherwise negative. Parents or caregivers might be dismissive of any concerns about learning or behaviour in the setting. Practitioners may have to be patient and take a long-term strategy, being realistic about what they can change quickly. As long as a parent is providing good enough care, we might not need to do anything, apart from provide in our setting an alternative world of positive interactions and fun, and helping the child adjust to it. But educators may have concerns about the child's care or welfare, in which case they do have a role in supporting families and helping them access help, or even taking steps for safeguarding.

Overprotective or Constricting

Since it has the same driving motivations, this pattern can be covered more briefly. In short, parents and caregivers work to make sure that no further harm can come to the child. To do this, they may become quite controlling, not just of the child, but of everyone who encounters them. Educators might experience this as setting out conditions for what a child does or how, be this meal times or play experiences. Alternatively, family members might be anxious about a child's progress, often coming up with ideas to "bring them on". Or they may go the other way and resist suggestions of ways to stretch and challenge their child, or come with concerns that their child was upset the day before at trying something new. These concerns may intensify at key times, such as an approaching transition to school or a new class. Finally, educators may encounter children with gaps in their development. For example, if parents or carers restrict their free outdoor play, perhaps out of fear for them, or feeling unwelcome in the space, there may be some catching up to plan with motor development or confidence.

Re-Enacting

The third pattern is in some ways the hardest to relate to as it comes from the deep impact of traumatic memories. Recall from Chapters 2-4 that memories of traumatic experiences can intrude into the present, almost as if they are another layer painted over what is happening. If you remember from the example given, my friend in a coffee shop also looked to me like the Loch Ness Monster. In the same way, families can get stuck in the scripts of a traumatic experience. This does not mean they literally re-enact it (although we might see some patterns that are similar such as unnecessary risk taking). But it does mean that the emotions and fight/flight/freeze/flop responses are to the fore in their interactions - either with the world in general or with their children. So parents may come across as frightening to their child, or to the practitioner. Alternatively, they may talk repeatedly about the experience, or become preoccupied with it, collecting similar news stories, or joining online discussion groups. It can be hard to let go of a traumatic experience, but it can have profound impacts on a child's recovery. These are reactions where educators may feel more intervention is needed, and they need to consider risks to the child in the present and future.

There is more material on how early educators can intervene to support families, and the boundaries around this, in the previous chapter. We will include considerations of safeguarding and child protection. But often there is much we can do to help in our everyday interactions with families. A key part of this is how we have conversations about issues and difficulties that arise. This is the topic for the next section.

Difficult Conversations

We have seen in earlier chapters that early childhood trauma can have a deep impact across a broad range of issues in learning, development, and behaviour. One thing this means for families is that they may well have many more conversations than others do about difficulties and problems. This can make it harder for early educators as we need to raise yet another unwelcome matter with them, when their lives are possibly already full of worries that seem unsolvable. However, there are few things in early education that we cannot do something about, so our conversations with families are also ways for them to experience the world differently - as containing solutions, people who want to understand and help them, and as a place where they and their perspectives are welcome.

The same goes for the practitioner. We might feel we are raising yet another problem for an overburdened family, worried about the effects on our relationships with them; as well as potentially being under pressure to get things sorted out so that everyone can learn better and with more harmony in the setting. The flip side of this is that the conversation can be a way to build mutual understanding and collaboration that might make everything easier going forward. Families do not always expect us to have all the answers, or indeed any answers. But the experience of working together to find a way forward can be a good one for educator, caregivers, and for the children too.

Key Elements

A trauma-informed approach to difficult conversations is about keeping as simple as possible. I will illustrate this first with an example, before looking at a particular conversation in slow motion to bring out the detail. It is a story that many readers will find familiar, of the annual service for the family car. If you don't drive or have a car, then similar stories of a trip to the dentist or to get an appliance fixed work just as well.

> Jack has taken his car in for what he expects to be a routine service. However, the mechanic needs to tell Jack that they have discovered a serious problem that will need time and money to fix.

Putting ourselves in Jack's shoes we can consider how he might want the mechanic to do this. When I do this as an activity with groups of professionals, they usually come up with ideas such as:

- Sit him down
- Explain the issue so Jack can understand it
- Say what can be done about it
- Be up front about costs and timescale
- Let Jack ask questions
- Give him time to take it in

The point of the story, and the activity, is that most people know how to have a conversation about difficult issues, because we know exactly how we would like someone to have one with us. But there is more going on. This is actually a trauma-informed conversation. To see this, recall the three elements that make up a traumatic, or potentially traumatic, experience:

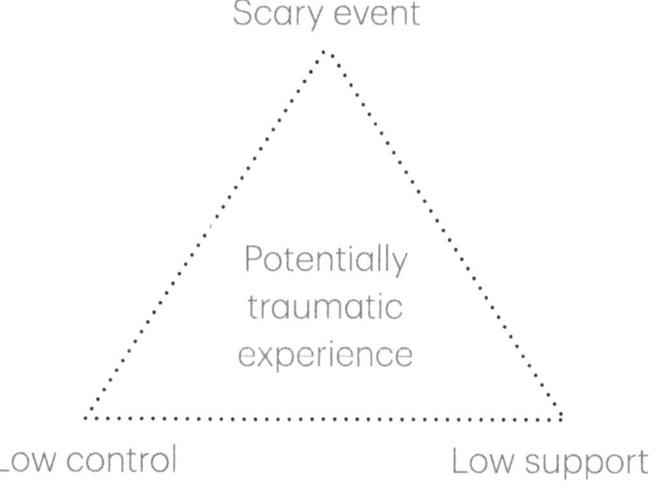

Figure 16.1 The trauma triad

Taking the car in for a service is not for most people a scary event. This is why I chose it as the example rather than a dentist visit (which would trigger me). But it is about to turn into one for Jack when he hears about the potential cost and inconvenience. He might well feel bewildered, or that things are getting out of control. Let's look at the conversation elements again though, to see how the mechanic manages to address and reduce each of the three difficult elements.

Increasing safety	• Sit him down • Explain the issue so Jack can understand it
Enabling control	• Say what can be done about it • Be up front about costs and timescale
Providing support	• Let Jack ask questions • Give him time to take it in

Providing clear and accurate information reduces uncertainty and puts limits around how bad the issue is. It might be quite bad, but explanation helps Jack not to imagine it is even worse than it is. Asking questions, and having them patiently answered, provides a lot of relational support as Jack feels heard and understood, and the mechanic is clearly wanting to do all they can to help. Knowing what can be done, and what it will take, gives Jack a greater sense of control over what is happening. This is not an insolvable problem about which nothing can be done, but an issue that can be fixed.

In Early Education

We have all we need to apply this to difficult conversations in an early education setting. Firstly we can reflect on how people might experience the conversation - either in advance or while it is happening. We can use these reflections to make sure the conversation feels as safe as possible, as well as increasing the parent or caregiver's sense of control and awareness of available support. Let's eavesdrop on Lee's conversation with Riley about her little girl Orla who is starting to bite other people in the setting.

Lee has spent some time building a relationship with Riley, making her feel welcome in the setting, and taking the time for an occasional cup of coffee. He has made clear how much Orla contributes to the setting, and shows Riley examples of her learning.

He knows that Riley is often in a rush in the mornings as she has to get her teenager to school and back in time to make breakfast for her elderly mother. But she often has time at pick-up, and Lee makes sure every so often they talk about Orla. He has from time to time raised low-key issues, such as how to persuade Orla to try bananas, in order to develop a partnership in problem solving. He took advice from Riley on these, and showed her how her ideas had worked, in order to demonstrate that he sees her as capable, interested, and involved.

All that has set the foundation for today, when they need to talk about a "big issue". Let's go through the conversation, and I will draw out the trauma-informed elements that make it work well. You will see lots of reflections in your own practice, so I invite you to reflect on your own, different, ways of doing this.

Lee	We've got another of those little problems to sort out together	*Safe* - labelling the issue as solvable *Control* - inviting collaboration rather than telling; recalling past success in doing this
Riley	Oh what's she done now!	
Lee	Ha ha, yes, raising kids can be one thing after another!	*Safety* and *support* - all families have issues sometimes
Riley	Just tell me how bad it is	
	It's not too bad at all, it's something we help a lot of kids with Look, is this a good time to talk for you?	*Safety* - providing scale "not too bad" *Safety* - a lot of kids do this *Support* - we help *Control* - question about good time; but also sharing control by moving the conversation on
Riley	If we must, we must	
Lee	Thank you	*Control* - thanking Riley for making the choice to talk
Lee	Let's just check through the window that Orla's ok - yes, she's happy making a huge tower; she's so much more confident since you suggested trying those blocks	*Safety* - Orla is ok *Control* - compliment on Riley's effective ideas *Support* - Lee is so happy that Orla is doing well
Riley	Mmmm	
Lee	So the issue is this. Some children go through a time, I don't think they mean to, but they sometimes bite people	*Safety* - it is a known childhood issue; also Lee is calm and matter of fact about it *Safety* - it's "sometimes" *Control* - it's not "Orla is a biter" but a problem she has
Riley	My, that's terrible!	
Lee	Well, yes, it does worry people; but usually it stops quite quickly once we work out why it's happening	*Safety* - ok to be worried; also indicates how worried to be (a bit but not a lot)
Riley	Well it must be those other kids, she's got it from them. I told you that Milo was no good	
Lee	In my experience, this isn't usually anyone's fault. Almost any child can do this It's usually one of three reasons - they are a bit stressed out generally, there is something they really don't want to do, or else she doesn't know how to say what she's feeling	*Safety* - does not get into a potential "fight" cycle *Safety* - Normalises the issue - this happens and isn't anyone's fault *Support* - information about causes helps to understand
Riley	Everything is fine at home	
Lee	That's great to hear. So I'd love to know what you think it might be. Is there anything you know that Orla really hates doing?	*Safety* - valuing what Riley says *Control* - asking for Riley's ideas to shape the conversation
Riley	I can't get her off the phone once she has it. She throws a tantrum and grumps for like an hour	

(*Continued*)

(Continued)

Lee	Sounds like she really knows how to tell you she's unhappy! Now I think of it, Orla does this biting when we try to get her to stop doing something - do you think it might be that?	*Support* - communicates esteem for Riley and her relationship *Control* - Riley as an expert on her child *Control* - offering her a chance to influence Lee's thinking
Riley	Could be	
Lee	So, can I ask, if you need her to stop playing with the puppy coz it's time to eat, how do you do it?	*Control* - asking to ask *Support* - conveys assumption Riley can deal competently with this example
Riley	Well, I say, Orla, hon, it's time for tea soon. And tell her what it is, my that girl loves her food!	
Lee	So some advance warning, letting her know the next thing is something she likes, giving her time I think those are great ideas. Do you think that might work if we try them here?	*Support* - reflecting back Riley's ideas so she can hear how good they are *Support* - labelling as good ideas *Control* - "I think" rather than "they are" invites agreement rather than tells what is what

This is just one conversation. It is important to realise that we cannot always expect parents or caregivers to share the whole picture in one go. People have to feel very safe sometimes before they can disclose relevant information. This might be about fear of what will happen if they do, not trusting us with the information, or as with Riley here an overwhelming sense of guilt. What if we think badly of them, and agree that whatever is happening is their fault? This fear can drive parents further into withdrawal, overprotection, or re-enacting. As might putting pressure on them to "tell it as it is", "just come out with it", or similar.

Lee, in this case, was fairly sure that things were fraught at home with frequent arguments, and it was likely that this could be raising Orla's stress levels generally. But it was also the case that the ideas they discussed were also factors, and the management ideas were still good ones. What happened subsequently bears this out. A few weeks later, when there was partial success in reducing Orla's biting, Riley asked to see Lee. She started to tell him about what was happening at home, and asked if there was any support locally she could access. Trauma-informed practice often gets us where we need to get to, but at the pace that families can cope with; and only by establishing sufficient safety, trust, and collaboration.

Noticing Stress Reactions

I mentioned in the commentary the idea of a "fight cycle". We've met this idea before in Chapter 10 when talking about co-regulation. Sometimes in a conversation we can find ourselves being drawn into patterns that reflect how the other person is feeling and acting, rather than our own thoughts and emotions. "Fight" is quite contagious, as we naturally respond to another human's higher arousal. But we can realise this, step back and reflect for a split section, and think how we can stay calm. All that is happening is that our brain systems have started to detect and assess an apparent stressor (a parent criticising us, for example) and have raised our arousal levels as a response. Our regulating systems know it is probably not a big threat, but are not quite sure enough to shut down our own fight response. So it is a time for us to take the wheel ourselves for a moment and deliberately turn down our reactions. There are some ideas for how to do this in Chapters 10 and 15. What goes for fight responses and cycles is true for the other reactions as well. "Flop" is particularly easy to catch from others, as we start to feel progressively helpless, bereft of ideas, or lacking beliefs that we can solve the problem. Skilled practitioners can start to forget everything they know. Again, a moment of reflection can help us interrupt the cycle before it becomes a whirlpool.

Here are some ideas to address fight, flight, freeze, and flop cycles in conversations:

Cycle	*What we notice in ourselves*	*Ways to interrupt*
Fight	Getting upset, feeling increasingly challenged, starting to respond more strongly, or even with blame	Take conscious control of regulation systems to relax (breathing, pause, move, etc.) Slow down, quieten down Convey friendliness even if not felt (smile, gentle body language)
Flight	Reluctance to raise issues, or minimising them	Have a plan for the conversation and stick to it Ask if it is ok to raise something Check with yourself that you are safe Remind yourself of your competence and experience
Flop/Freeze	Running out of ideas, feeling helpless or hopeless Deciding a parent cannot and will not change, etc.	

Concluding Reflections

Family engagement is now a core part of the role of early education settings. There are many different frameworks and models to support it. Any of these can be combined with trauma-informed principles to enhance their effectiveness for all families, and especially for those affected by trauma. Here, the last word goes to Janis Keyser, from her excellent and practical book *From Parents to Partners* (2006, p. 5):

> even when they seem most unreasonable, parents are also showing healthy impulses. For example, complaining, accusing, overprotective, or critical parents might not have the words to express feeling left out, concerned, worried, or guilty. Continually late, absent, or uninvolved parents may be feeling overwhelmed or uncomfortable at the school. Talkative, questioning, or lingering parents may want to learn from you about how to be a better parent.

Chapter summary:

- Engaging positively with families can be complex and daunting, but taking a trauma-informed approach can make it easier
- Both practitioners and families may have assumptions that make engagement easier or more difficult
- Being aware of these and using the trauma triad can make engagement more positive and effective

Practice points:

- Reflect on your own assumptions about families and family engagement
- Do not take reactions personally or blame families for their responses, which may make sense in their situations
- Use the trauma triad to plan and reflect on engagement processes and encounters

17

Staff Stress and Secondary Trauma

This chapter will provide:

- Reflection on why working in early education can be stressful as well as rewarding
- Information about secondary traumatisation
- An ecological model for wellbeing that avoids blame and inspires positive action

We saw in Chapters 8–10 how children use adult brains and capacity in order to manage difficult feelings and challenges. By "borrowing" our capabilities, they gradually come to develop their own. They also need carefully judged experiences of manageable and resolved challenge both to develop their emotional resilience and to make progress with learning. By being surrounded with adults who can see the minds behind behaviour, understand the needs being expressed, and then support children's developing abilities to solve their problems, children develop a toolkit of effective actions and schemas about themselves and the world that set them up for a lifetime.

It is therefore essential to pay attention to those adults. On the one hand, if the adults and caregivers are themselves stressed and frazzled, or feeling helpless, they are that much less available to provide the capacities that the children need to borrow (Buettner et al., 2016; de Schipper et al., 2009). And on the other, as we will see, providing this kind of environment of positive relationships and "just right" levels of stimulation is hard work that can be tiring and taxing (Lee & Brotheridge, 2011). So if we are to be effective in early education we have to consider staff wellbeing. And if we are to be trauma-informed that also means considering this as an end in itself, as something staff have a right to. We will have a setting where children are flourishing if the caring adults are also themselves flourishing. The alternative can be a vicious circle whereby children's behaviours lead to higher levels of practitioner stress (Friedman-Krauss et al., 2014), impacting their ability to support the children, resulting in more stress-inducing behaviours from the children (Kwon et al., 2019). Less dramatic, but equally taxing on professional identity and self-esteem, can be when the stress reduces the sense of closeness to the children that is part of the reward of the work (Whitaker et al., 2015).

DOI: 10.4324/9781003563808-22

Being trauma-informed adds further depth to this. It helps us see why providing early education can be a stressful occupation and how this can be managed. And it helps us understand the additional impact of working with children who have experienced trauma and how even the most experienced practitioners in the best run settings can sometimes experience a secondary form of trauma.

This chapter covers both of these layers. We consider the day-to-day stressors of working with young children, along with some of the signs that a practitioner - or a whole setting - is getting overstressed. And we will look at how secondary traumatisation is a common experience for early educators and how this can be addressed and prevented. There are complex debates about the different ways to describe this, so you may have heard about "burnout", secondary stress, or other terms. For our purposes we can talk generally, as these generally overlap (Cieslak et al., 2014).

A central theme of the approach offered here is to question assumptions that wellbeing is down to the practitioner and is something about individuals. For example that it is up to staff to "look after themselves" and ensure they are fit for the job, without also considering the working conditions, the ethos of the setting and the levels of demand in the work. Or that simple fixes such as the occasional "wellbeing day" are either effective or all that is needed. We will be paying just as much attention to the working context as to the practitioner's skills in what follows.

One final note. People who work in early education are no different from people in general, which means that many of us have experienced trauma in our own lives. As you go through this chapter, you may find yourself also wanting to review some of the material in Chapters 6 and 18 on living well after traumatic experiences, and please make sure you seek help if that is what you need.

An Ecological Model for Wellbeing

This chapter is based on the same ecological model for stress and wellbeing that we saw in Chapter 15. This ties together factors relating to the individual practitioner, the children, the setting, and even the wider world of politics and policy.

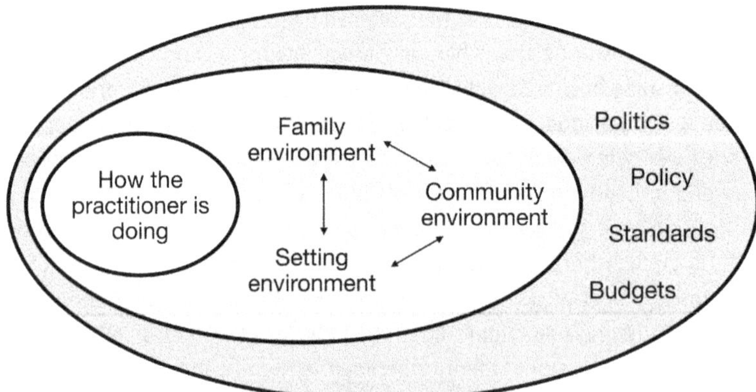

Figure 17.1 An ecological model for staff wellbeing

Wellbeing is not just about any individual – we live in a big "onion" of overlapping factors. So when a practitioner is getting stressed and finding that the work is starting to get them down or they are struggling to cope with it then it is likely not just to do with them "lacking resilience" or needing to work harder. The solution may not lie in them learning to relax or toughen up, but in addressing stressors in the setting or wider environment.

Why Is Early Education Stressful?

With the ecological model, we can give a fuller answer to this question, and therefore find the solutions that might work in a complex situation. In Chapter 11, we met Jan and Mia, who helped us to think about reflective practice using an everyday kind of incident.

> Mia (4) is wobbling across the setting floor with a tray piled high with loose parts. She is nearly at the table, when two other children bustle past carrying a large box. The corner of the box nudges her elbow and acorns, twigs, and small pebbles fly everywhere. Jan, an experienced educator, opens her mouth to say . . .

We saw that Jan has a wide range of options from how she responds, ranging from doing nothing at all to shouting at Mia to tidy the mess up. We also saw how much goes on in Jan's brain to produce the most helpful response that is most tuned into where Mia's brain is. This means that Jan's brain is working hard and using energy. There is a prompting event, a stress system reaction, and then a balancing towards appropriate action. Her brain is also gathering information about the environment. The occasional "alarm" experience is no big deal, but what if this happens often? Perhaps Jan's brain needs to make some adjustments to deal with this.

And one thing that is certain about an early education setting is that there is a lot going on! Lots of children are busy doing lots of things, which means that at any moment something might happen that requires Jan's attention. She is also a professional educator, so she is keeping an eye on all the children in turn, constantly assessing their state of wellbeing, what they are learning, and whether scaffolding or some other intervention is needed – as well as beginning to form plans about tomorrow. Nor would it be an early education setting if there were not also some paperwork (or screenwork) at the back of her mind or even requiring her attention now as a deadline for implementing some new guidance has passed.

Of course it is a lot easier for Jan because over the other side of the room is Jim. He has already noticed that the room is starting to get a bit frenetic, throws Jan a smile of understanding, and opens the door into the setting garden to let some children out to let off steam. This also gives Jan a bit of space to clear up the crunchy mess on the floor. Jim was able to do this because all the practitioners have agreed that while the children meeting their writing targets for this year is important, every so often these particular children just need to move about more, so they can abandon the tables. Meanwhile, the manager sits in her office, looking at the attainment spreadsheet, wondering how she will explain the slow progress this year with curriculum performance indicators when the next inspection is due.

We started this scenario with the minor stress of a child dropping some loose parts, and suddenly we are considering the whole education system, with its targets and scrutiny. This illustrates the point of the ecological model. Without this, we might just say:

> "The children are difficult - Jan is stressed".

In which case we only have two options to improve things. Either we change the children, which is difficult over short timescales, or we send Jan on a course to build her resilience. We are also a little way from being trauma-informed, from an understanding that how people feel in a situation is not so much about them being weak as about the fact they are dealing with a situation that, for them, is difficult.

A trauma-informed approach to staff wellbeing involves looking at the whole picture, and the "onion" can help us do this. Let's visit a different setting where similar things go on, but in a very different context:

> June is working on completing an online tracker of the children's literacy skills to show that the setting is meeting its attainment targets. It was due yesterday but a colleague was off sick with stress. She looks up at a crashing noise and sees that Mike has dropped a tray of loose parts. She opens her mouth and says . . .

It seems likely that June might say something a little more critical or disciplinary than Jan did. If we were watching, we might say to ourselves:

> "June is already stressed out by a high stakes, low support situation, so she finds the children much more stressful than she might".

If we set this out as a diagram, we might have something like this:

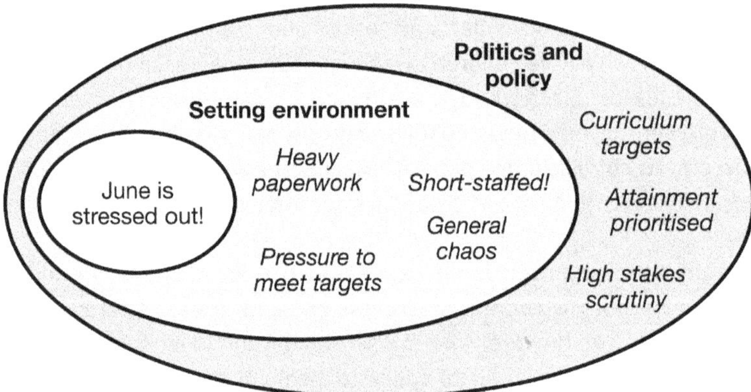

Figure 17.2 The pressures on June in full context

The ecological approach tells us something else as well. Both Jan and June are highly skilled and motivated practitioners. But June is starting to think that she is not the right fit for this job (McMullen et al., 2020). She is, she thinks, far too impatient and just isn't as good as she thought she was with young children. Looking from the outside, we can see something different. June is not that different to Jan, but she is working in a very different context, one of high pressure and low support. This makes her more stressed than Jan, and therefore more likely to respond to the daily ups and downs in a less measured way. If June does not realise this, then she may think that this is to do entirely with her, about her skills and attitudes. Then a vicious spiral might start of falling confidence, less well-judged responses, reduced creativity, leading to further reduced self-image and lower confidence. So June eventually becomes what she thought she was, even though she really wasn't and only seems so because of the wider context.

Secondary Trauma

There is one more "wider world" factor to add. As we now know, many of the children in our care have experienced trauma and adversity. This has many consequences that mean more demands on practitioners, including the need to plan and individualise their care and learning. One with particular relevance for this chapter is the way the children's stress systems respond to apparently ordinary difficulties.

> Jakob screams with fear and runs to the nearest adult whenever a fly or other insect buzzes past him.
>
> Hans has an "all or nothing" stress response. He is often quite calm, but produces enraged tantrums whenever he can't do what he wants.

We can recognise both these children from our work in Chapters 3 and 5. Jakob has a particular trigger, which may well be linked to a difficult experience. It is not hard to manage in itself, but every time an adult hears a child scream, their own stress system briefly goes into high alert. Hans, for whatever reason, has not yet developed a stress system with graded responses, and also seems to be developmentally similar to a younger child in his reaction to frustrations. So he is spending a lot of his time in a "high alert" state and also unpredictably setting off the adults' stress systems too.

We saw above how Jan's stress system might briefly go into higher arousal during a fairly routine incident. This is even more the case working with Jakob or Hans. Neither of these children is a threat or a danger to Jan. But she is a practitioner with two key attributes. She cares very much about the children and helping them. And she is good at empathy, which means that she feels what they feel. So when Jakob or Hans have difficulties, Jan's stress system spikes in response. She feels a version of what they feel, and she also feels high levels of concern for them. This is why those who work a lot with traumatised people can start to develop "secondary trauma". They have not themselves been traumatised, but they start to feel, think, and even act as though they have. Their stress systems are adapting so as to cope with the experience of being often exposed to high levels of distress.

Why is early education stressful then? It is the interaction of a wide range of factors (Tebben et al., 2021). The ups and downs of children's learning and emotions mean that our stress systems are constantly engaged and we spend a significant amount of time in a state of higher arousal. That's not a problem in itself, and as we will see below can actually be good for us. But if we don't get chances to "power down", both within the day and between days, then this can lead to longer term changes in our stress systems that we will explore below. In addition, early education can be a place where there are not enough resources, or people, or where there are high demands. If this is so, then what would otherwise be a series of interesting and enjoyable challenges can start to become overwhelming.

The good news is that there are lots of ways we can prevent this. We will start by considering what is "too much stress" and how we can recognise it.

What Is Too Much Stress?

In Chapter 1 we looked at how the brain handles one-off stressful events. In this chapter we will extend this to see how our stress systems change and respond in the face of ongoing stressors. It is one thing dealing with an isolated event, and another being ready for these things happening over and over again. It is a bit like if I have gone into town to do some shopping on a bright summer's day and there is a sudden rain shower. I can easily take shelter in a shop, or just head home. But suppose we are going through a season where it rains often. I could still do those short-term responses, but they are a bother and they prevent me getting the shopping done. So I make some longer term adjustments, such as taking an umbrella or a hat.

In the same way, our brains have a short-term (or acute) set of stress reactions, and a longer term (chronic) set of adaptations. In the short term, our brains make sure that we are stressed just enough to deal with whatever is happening and that we then calm down as soon as we can. When we talk about "being stressed" we usually mean that this smooth up-and-down pattern is disrupted. We start feeling overwhelmed and to worry about coping, as well as feeling emotional strain. This is both unpleasant in itself and can lead to difficulties if prolonged. Equally, so is constant low stress, as most people have experienced. For example, we plan a relaxing evening, with a takeaway to eat and a TV show to binge-watch. A nice change, but if this goes on evening after evening, we might start to feel something is missing and we get less and less relaxation benefit. Perhaps we might naturally start to seek some interest and excitement, for example having a chat with a friend, or going bowling with the kids. It turns out that in order to recover from the stresses of the working day, we need a little bit of stress!

This is not as odd as it sounds. We have met this before when thinking about the contrast for developing children between toxic stress and the kinds of everyday moderate and resolved stresses that help them grow and flourish. This is simply the adult version of the same point. If we are engaged in something that is enjoyable, worthwhile, and that we believe we can accomplish even if it is at the moment a bit out of our reach, then this is good for us. It expands our capacity just as enough but not too much training can build our muscles. We can even call this "good stress" (Selye, 1978) in contrast to distress (too much) or inadequate stress (not enough).

Are there some ways we can tell if we (or colleagues) are experiencing distress rather than good stress? And are there ways to turn distress into good stress or to recover from its effects? There certainly are, and this is the topic of the next section.

The Effects of Too Much Stress

One reason why high levels of stress can persist in a setting or in an organisation is that the effects are difficult to talk about. As we will see, they are nearly all things that people feel they, or others, should not be doing. There might be a sense of blame or shame, either of ourselves or others. It is important to realise and recognise, however, that all of these behaviours and attitudes are symptoms not truths about us. They are what happen to people and systems when they get overstressed, and as is often the case when we think in a trauma-informed way, they turn out to be our brains doing their very best to help us.

To show this, I need to take you back to the example of an adverse context that we used in Chapter 5. I asked you to imagine you had been abandoned on an island full of dinosaurs. We looked at this from the outside to see what kinds of people would do well in this context and therefore how children might develop when they experience early adversity and trauma. This time, let's consider your adult brain on the island and what it might do for you to help you survive. This is not Jan facing the occasional minor mishap in an early education setting, but the continual presence of high levels of danger.

We know already how the brain starts to cope. Arousal levels rise, and we find that fight, flight, freeze, or flop are at the top of our behavioural agendas. But there are other necessary adaptations too. In fact we are caught in something of a bind. All that fighting, freezing, and hiding is tiring, so we need to be able to rest. But while we sleep, we might get eaten, so we need almost half an eye open for danger. And it is probably quite hard to settle to rest at all. We need fuel for our bodies, so we might grab food when we see it, and also prioritise the kinds of foods that give us quick energy or fill us up fast. Finally, we might preserve our energy as much as possible. If someone suggests a sing-song round the camp fire, we might prefer to rest for the next day. And we will find ourselves spending less time being interested in our usual hobbies, be it spotting butterflies or writing poetry.

All of these reactions are created by the stress systems in our brains so as to adapt to circumstances. These work fine when we are faced with constant major threats and an actual need to survive. But they cause us problems when it is day-to-day stressors and we end up in this kind of survival mode over things that are not actually matters of life and death (for a more formal account, see Henderson et al., 2023). We start to see the same signs though, including:

- More fight, flight, freeze, flop type behaviours
- Reduced or disrupted sleep
- More seeking of rest
- Increased consumption of food, especially carbohydrates, and/or alcohol
- Reduced social activity
- Less engagement with previous interests

Looking at the last two of those, there can be an impact not just in our personal lives as we get less interested in meeting friends or gardening, but also at work. Often staff will find themselves feeling generally less effective, getting less done, or detached from the work, like they are caring less or it does not matter (Maslach & Leiter, 2016).

Some people feel "wired all the time" and others feel "tired all the time". Often, we tend to be just keeping going, without a lot of awareness about how we are feeling. But what we do can be a good indicator as well. A sure sign that someone is getting overstressed is the appearance of our old friends fight, flight, freeze, and flop. Of course it is rare for early educators to actually hide under tables or in cupboards, let alone start to throw mud pies at people.

But we might sometimes feel the urge to! More commonly, we notice ourselves getting more fight-y, flight-y, freezy, or floppy. Here are some examples of each in an early education setting:

Stress behaviour type	*Examples*
Fight	Stronger than desired reactions to children or adults More conflict between staff Blaming others - children, colleagues, families
Flight	Avoiding tasks Avoiding individuals or situations Overextended breaks Absence from work
Freeze	"Jamming" when something happens Going blank faced with a challenge Struggling with decision making Emotional disconnection Sticking to routines or the plan no matter what
Flop	Becoming helpless Stuck in feeling nothing can get better Lack of control or agency

The point of that list, and of everything that has come before it is this. Working in early education is stressful, and working with high levels of trauma among the children only adds to this. All, or nearly all, of the effects of this are a result of how the human stress system works. And much of it is driven or exacerbated by surrounding factors. If we notice these signs in ourselves or in others, then it is not our fault, or their fault. But this does not mean we cannot make changes to prevent or reduce it - and that is what the next chapter is about. We will start by looking at factors to do with the setting, the immediate environment, then what individuals can do, before finishing with some thoughts about the wider world of politics and policy.

But the main message of this chapter is really the first intervention. Realising how we are feeling, thinking, and acting, and that this is a natural reaction to high levels of demand, means we do not have to feel guilt or shame either for ourselves or others. With this foundation, there is much that can be done, within an ecological approach, to improve staff wellbeing. This is the topic of the next chapter, and the following considers the specific case of when practitioners are carrying their own traumatic memories.

Chapter summary:

- Working in early education is rewarding, but also emotionally taxing and sometimes stressful
- Most sources of stress are in the environment and wider system rather than being the practitioner's weakness or incapacity
- There are known, common effects of high levels of stress that are normal and preventable
- Working with traumatised children can lead to secondary traumatisation

Practice points:

- Be aware of the impacts of working in highly stressful environments or with children who have experienced trauma
- Understand these as effects of stress rather than personal weakness
- Reflect on the impacts of the setting, and wider ecology, on staff and how to address these

18 Promoting Staff Wellbeing

This chapter will provide:

- Practical strategies to promote staff wellbeing at all levels of the system
- Information about common signs of overstress or secondary trauma
- Trauma-informed ways to care for teams and individuals

In the previous chapter we met June, and looked at the multiple interacting factors that place her in a state of chronic stress.

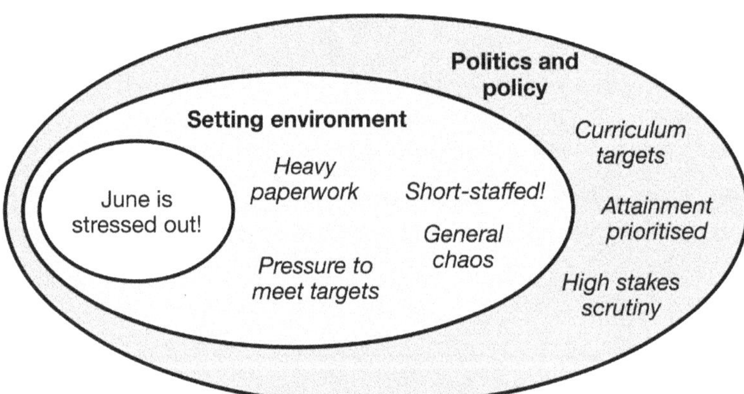

Figure 18.1 The pressures on June in full context

Just a glance at this picture can show us that the main emphasis on how to promote staff wellbeing is sometimes put in the wrong place – or rather that the first thoughts for how to promote it do not always land on the main causes. For example, we might coach June on how to handle stress and emotions better; suggest she takes up yoga or sees a therapist. Or at the setting level we might put on a "wellbeing day" or assemble a bank of self-help resources.

DOI: 10.4324/9781003563808-23

Effective promotion of staff wellbeing needs to consider all the levels and how they interact. We can see that while perhaps June might have some things to try to help her handle the stress, the main drivers do not come from here. Instead there are processes in the whole setting that are being created or reinforced by a high pressure wider environment of policy and practice. This chapter therefore considers how to promote staff wellbeing at all three levels - the whole setting, the individual, and the world around us.

Looking at the Whole Setting

There has been a lot of research into what supports wellbeing and stress recovery in education, and some of this has been about early years settings. McMullen and colleagues (2020) suggest that practitioners need to feel comfort, security, feeling connected to their group, self-respect, feeling understood, engagement in the work, feeling one makes a valued contribution, feeling confident and in control of the work, and being able to make choices. Other factors include fairness in workloads and feeling a sense of "flow" in what we do (Jones et al., 2019), and the work having a sense of meaning (Duffy et al., 2013). The latter point is relevant for this book since practitioners who regard themselves as trauma-informed can have decreased levels of compassion fatigue and secondary stress (Ormiston et al., 2022). To this wider research I would add having a sense of control over what happens, being able to influence a stressful environment, rather than responding by shutting down emotions (Lazarus, 2006). And relational support in the form of supervision where practitioners can reflect in a safe space on the impact of the work on them and consider solutions (Huffhines et al., 2023).

These factors suggest an overall recipe for what aspects of an early education setting can protect against secondary traumatisation, and how recovery can be supported within the role. Some of the ingredients in this recipe are suggested below under some summary headings. There are many other possibilities and some of these may not fit a particular setting. The key strategy is to involve staff in regular reflection on what they need in a process where everyone can take part without blame or shame.

Comfort:

- Pleasant work spaces, with quiet and dignified areas for breaks or off-floor work
- Regular and sufficient breaks with encouragement to use them well
- Physical needs, such as hydration, snacks, comfortable temperature, clean facilities
- Interactions between people are respectful and kind (see Chapters 8 and 9)

Security:

- Clear roles, so everyone knows what they are expected (or not expected) to do
- Leadership that provides psychological safety in interactions
- Fair and secure employment conditions
- Everyone allows each other to make or admit mistakes, and to question or doubt
- Safeguarding and risk policies and procedures are up to date and followed

Belonging:

- A warm and inclusive, but not intrusive culture, that welcomes everyone
- Leaders keep contact with everyone, checking they are ok and offering positive encouragement
- Collaborative decision making with everyone consulted and able to contribute
- Celebrations of individual significant events (birthdays, child passing driving test) and team milestones
- Relaxed time together with voluntary attendance, such as evenings out or team breaks
- Understandings that staff can chat and support each other - and that this is not always "time out"

Self-efficacy:

- Access to professional learning that fits both the setting's priorities and the needs of each individual staff member
- Competence building feedback. Successes are celebrated and attributed to staff efforts, and setbacks are analysed for what can be learned
- Autonomy and choice. Within guidelines, staff can make decisions and have these supported by managers and others
- Leadership development. Chances to take a lead on areas of interest, and to develop career through either job progression or specialisation
- Expertise is recognised. Ideas are listened to and explored, with acknowledgement of staff knowledge of children and families

Meaning:

- Shared and agreed values (preferably trauma-informed ones) that underpin setting policies and practices
- Chances to tell stories of good moments, successes, and reflect on the impact on children, families, or staff
- Understanding that working with children affected by trauma can be difficult, with time and space to reflect on the accompanying rewards
- Everyone in the setting sees that their cultural background is included, respected, and reflected in practice

It is easy to take the items above in one of two unintended directions. The first is a "them and us" framing, setting the general staff against managers who have a duty to provide all these things and are to be criticised or even opposed if they do not. The trauma-informed version of this would be to acknowledge that managers are people too, and subject to some or more of the same constraints and pressures in the overall "onion". Indeed the political, resources, and policy context might make them more vulnerable to excessive stress. This is not to excuse poor management practice, or suggest that staff should put up with denials of their workplace rights. But it is the case that if the general staff group are overstressed, so probably are the managers, since all are swimming in the same seas.

The second unhelpful turn to become aware of is a tempting path when under stress. This is to become helpless and put all the causes outside oneself. "No wonder I can't cope, look at all the things that aren't in place". "I won't perform well at work unless . . ." As with all negative thoughts, there is a grain of truth to this. But it is not the whole picture. Nearly all the items in the table are within the scope of anyone within the setting. I can in a conversation acknowledge the perspective of a colleague that I disagree with - "I can see why X is important to you". I can take the time for a short chat while we clear up the devastation of snack time to ask after the pet that was ill. I can notice and celebrate something a co-worker has done - "I like the way you've re-organised the outdoor boots". If enough individuals in a group do this, then it can become more of the collective culture.

But to do this, they have to be reasonably ok in themselves, and the wider culture has to support it. So we will move on to considering the political and policy context before a section on individual wellbeing.

The Wider World

It is difficult to move on from traumatic experiences unless we are feeling safe. Similarly, it is difficult to create and maintain a trauma-informed setting in a wider context that is hostile to it. It is also easy to feel helpless. Most of us are unlikely to become senior local administrators, or get ourselves elected to a legislature and then be able to change the whole system! But there are things we can do, and this section sets out some ideas. Again, as with a lot of this chapter, the individual ideas may not suit all circumstances - the point is about self-efficacy. We are not helpless. So if you think of other problems than these and better ideas to address them, that is great.

Accountability and Outcome Measures

There is nothing wrong with having outcome measures for early education. We are often spending the public's money and they have a reasonable expectation to know if this makes a difference. We are also accountable to the children to show we are providing what they need. But this can result in some very narrow measures and restrictive frameworks. For children who have experienced adversity and trauma it can also mean targets and expectations that are unrealistic and that pull settings away from providing what we know they need. Here are some ways we can mitigate this:

- Do the measures and reporting we have to do, but set this in a context of reasonable expectations of the children. Emphasise the progress over time rather than the snapshot score
- Keep a focus on the children and where they are. Some will need a lot of time on developing a sense of safety before they can do "formal" learning
- Build evidence for children's progress in important areas of development that are not covered in mandated frameworks, or that need to be covered differently
- Consider what and how to share with families, setting the context and focusing on progress in areas relevant to the child's situation

- Agree and keep refreshing a clear trauma-informed rationale for what you do in your setting, and why you prioritise what you do
- Get involved in campaigns to reform early learning curriculums and frameworks to make them more child-centred and trauma-informed

Under-Resourcing of Early Years

Many national and local governments talk of the importance of early years and of early intervention, but the funding and esteem does not always match this. The impact can be on what we are able to provide, but also on staffing ratios and possibilities for professional learning. In the face of this we might:

- Develop partnerships with families and local businesses to share resources (e.g., unwanted cardboard boxes, tyres, outdoor clothing, food items, etc.)
- Explore funding opportunities from foundations or from short-term government projects for either material or staffing
- Look out for free webinars or online book groups to provide professional learning
- Campaign for better funding and higher esteem for early years education

Policy Focus on Compliance and Behaviour Management

This comes up often when I do training. "We get this, but we have to make them behave", "We are told we have to have behaviour charts". It is true that we have to do what is mandated, but we can also do our best to do so in a trauma-informed way. For example:

- A clear setting rationale for behaviour management that sets out trauma-informed principles and practices
- Work within local administration and quality scrutiny to spread the trauma-informed messages and evidence
- Keep reframing behaviour language from punitive models to trauma-informed thinking
- Link the recording of progress with children's learning and development to the co-regulated scaffolding provided
- Use setting communications (newsletters, social media) to show the impact of the approaches adopted (e.g., lots of happy children playing with mud and learning!)

Fragmented Services

This book concentrates on what we can do in early education rather than covering what other services such as health or social care might do. Often settings can feel isolated either because other services are not available locally, or because they are not well joined up. We might try:

- Building and maintaining personal relationships with other professionals. Invite them in to play! Or include them in setting celebrations or events
- Recognise and communicate the understanding that they might not be available or integrated because of their own resource constraints rather than a lack of willingness to help

- Focus on what can be done together, even if it is just accessing advice from them or providing them with information
- Where there are joined up processes such as a Team Around the Child or similar, try to make staff available to take part in these with their invaluable knowledge and perspectives
- Help families to find and access services, and advocate for them if they wish
- Make sure your own practice and recording is holistic, thinking of the whole child and their situation

What We Can Do Ourselves

In order to manage and address all the systemic factors, we need to be doing as well as possible ourselves. And there is a lot we can do to help us manage stress and working with trauma. Some more in-depth resources for this are in the reading list at the end of the chapter, but here are some of the outlines that are usually recommended.

Lifestyle

As we saw above, our built-in survival mode for chronic stress involves changes in how we eat, sleep, and spend our time. In particular, the following are common and normal in the face of ongoing high stress:

- Reduced or disrupted sleep
- More seeking of rest
- Increased consumption of food, especially carbohydrates, and/or alcohol
- Reduced social activity
- Less engagement with previous interests

These may be our natural built-in responses but like all stress responses they are about survival rather than flourishing. We can become aware of them and make choices about which of them are really helping us. For example, seeking rest. While the occasional evening on the sofa with a takeaway watching boxsets can be just what we need, if it becomes a habit we might find we don't recover so well. We get more into a "sludgy" flop mode where rest isn't actually restful. Similarly, once in a while we might not be able to face the evening out with the in-laws and instead bicker for hours with friends on social media. Nothing wrong with it, but again if it becomes habitual, we won't get so much benefit and even get stuck.

In the next chapter, on trauma recovery, we look at living positively. The same kinds of elements can prevent secondary stress too, and the following list sets some of them out. This is only a summary to help consider what to prioritise. In outline, though, it is the age-old advice about a healthy and active lifestyle:

- Reduced or disrupted sleep:
  - o Set regular bed and rise times, and stick to them
  - o Don't work in bed, and reduce watching films or social media – let your body associate it with sleep

- Make where you sleep cozy and attractive but not over-cluttered
- Have a calm wind-down routine for the hour or so before bed with reduced activity and screen use
- Remember most people have sleep issues from time to time, but re-learning the habits can resolve these
- If waking in the night, do something restful, like reading; accept waking periods as normal
- Address negative thoughts that keep you awake (see "Cognitive Restructuring" below)
- Be aware sleep problems can be caused by physical health issues so seek medical advice if you suspect, e.g., apnea, asthma, chronic pain, reflux, thyroid issues, or (for men) frequent needs to urinate.

- More seeking of rest:
  - Put some boundaries around rest - e.g., have a sit and a cuppa for 30 mins, and stick to it
  - Alternative rest and (gentle) activity. After a sit down, do some stretches or make a meal
  - Make a list of the things you enjoy doing or find meaning in - which would you like to do more of, or get into a routine
  - Break tasks up into steps. Clean one window a day rather than all of them in one go; wash some dishes rather than none
  - Make small and do-able steps of progress. Better to have a 30 minute walk every weekend than resolve and fail to run a marathon a day
- Increased consumption of food, especially carbohydrates, and/or alcohol:
  - Be aware of changes in consumption and/or when eating or drinking is used as comfort
  - Avoid self-blame around food or alcohol consumption
  - Be aware of, and make choices about, bargaining. "Just one more biscuit" or "I'll burn this off with a bike ride next week"
  - Substitute healthier alternatives for comfort consumption. Munch carrot sticks instead of a chocolate bar; enjoy sparkling water with some lemon slices rather than a gin and tonic
  - Swap processed foods for whole grains (e.g., not white bread, rice, etc.) for some meals - they give fullness and comfort for longer
  - Make small achievable changes each week
  - Seek help if you are feeling stuck or food/drink are associated with anxiety or low mood
- Reduced social activity:
  - A bit of withdrawal if one needs it will do no harm over the short term
  - Sometimes the things we least feel like doing are what we most need
  - Focus on the pleasure you might give valued others as a motivation
  - Put some boundaries around experiences. Go for half an hour, or just the movie and not the meal. Setting a timer or having a booked lift to pick you up depersonalises it

  - Be up front with friends and family that you are having a difficult time. They may well be sympathetic and offer help
- Less engagement with previous interests:
  - Accept it is natural to feel this if overstressed or tired
  - Consider what interests are higher reward and lower effort, and devote some time to those
  - Re-start small and build up. You might not get back to painting masterpieces in a week, but perhaps you can clean the brushes
  - Allow time for habits to rebuild and accept setbacks along the way, especially if trying too much too soon
  - Include others who can encourage (e.g., a park run or walk with a friend)
  - Describe your enjoyable activity as being restorative healing rather than either a chore or self-indulgence

All of these, and any other ideas that the list prompts, can help. They depend however on having safe spaces and times where they can have effect. The next short section is about establishing these.

Making a Boundary

The onion diagram shows us how stresses in different areas of our lives can interact and influence each other. Many people find that if they are having a stressful time at work, this can spill over into family and home. They might be more grumpy over mealtimes, or less inclined to pretend to be interested in their teenager's current opinions. It can go the other way, too. Stress at home can influence how we are at work. And it can become a circle of stress.

One set of solutions to this is to create some boundaries and distance between the different contexts so we can "switch off" or "switch on" (Sonnentag & Bayer, 2005). People vary in how easy they find this, but it is a set of skills that can be learned as long as this is in a self-care way rather than "one more thing" to do (Ludick & Figley, 2017). I learned a lot about this during the Covid lockdowns in 2020, when work was at home and harder to switch off from. A wise friend advised me to put a towel over the laptop at the end of the day – and strangely this little ritual made the difference between living at work and working at home.

Here are some ideas to create an "airlock" between home and work so that problems in one cross over less to the other.

- Routines and rituals:
  - Create boundary rituals for arriving at work from home:
    - Changing clothing
    - Making a drink
    - Greeting colleagues
    - Stretching
    - Planning the day
  - Create boundary rituals for arriving at home from work:
    - Changing clothing
    - Having a cup of tea or coffee, or water

        - Doing something social and enjoyable
        - Getting some exercise
        - Doing something soothing such as reading for a bit or playing music
- Physical separation:
    - Make the commute a deliberate and mindful separation. Count off the stops, or landmarks
    - Do something you enjoy when travelling (music, a podcast, an audiobook, or, if not driving, reading)
    - Consciously and mindfully "arrive", talking yourself though it (see Using Self-Talk in Chapter 19)
- Putting it aside:
    - If worries about home/work arise, write them down and fold the paper to deal with it when you are there
    - Mention the problem to someone you can trust with it and have a brief chat about how to solve it
    - If it sticks with you either try "reworking ruminations", or finding an adaptive way to express the feelings (a brisk walk, drawing a picture)
    - Be aware of if you are getting to the top or bottom of your window of tolerance and try one of the stress regulation ideas below
- Reworking ruminations:
    - When time at home is full of thoughts about work churning around, consider more steps for making a physical separation or putting thoughts aside
    - Deliberately devote time to problem solving the worries - what are you going to do about it tomorrow? Write them down and put the paper in your pocket to take
    - Reframe the negative ruminations using cognitive restructuring (see below)

Finding Meaning

Working in early education can be difficult and stressful, and it can also be rewarding as we know the differences we are trying to make for children and families (Berlin et al., 2020). Under chronic stress, we might naturally focus more on the difficulties and start to forget about the rewards. That's how people respond to repeated stressful challenges - it is their brains doing their job of checking the environment for more things to guard against. The psychological effect can be a spiral of exhaustion and lower mood, concentration on negative information, leading to negative thoughts and then lower mood (Southall, 2024). This can take us eventually into a more fixed pattern of thinking and feeling that is an actual mood disorder such as depression (Clark & Beck, 2010). If this is so, it is not a sign of weakness but simply the brain overdoing its job, and it is always ok to seek help.

However, the good news is that there is a lot we can do to stop the cycle, and to help us be more aware of the upsides, and to enjoy being with the children (Lee et al., 2011). One way to do this is to deliberately practice compassion satisfaction (Oberg et al., 2023). This means reframing the difficulties of the work we do in terms of the satisfaction we can get from trying to do it as well as we can. That includes the limits of what we can do. Not everything we try will work, we are not going to be winning the gold medal for co-regulation everyday - but we have done our best. And we are entitled to be pleased about that.

We can apply this more generally by again deliberately focusing attention onto any other rewards from what we do that balance the stress and exhaustion (Brophy-Herb et al., 2023). This is not about pretending everything is fine. It is not fine. But it is not all bad, and seeing some of that can help reduce the thought-mood spiral. Some ways to do this include:

- Make a list of what went well today. What did you do to bring that about? What difference did it make? What does it say about you that you managed this? (No "buts"!)
- If things go wrong, ask yourself what good thing you were trying to do. What have you learned from this experience for next time?
- Think of something that a child did in the last week or so that made you laugh or was a pleasant surprise. What happened? What was so good about it?
- Reframe the exhaustion. It is not that you are weak, but that you have worked hard. And you've done this because you care.

Cognitive Restructuring

Finding meaning is one aspect of a wider set of strategies sometimes called cognitive restructuring, or reappraisal. The basic idea is that we have all kinds of thoughts about what is going on or what it means. Much of the time, this matches reality. I think I am late for the train, and indeed I am. But often, it is a shortcut assumption that does not match reality. I think I am an unreliable idiot for missing the train. And I think my friends are going to give up on me because I am late to the party. But actually, the traffic was worse than usual due to a breakdown that I couldn't have foreseen. And my friends are used to me being late and won't mind at all.

Thoughts are not reality. They are our brain's first go at interpreting what is going on. When we are stressed and under pressure, these proposals often involve some negative ideas about ourselves. But they are just that, proposals, and we do not have to accept them. They have arisen because that's what our brains produce under stress - they are called negative automatic thoughts. Putting them through a gentle process of assessment against the actual evidence can reduce the distress they cause. There are six steps to this:

1	Noticing the thought	I'm late for the train. I'm an unreliable idiot
2	How do I feel?	Terrible
3	What's the evidence for the thought being true?	Well, I missed the train, and it's not the first time
4	What's the evidence against the thought?	I allowed plenty of time. The road was blocked by a broken down van. I couldn't have known that
5	What's a more balanced view?	I'm not totally reliable, but this time it really wasn't my fault. My friends will understand
6	How do I feel now?	Embarrassed still but not so bad

Working in early education can give rise to any number of negative thoughts. I'll give some examples here. The key thing to remember is that just because I might think them, this does not make them true (a difficult concept for me to grasp a lot of the time!).

I'm really bad at this
If I ask for help, they will think I'm weak
The setting manager was annoyed with me
Everyone else manages better than I do
I shouldn't feel like this
I have to get this (or everything) right
It's all my fault
It's all their fault
I can't do another day like this
I can't stand these children
I am not suited to this work

There are many more, and each person has their own small menu that comes out at times of difficulty. But they also all respond to a degree to the restructuring process. Another example from my experience. A training event with 100 people has just been rather flat, with no questions asked:

1	Noticing the thought	That went really badly. I'm terrible at training
2	How do I feel?	Sad and incompetent
3	What's the evidence for the thought being true?	There weren't any questions
4	What's the evidence against the thought?	It was the same training that has always gone well before; there were nods and smiles while I was talking. Also few people in the group knew each other
5	What's a more balanced view?	Maybe I covered everything; or maybe it was the group dynamics; some maybe didn't want to be there
6	How do I feel now?	Having some ideas for reluctant participants if it happens again (e.g., Post-Its for questions)

Cognitive restructuring is often effective, but it can be difficult to do especially at first or on one's own. A very useful and comprehensive guide is *Mind over Mood* by Greenberger and Padesky (2015). In a fast-moving context as well, one may not have time to sit down with pen and paper and negotiate with the thoughts. I sometimes use a much simpler version for myself based in a broader base of evidence called attribution theory (Seligman, 1990; Weiner, 1985). This shortcut again takes the negative thought seriously. But it looks for explanations or responses that are not about me. For example:

The manager was annoyed with me	They have a lot on their mind
I shouldn't feel like this	We are all getting a bit stressed
I have to get everything right	We are doing difficult things
I can't do another day like this	What do we need to change? Who can help?

Reducing Stress Reactions

Sometimes when we are very stressed, or under a long-term burden of cares, it can be hard to think. So cognitive approaches do not work for everyone, or for anyone all of the time.

Remembering the way our stress systems work, however, we can instead try soothing the stress reactions. We will look at these first in terms of strengthening our sense of safety, and then some ideas for managing in a difficult moment.

Practising Psychological Safety

In order to return the brain to safe state from stressed state, we need to have that safe state well established. This can be difficult if life is a helter-skelter of one thing after another or if we are not able to meet our basic needs. Our own experiences of trauma can also make it harder, and the following chapter offers some ideas for managing traumatic memories.

Apart from this, the most effective ways to reinforce our basic sense of safety are to review the practical ingredients in the section above on lifestyle. Restoring and maintaining a routine and rhythm to our lives that includes sleep, good nutrition, exercise, interest, meaning, and social contact helps maintain the safe state as the brain is able to spend more time in it, and less time monitoring unmet needs.

There are also some practices that can develop the safe state further including mindfulness and yoga. It is best to approach these with guidance (for example classes) so we are practising them safely and can discuss whether they are right for us. I find both useful, but please be aware that they can bring forward traumatic memories so they may not be for everyone - best to discuss with providers and to stop if they are difficult or distressing. Just as effective, if practised regularly, are any of the soothing and grounding ideas set out for children in Chapter 12.

Coping in the Moment

If we devote some time and energy to practising psychological safety, we may notice over time that difficult moments become either more rare or easier to deal with. What has happened is not that the world has decided to be less stressful but that our brain is automatically dealing with them more smoothly. The stress system is labelling the events as less big or urgent, and the regulating systems have got smoother at soothing our reactions. But there are often still things that happen that catch us out, and it is useful to have some strategies for managing in a "hot" moment. Again this is very individual but some of the most common ideas include the following:

- Stop and pause! Even a couple of seconds before we do whatever the first impulse was can be enough to reset a little.
- Breathe! This can be a slow breath in and out, or the famous "count to ten". Some people like more structured breathing such as inhaling for 4 counts, holding for 4 and then exhaling for 4 before holding for another 4 before breathing in.
- Quick grounding. Press your feet into the floor and/or straighten your back. Or use an object such as something to grasp like a small stone or a rubber band - or your own finger tips.
- Distractors. Count back from 100 in sevens, or do something deliberate like have a sip of water or move about. Use a grounding strategy such as notice something blue, red, and

green nearby, or track the four corners of the room. Or conjure a visual in your imagination (anything calming will do such as a favourite place or plant).

- Connect. Look at a colleague and make eye contact. This may move them to help, or else just the connection can be calming.
- Create distance. If you feel the need, it is always ok to just put in some actual distance. It might be a single step back, or if you need to remove yourself from the scene entirely, then as long as there is someone supervising the children that is ok.

Conclusion

Promoting staff wellbeing is a big and complex topic, but an important one. Different things work for different people, but the overall structure needs to be systemic considering the pressures that drive chronic stress at work and how they can be mitigated. We need to be aware of, and avoid, an understandable tendency to hope for short-term and easy fixes. Having said that, an ecological approach that addresses everyone in a sensitive and mind-minded way can improve things quite quickly.

The last element to consider is how we can manage traumatic memories, and this is the topic of the next chapter.

Chapter summary:

- Promoting staff wellbeing is about developing the working context as well as individuals "looking after themselves"
- Everyone can have a role in creating a positive working environment
- There is also much that individuals can do to be aware of their needs and support their wellbeing

19

Staff Traumatic Memories

This chapter will provide:

- Material to support staff to reflect on any traumatic memories they may have
- Ideas that may support both coping and recovery
- An account of safe and effective trauma-focused therapies

People working in early education, as well as the stressors and rewards of that occupation, are as likely to experience traumatic events in daily life as anyone else. Traumatic memories can persist and stay fresh for years. But as we gain confidence and control in noticing and managing their impacts, these can gradually reduce in depth or frequency. And, although they are not as widely known about or available as they should be, there are safe and effective therapies that for many people can help considerably.

While it is impossible in this book to provide a comprehensive guide to living with, and resolving, traumatic memories, this chapter aims to provide some pointers and signposts. These are not a substitute for professional help and advice, so please do seek that if you need it. We will look first at coping with triggers, then at how living as full a life as possible can help recovery. In a final section I'll describe some therapeutic methods that have evidence for safety and effectiveness.

Coping with Triggers

Before we look directly at triggers, we need to establish as much of a basic sense of safety as we can – just as we saw with the children in Chapters 6–13. The methods for adults are not that different. We can look at our overall "diet" of stimulation. Are we getting enough interest and pleasurable stress – or not enough? Is our world and lifestyle more or less stable and predictable? Then we can consider the internal generation of a sense of safety. Just like children, adults benefit from repeated and rhythmic activity. This tends to take adult forms rather than playing with foam, and could be things like a regular film night, or the satisfaction of smoothing a plank to be part of a shed, or digging in a row of potatoes, or even washing the dishes.

It may also help if we deliberately practise soothing and grounding activities. Any of those in Chapter 12 that appeal will do. This is important because when we encounter triggers what we need to do is draw our brains back into the safe state from the triggered state. It is the

DOI: 10.4324/9781003563808-24

same as if we want to get out of a swimming pool; we need a firm surface to get onto, and a ladder to help us get there. Practising soothing and grounding when we do not need it helps to establish that firm ground and a path to take us there. The stronger and more well established that safe state is, the more easily we can find it at need.

With this established, the first step in managing trigger experiences is to become aware of them and how they affect us. This can be quite individual and specific, as we have seen.

> For most of my young adulthood, I used to get anxious and irritable in supermarkets, especially at the checkout. I would complain about having to wait, become impatient with slow people in front of me; and sometimes even abandon the shopping altogether and leave the store.

With the expertise on trauma we now have, we can easily see some elements of fight and flight here! But being a typical human being, despite already working as a trauma psychologist, it was years before I realised that there was something about supermarkets that created a "flight" and "fight" reaction in me. In fact, I didn't realise at all – it was pointed out by my long-suffering partner who was fed up being left at the checkout with the shopping (and the bill).

The second step is equally difficult, and slightly more counter-intuitive. We have to accept the fact of a trigger. I need to explain that carefully. I do not mean we pretend everything is fine, and I certainly do not mean that it is ok that people live lives with traumatic memories in them. What I do mean is to remember that all that has happened is that we have found an aspect of life that, for whatever reason, we find difficult. And none of those reasons include us being weak, or it being our fault.

> Of course I felt bad about this. I started to think that everyone in the queue could tell I was getting impatient and knew I was a bad and grumpy person. But then I realised it was as much about the situation as it was about me. Just like I shiver when I go out in the snow without a coat, so I feel anxious in a queue at the checkout.

Adjusting the Experience

Once we have got this far, how to cope with the trigger can become as much common sense as putting a coat on before going out into a blizzard. In fact, we have even more options. Remember the three elements that make an experience traumatic:

- High levels of stress or threat
- Low control over what is happening
- Low or inaccessible support from others

Again we have to remember that the first element is in the eye of the experiencer. There is nothing intrinsically threatening about a supermarket checkout. For most, it is a boring experience, or one of mild anxiety as we wonder what we have forgotten. But my reactions were telling me that for whatever reason, it was highly stressful for me.

Having noticed and accepted that this was a trigger experience, I can start to think how to make it easier. You might like to pause and think of how, if you were around to give advice, you might suggest I make it less stressful, or more under control, or feel more supported. Here are some of the ideas that occurred to me:

- Reducing stress or threat:
  - Going when it is quieter so queues are shorter
  - Making sure I have enough time and am not in a hurry
  - Using positive self-talk (see the next section)
  - Any of the soothing or grounding strategies in Chapter 12
  - Distracting myself with phone, product labels, newspaper headlines
- Increasing control:
  - Choosing a queue to join
  - Using a self-service checkout if available
  - Waiting until the queue is shorter
  - Working to a shopping list rather than piling up stuff
  - Organise my items in a particular way (fridge things first, or whatever)
  - Focusing on what I can control (see "Reflecting on Control" below)
- Increasing support:
  - Going with someone else who can chat and distract me
  - Agreeing that I can bail out at the checkout and meet outside
  - Smiling at the checkout staff – they usually smile back which is helpful

One of my ideas was actually about avoiding the trigger. In earlier chapters we have looked at avoidances as a problem because often they get in the way of things we need to do, or that would help us, or that are an unavoidable part of childhood. At some point, a child has to have their teeth checked, or pick up a pencil, so we want to manage avoidances rather than reinforce them.

But in daily life, often we can just go ahead and avoid. The difference is that we are doing this consciously and deliberately, taking control and making choices about what is important to us. So if I can avoid the checkout because someone else is happy to do that bit, why not? The fact that I can do this, and take a degree of control over whether I experience a trigger or not, might make that trigger easier to bear when I do have to face it. If I am there in the queue all by myself, I can tell myself this is not how things always are and all I have to do is get through this one time.

Reflective Activity

Think of a day-to-day activity that often mildly raises stress levels. Do not go for an actual trigger at this stage or for something high stakes like a child late for football practice. I might pick something like not being able to find my car keys, or being slightly late for a meeting.

What are some ways you could adjust or approach this next time so as to (any or all of the following):

- Make it less high pressure?
- Have more control over what happens?
- Access more support and help?

I might phone or message ahead to say I'll be a bit late (reduce stress), plan my diary with more gaps for travel (control), or set up a reminder to set off (support).

Try your ideas out and see if they help!

When we do have to face a trigger though, alongside the general principles of reducing stress, and increasing control and support, there are two clusters of strategies that might be helpful. Both of these use the top-down, deliberate, self-regulation systems so are best if we are calm enough to use them. If we are feeling ourselves moving out of our "zone of tolerance" into higher stress, then starting with soothing and grounding to lay a foundation might work best. But given that, we might try some cognitive strategies. These include using self-talk and reflecting on control.

Using Self-Talk

On the rare occasions that I go to the dentist, one of the ways I get through it is to repeat silently to myself over and over again the same phrases, such as "it's not going to last long", "it's not nice but it's necessary", "the dentist knows what they are doing", and so on. This is a version of what is sometimes called "positive self-talk". How and why this works has been extensively studied (Kross et al., 2014; Oleś et al., 2020) but it is basically the deliberate practice of saying to ourselves what a friend might say when coaching us through an experience. As such, it is hard to script since what one person finds motivating and helpful might be irritating to someone else. But common phrases include things like:

I'm trying my best
It won't last long
I managed this before
Everyone makes mistakes
I can learn from this
Just one small step
It's ok to do this my way

Reflecting on Control

We sometimes bear the whole burden of responsibility for events that we actually have little control over. I used to be scared of flying and a big part of it was an irrational sense that I was somehow influential on keeping the plane going - by force of will and worry, and by making sure I always had my water bottle, and my things in the same order each time. It is how human beings make sense of what is happening and strive for a feeling of control over things too big for us. But it also can trap us in the negative feelings.

What can help is deliberately to reflect on what we can control about a situation and what we can't. In my flying example, I eventually persuaded myself that aircraft are actually flown by people who know what they are doing and train extensively for any scenario. I told myself that I cannot control whether the air will have turbulence, but I can try to relax when it happens and believe the pilots when they say it's no big deal.

The same process can help with trigger experiences. In my supermarket example, I could control my waiting time to an extent by picking the shortest queue. But perhaps the person in front has a lot of items and wants to pay in the smallest coins possible along with 100 coupons? Nothing I can do. But I can control my reaction – including remembering that it isn't my fault, it is just one of those things. More generally, it can help to think about a situation and what bits of it go into each of these different boxes:

Aspects I have no control over	Aspects I could change with help	Aspects I can control

The purpose is to reduce the stress by worrying less about what can't be changed (the dentist), increasing my awareness of control where I have it (trying some self-talk) and raising the awareness of help that is available (let the dentist know if it hurts).

Grow the Rest of Life

There is an excellent book, now quite old, by Maggie Dolan for people who experienced abusive childhoods. It is called *Beyond Survival: Living Well Is the Best Revenge*. Without going too far into the vengeance theme, the basic idea is that we can overemphasise "getting over" past trauma and therefore miss opportunities to create and live a fulfilling and rewarding life.

Sometimes we cannot process the trauma, for lots of different reasons. But we can grow the rest of life. In therapeutic conversations I have often used this diagram (which I learned from a colleague, David Murray):

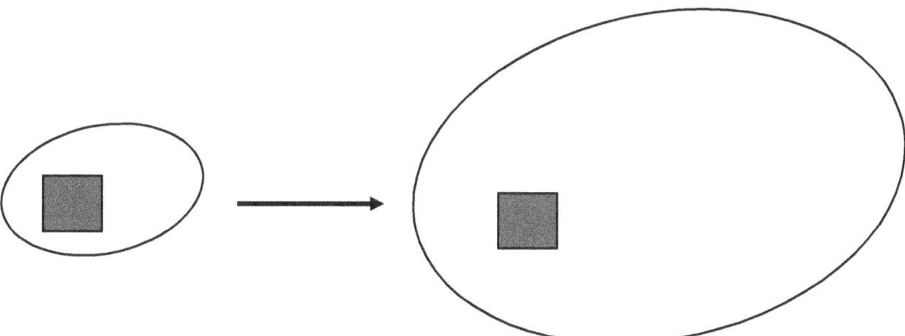

Figure 19.1 An intuitive depiction of reducing trauma's impact

The idea is simple. The traumatic memory remains, and with it some triggers and avoidances. But we can put a focus on aspects of life where the trauma is not, and where it has less influence. If we try to grow and develop these, then the trauma stays the same, but it becomes much less of our lives. I'll cover two ways of doing this – firstly developing oases of safety, and secondly addressing some of the common post-traumatic cognitions.

Developing Oases of Safety

One of the most useful discussions I have with children and young people is to make a map of safety. This can be an actual map - we draw together where in their world they feel most safe. It might be at a friend's house, or with a trusted teacher, or when they are by themselves in their room under a duvet. It's different for everyone. The point is partly to gain a sense of how safe they actually are, but it does two other things as well. Firstly, it loosens the grip of the traumatic memories as they try to tell the youngster they are not safe. The world is still scary, but not all scary. Secondly, once we know this we can look at how to make best use of those "oases", and whether there are other places that with small changes could become oases as well.

I use the word "map", but it needn't just be places. It could be people, or it could be activities, or when we have a familiar object to carry around. Anything will do. Once we know what or where or who they are, we can access them more, or just be more aware of the feelings of safety they provide.

Reflective Activity

Have an imaginary "walk through" your life - maybe a typical week, or even a whole year if you want a longer cycle.

- Where do you feel most comfortable and relaxed?
- What activities give you most pleasure or satisfaction?
- Who do you feel happy and safe to be with?

Draw it as a "map" if you like!

Having looked at this, are there ways you could make life feel even better or safer? What do you want to do more of, or less of? Or are there new ideas?

Post-Traumatic Cognitions

Back in Chapter 2 we saw that during overwhelming experiences the brain prioritises fight, flight, freeze, and flop actions, and the strong feelings and body states that support these. Thinking and reasoning is more turned down. However, traumatic memories often do contain cognitions or thoughts - either fragmentary memories of the time or else subsequent attempts by the brain to make the memories more meaningful and part of our general biography. Exactly which cognitions can depend both on the experience and on the individual. With complex trauma, there are often many and they intertwine with each other. Some examples include:

I am bad
I always mess things up
I'm not safe
It's all my fault
I am weak
I am broken

I am unlovable
I can't be trusted
I am disgusting
I'm not good enough
I'm different or weird
I don't exist

Before we go any further, please just be aware that addressing these cognitions can be quite an emotional experience. There is a direct link from what we think about ourselves to how we feel, and changing built-in negative assumptions about ourselves can be quite poignant. You might want to review the Safety Notice at the start of the book and think about whether you want to read on, or leave this part for another time. I'll put in a page break here for that reason. When you are ready, turn the page.

These cognitions can be horrible, and can influence our lives and how others react to us. If someone goes through life thinking they are weak, for example, they might avoid challenges, be reluctant to try new things, become helpless unexpectedly. People might start to treat them as unreliable, or offer them lots of help they didn't actually need, which further convinces them that the thought is true.

But it is not true. It is not true. It isn't true. The very fact that this person has lived through a traumatic experience and is still more or less here shows that they are strong, not weak. Or yes, maybe they are weakened by it – but they also have some strength too. So here are the first three responses to negative cognitions like these:

- They are a natural consequence of a difficult experience.
- They are not true, any more than the original experience is happening all over again when we meet a trigger.
- But they feel true. And that's just the way our stress systems are wired. We are not being silly or mad.

But we also don't have to put up with it. We can challenge these thoughts. Or better, we can get into a dialogue with them and about them, and come to a more balanced view. One way to do this is by the kind of cognitive restructuring we saw in Chapter 17. In this process, we become aware of the thought, take it seriously, and weigh up the evidence for and against it. And then decide what we think on the whole. Here's an example:

What's happening?	I'm in the car park, despising myself because I abandoned my partner at the supermarket checkout
What negative thoughts have I got?	I can't be trusted I let people down
How strong is that (0–100)?	90! What a loser!
What's the evidence for it?	I'm here hiding by the car
What's some evidence that it might not always be true?	I do a complicated job looking after children's welfare and get more right than wrong mostly
What's a balanced view then?	I just don't like supermarkets!
How strong are those negative thoughts now (0–100)?	40; feeling better

We can also come at this another way – through actions. I personally find this more powerful as I tend to live too much in my head anyway. Whatever the cognition, there are things we already do that show it isn't true. It can help to become more aware of these. And we might have some ideas for new things as well. In other words, we do our best to deliberately live as though the cognitions are untrue. Suppose, for example, I have a persisting thought that I am a bad person. I can gently challenge this by looking for ways to do good things, either for myself or for others. I might prepare a cup of coffee for my partner who is busy with a long online meeting. The smile tells me I have done something good. Or if I have a sense sometimes that I'm not good enough, I might choose a small challenge (get the dishes washed!)

and notice if this changes how I feel in the moment. Building these kinds of actions deliberately into each day can shift our thoughts over time.

What exactly these "opposites" are varies from person to person, but I've put my own versions below to start some ideas. These were the ones I had stuck in my head for a long time.

Negative cognition	*The opposite*
I am bad	I can do good things
I always mess things up	I can get things right
I'm not safe	I can feel safe
I don't matter	I can make a difference
I am weak	I can do things
I am broken	I'm not finished yet
I am unlovable	There are people who care about me
I can't be trusted	I am mostly reliable
I am disgusting	It's ok to be me
I'm not good enough	It's enough to do my best
I'm different or weird	Yes, in a good way!
I don't exist	There are people who are glad that I do

So the task for me is to live as though all those things in the "opposite" column are true. What would you advise *me* to try? I've left it blank to support reflection.

The positive cognitions	*To show these are true, James could . . .*
I can do good things	
I can get things right	
I can feel safe	
I can make a difference	
I can do things	
I'm not finished yet	
There are people who care about me	
I am mostly reliable	
It's ok to be me	
It's enough to do my best	
Yes, in a good way!	
There are people who are glad that I do	

Here are some of my ideas. I make the effort to keep in touch with my widely dispersed family. I might start with the thought that they don't really want to see me and are just being kind for family's sake. But halfway into the chat on social media I feel a bit more like there are people who are glad that I'm here, and who care about me. In the evening, tired after a day at work, and feeling I am a bit broken, I make a list of what's on tomorrow and the minimum I hope to achieve. Ticking this off the next day (and I have learned to carefully choose my list so it is almost bound to happen!) I start to realise I can make a difference and that I am far from out for the count yet.

It is very individual and personal and does not work for everyone. I've left a blank version of the basic idea in case it is helpful for a reflection:

What would I like to think about myself?	*What do I already do that might show this is true?*	*What other (small) things could I try doing?*

Here are just a few ideas to start with to prompt others – remember this is very individual:

- Helping a friend with something
- Volunteering for a cause you care about
- Any kind of hobby you enjoy
- Managing some exercise, or creating a new goal
- Something you did recently that you thought you wouldn't manage
- Making something (a meal, a cake, a picture, a hideous clay statue)
- Make a list of what went well today, or this week
- Make a deal to give yourself a treat tomorrow, and do it
- Spend time with someone who cares for you (a person, a pet)
- Deliberately care for yourself, nice food, some pleasant soap – you *are* worth it
- Ditto for another – a meal, a surprise gift, a call or visit
- Make a den or cosy corner, your own space to be nurtured
- Tidy up, clean a window, wash the car, weed a window box
- Tell someone it is good to see them
- Have a walk or a swim
- Anything, really, that is good to do

If those just sound like an ordinary life lived well, that is the point. The effect of trauma is to dissociate, to make life feel less ordinary, less good – to cut us off from those feelings. Living well is the best recovery.

Trauma-Specific Therapies

There are many things on offer that claim to "heal trauma". In terms of evidence, there are two main approaches that are known to be both safe and effective. As noted above, neither of these are necessarily widely available or known about, even by healthcare providers. So this section will describe them briefly so that readers know what to ask for, either for themselves or for others. Both approaches have the same aim, even if they get there quite differently. This is to enable and support the natural processing of memories that the brain does, but which has been blocked because the memory in question is so overwhelming. The principle is simple – to process anything, we have to think about it, sometimes many times. We know this, for example, if we get unexpected good news. It can sometimes take days for this to "sink in". Similarly, the way the brain stores memories is through processing over time, a bit like sorting all the papers into a file so they are facing the same way and stacked neatly and can then be stored. In trauma, because the memories are so strong, the brain does not process them in the same way. So they stay "unfiled", which is why they feel like *now* rather than the past when they are triggered.

The evidence base for children is less extensive but I'll also indicate as well if and how these therapies can be adapted for use with young children. An essential note is that these are both complicated processes and should only be offered by, or done with, providers who have had sufficient training and ongoing supervision.

Trauma-focused cognitive behavioural therapy is a version of standard cognitive behaviour therapy adapted to include an element for processing traumatic memories. It is essentially a form of guided exposure, where the person is carefully prompted to recall the traumatic experience and the feelings that come with it, but in the safe context of the therapy. The cognitive behavioural element is a preparation for this, so that the person can cope with it. For example, people learn relaxation techniques, or how to deal with upsetting thoughts. Over time, the memories become less powerful and start to fade. People also acquire useful skills for managing triggers and avoidances, and preventing future traumatisation. Obviously, this form of therapy draws quite heavily on cognitive abilities, so it is less suitable for young children by themselves, in which case the intervention also involves parents and carers.

Eye movement desensitisation and reprocessing (EMDR) is rather different, and it is still not entirely clear how it works even if there is plenty of evidence that it does. The person is guided to recall the experience, meanwhile the therapist administers what is called "bilateral stimulation". In practice this is either repeated alternate taps to left and right hands, alternate lights on left and right, or else (hence the name) asking the person to follow a finger with their eyes from left to right. This keeps the person in a state of dual attention, where they are grounding in the safe present and looking at the memory. What tends to happen is the memory develops and gradually becomes less upsetting. People often have new insights ("it wasn't my fault") or find new meaning in their experience. The simplest explanation for how this works is that the left/right stimulation keeps the brain alert and aware that the person is in a safe place – and so the traumatic memory processes just like an ordinary memory. EMDR can be adapted for young children as it has versions involving play and storytelling that children often, strangely, end up enjoying!

> I had EMDR for my supermarket problem! The trigger turned out to be the "beep beep" of the checkout tills taking me back over ten years to the machines in a hospital where I visited my father who had been suddenly taken ill.

If you want to know more about these therapies, then there is a good page on trauma-focused cognitive behaviour therapy on the American Psychological Association website; and EMDR Europe is an authoritative source on that therapy. What is essential for both of these is that the therapist is properly trained and supervised, so it is always worth checking their qualifications and experience.

Closing Reflections

Living with the impact of traumatic memories can be difficult, but it does not mean we are broken or beyond hope. By understanding our triggers, creating moments of safety, and gently challenging the negative beliefs we carry, we can begin to reclaim our sense of safety and control. Small, deliberate actions - and practising safety and grounding - can gradually shift how we feel and think. For many, trauma-focused therapies may offer additional relief.

A consistent theme throughout this book is that psychological trauma is both common and an adaptive response to overwhelming experiences. So we can know we are not alone and we are not broken - even if it may feel like that at times. Many people experience not just recovery but what is called "post-traumatic growth", as they realise the strengths they have shown in doing as well as we are. And we might be able to bring that insight to the work of early education, as we can better understand children's experiences and take satisfaction in helping them lay the foundations for a full and flourishing life.

Glossary

Action System	Brain areas that generate physical or behavioural responses to stress or needs.
Adverse Childhood Experiences (ACEs)	Potentially traumatic events that occur in childhood (0-17 years), such as experiencing violence, abuse, or neglect, which can affect long-term health and development.
Affect Tolerance	The capacity to experience and manage emotional states without becoming overwhelmed or shutting down.
Amygdala	A part of the brain involved in processing emotions, especially fear and threat detection.
Attachment	The emotional bond formed between a child and caregivers which provides the foundation for emotional and social development.
Attachment Styles	Patterns of how individuals form and maintain relationships, often shaped by early interactions with caregivers.
Avoidance	A coping mechanism where a person tries to stay away from reminders of a traumatic event.
Buffering	Adult actions that protect children from overwhelming stress, reducing the impact of potentially traumatic experiences.
Buffering Stress	Providing relational and emotional support to a child during or after a stressful event to reduce the negative impact on development.
Co-Regulation	A process where a caregiver helps a child manage emotions by providing calm and responsive support.
Complex Trauma	Trauma that results from repeated or prolonged exposure to distressing events, often involving interpersonal relationships.
Core Self	The foundational, pre-verbal sense of identity built from early repetitive and rhythmic interactions.
Cortex	The outer layer of the brain responsible for higher-level thinking, reasoning, and decision making.
Decentring	The ability to see a situation from another person's point of view, particularly useful in managing conflicts and understanding behaviour.

Developmental Trauma	Trauma that occurs in early childhood and alters the development of the brain and body to respond to repeated or prolonged stress.
Dissociation	A process where a person disconnects from their thoughts, feelings, or sense of identity, often in response to trauma.
Emotional stuck point	A term describing when a person re-experiences a traumatic event as though they are the same age or in the same state as when it happened.
Executive Function	Cognitive skills including attention, memory, and self-control that help children plan, focus, and manage tasks.
Fetal Programming	The process by which conditions in the womb, such as maternal stress, influence the development of the baby's brain and body.
Fight Response	An instinctive reaction to confront or defend against danger.
Fight, Flight, Freeze, Flop	Common automatic responses to danger or stress. "Fight" means to confront, "Flight" to escape, "Freeze" to become immobile, and "Flop" to shut down.
Flight Response	An instinctive reaction to escape from danger.
Flop Response	A less commonly known reaction where the body collapses or shuts down in response to extreme threat.
Freeze Response	An automatic reaction to threat where the body becomes still, often to avoid detection or harm.
Heuristic	A practical method or approach to problem-solving that simplifies complex issues for effective action.
Hippocampus	A brain area involved in memory formation and linking memories to emotions.
Hypervigilance	A heightened state of sensory sensitivity and alertness, often seen in children who have experienced trauma.
Interconnections	Links between brain areas that allow for communication and coordination of responses.
Intergenerational Trauma	Trauma that is passed from one generation to the next, affecting family systems and child development.
Intrusion	When a traumatic memory comes into a person's awareness unexpectedly, often with intense emotions or physical reactions.
Limbic System	A group of brain structures involved in emotion, memory, and motivation.
Neurodevelopment	The process by which the brain grows and develops, particularly in early childhood.
Neurons	Nerve cells in the brain that communicate with each other to process information.
Post-Traumatic Stress	Persistent physical and emotional symptoms that occur after experiencing a traumatic event.
Prefrontal Cortex	The part of the brain responsible for reasoning, decision making, and self-control.

Proprioception	The internal sense of body position and movement in space.
Regulating Systems	Brain regions involved in controlling impulses, reasoning about consequences, and managing emotions.
Regulation	The brain's process of managing emotional responses and impulses to behave in socially appropriate ways.
Relational trauma	Trauma that results from disruptions in caregiving relationships, especially when the caregiver is also distressed.
Secure Attachment	A strong and healthy emotional bond between a child and caregiver, leading to better resilience and emotional regulation.
Self-Efficacy	One's belief in their own ability to achieve goals or influence outcomes.
Self-Regulation	The ability of a child to manage their emotions, behaviours, and attention, developed through responsive caregiving.
Sensory Processing	How the brain interprets and organises sensory information from the environment.
Shame	A painful emotion stemming from a negative self-view, often linked to early trauma.
Simple Trauma	Trauma that stems from a single, clearly identifiable event.
Stress Regulation	The body and brain's ability to return to a calm state after experiencing stress.
Stress System	The network in the brain that detects threats and activates responses to help an individual stay safe.
Survivor Guilt	Feelings of guilt experienced by someone who has survived a traumatic event while others did not or were more seriously harmed.

References

Alamos, P., & Williford, A. P. (2020). Teacher-child emotion talk in preschool children displaying elevated externalizing behaviors. *Journal of Applied Developmental Psychology*, *67*, 101107.

Aldrich, N. J., Chen, J., & Alfieri, L. (2021). Evaluating associations between parental mind-mindedness and children's developmental capacities through meta-analysis. *Developmental Review*, *60*, 100946.

Alvidrez, J., & Tabor, D. C. (2021). Now is the time to incorporate the construct of structural racism and discrimination into health research. *Ethnicity & Disease*, *31*(Suppl 1), 283.

American Psychiatric Association (APA). (2013). *Diagnostic and statistical manual of mental disorders: DSM-5*. APA.

Astle, D. E., Holmes, J., Kievit, R., & Gathercole, S. E. (2022). Annual research review: The transdiagnostic revolution in neurodevelopmental disorders. *Journal of Child Psychology and Psychiatry*, *63*, 397–417.

Atkinson, L., Jamieson, B., Khoury, J., Ludmer, J., & Gonzalez, A. (2016). Stress physiology in infancy and early childhood: Cortisol flexibility, attunement and coordination. *Journal of Neuroendocrinology*, *28*(8). https://doi.org/10.1111/jne.12408

Australian Government Department of Education. (2022). *Belonging, being and becoming: The early years framework for Australia*. Australian Government Department of Education.

Baldwin, J. R., Caspi, A., Meehan, A. J., Ambler, A., Arseneault, L., Fisher, H. L., & Danese, A. (2021). Population vs individual prediction of poor health from results of adverse childhood experiences screening. *JAMA Pediatrics*, *175*(4), 385–393.

Barger, M. M., Kim, E. M., Kuncel, N. R., & Pomerantz, E. M. (2019). The relation between parents' involvement in children's schooling and children's adjustment: A meta-analysis. *Psychological Bulletin*, *145*(9), 855.

Bartlett, J. D., & Smith, S. (2019). The role of early care and education in addressing early childhood trauma. *American Journal of Community Psychology*, *64*(3-4), 359-372.

Baumeister, D., Akhtar, R., Ciufolini, S., Pariante, C. M., & Mondelli, V. (2016). Childhood trauma and adulthood inflammation: A meta-analysis of peripheral C-reactive protein, interleukin-6 and tumour necrosis factor-α. *Molecular Psychiatry*, *21*(5), 642–649.

Bellis, M. A., Hardcastle, K., Ford, K., Hughes, K., Ashton, K., Quigg, Z., & Butler, N. (2017). Does continuous trusted adult support in childhood impart life-course resilience against adverse childhood experiences? A retrospective study on adult health-harming behaviours and mental well-being. *BMC Psychiatry*, *17*, 1-12.

Bergman, K., Sarkar, P., Glover, V., & O'Connor, T. G. (2010). Maternal prenatal cortisol and infant cognitive development: Moderation by infant–mother attachment. *Biological Psychiatry*, *67*(11), 1026–1032.

Berlin, L. J., Shdaimah, C. S., Goodman, A., & Slopen, N. (2020). "I'm literally drowning": A mixed-methods exploration of infant-toddler child care providers' wellbeing. *Early Education and Development*, *31*(7), 1071-1088.

Bernier, A., Carlson, S. M., & Whipple, N. (2010). From external regulation to self-regulation: Early parenting precursors of young children's executive functioning. *Child Development*, *81*(1), 326–339.

Berntsen, D. (2001). Involuntary memories of emotional events: Do memories of traumas and extremely happy events differ? *Applied Cognitive Psychology*, *15*, S135–S158.

Biringen, Z., & Easterbrooks, M. A. (2012). Emotional availability: Concept, research, and window on developmental psychopathology. *Development and Psychopathology*, *24*(1), 1-8.

Bishop, D. V. M., Snowling, M. J., Thompson, P. A., Greenhalgh, T., & The Catalise Consortium. (2017). CATALISE: A multinational and multidisciplinary Delphi consensus study of problems with language development. Phase 2. Terminology. *Journal of Child Psychology and Psychiatry*, *58*, 1068–1080.

Bogat, G. A., DeJonghe, E., Levendosky, A. A., Davidson, W. S., & Von Eye, A. (2006). Trauma symptoms among infants exposed to intimate partner violence. *Child Abuse & Neglect*, *30*(2), 109–125.

Bornstein, M. H., & Esposito, G. (2023). Coregulation: A multilevel approach via biology and behavior. *Children*, *10*(8), 1323.

Bornstein, M. H., Arterberry, M. E., & Mash, C. (2004). Long-term memory for an emotional interpersonal interaction occurring at 5 months of age. *Infancy*, *6*(3), 407–416.

Breslau, N., Chilcoat, H. D., Kessler, R. C., & Davis, G. C. (1999). Previous exposure to trauma and PTSD effects of subsequent trauma: Results from the Detroit Area Survey of Trauma. *American Journal of Psychiatry*, *156*(6), 902–907.

Brewin, C. R. (2015). Re-experiencing traumatic events in PTSD: New avenues in research on intrusive memories and flashbacks. *European Journal of Psychotraumatology*, *6*(1), 27180.

Briggs-Gowan, M. J., Carter, A. S., Clark, R., Augustyn, M., McCarthy, K. J., & Ford, J. D. (2010). Exposure to potentially traumatic events in early childhood: Differential links to emergent psychopathology. *Journal of Child Psychology and Psychiatry*, *51*(10), 1132–1140.

Brophy-Herb, H. E., Brincks, A., Cook, J. L., Stacks, A., Vallotton, C. D., Frosch, C., & Jennings, P. A. (2023). Stress intensity and exhaustion among infant and toddler teachers: Descriptive analysis and associations with sources of stress and coping strategy use. *Early Education and Development*, *34*(7), 1545–1564.

Brown, L. A., Belli, G. M., Asnaani, A., & Foa, E. B. (2019). A review of the role of negative cognitions about oneself, others, and the world in the treatment of PTSD. *Cognitive Therapy Research*, *43*, 143–173.

Brunzell, T., Stokes, H., & Waters, L. (2016). Trauma-informed positive education: Using positive psychology to strengthen vulnerable students. *Contemporary School Psychology*, *20*, 63–83.

Bryant, R. A. (2019). Post-traumatic stress disorder: A state-of-the-art review of evidence and challenges. *World Psychiatry*, *18*(3), 259–269.

Buchanan, T. W. (2007). Retrieval of emotional memories. *Psychological Bulletin*, *133*(5), 761.

Buettner, C. K., Jeon, L., Hur, E., & Garcia, R. E. (2016). Teachers' social-emotional capacity: Factors associated with teachers' responsiveness and professional commitment. *Early Education and Development*, *27*(7), 1018–1039.

Buhle, J. T., Silvers, J. A., Wager, T. D., Lopez, R., Onyemekwu, C., Kober, H., & Ochsner, K. N. (2014). Cognitive reappraisal of emotion: A meta-analysis of human neuroimaging studies. *Cerebral Cortex*, *24*(11), 2981–2990.

Bundy, A. C., & Lane, S. J. (2020). Sensory integration: A. Jean Ayres' theory revisited. In A. C. Bundy, & S. J. Lane (Eds.), *Sensory integration: Theory and practice* (3rd ed., pp. 2–20). F. A. Davis.

Burnley, A., St Clair, M., Dack, C., Thompson, H., & Wren, Y. (2024). Exploring the psychosocial experiences of individuals with developmental language disorder during childhood: A qualitative investigation. *Journal of Autism and Developmental Disorders*, *54*, 3008–3027.

Cairney, J., Rigoli, D., & Piek, J. (2013). Developmental coordination disorder and internalizing problems in children: The environmental stress hypothesis elaborated. *Developmental Review*, *33*(3), 224–238.

Cesario, J., Johnson, D. J., & Eisthen, H. L. (2020). Your brain is not an onion with a tiny reptile inside. *Current Directions in Psychological Science*, 0963721420917687.

Champine, R. B., Lang, J. M., Nelson, A. M., Hanson, R. F., & Tebes, J. K. (2019). Systems measures of a trauma-informed approach: A systematic review. *American Journal of Community Psychology*, *64*(3–4), 418–437.

Chang, M. T., Bradin, S., & Hashikawa, A. N. (2018). Disaster preparedness among Michigan's licensed child care programs. *Pediatric Emergency Care* *34*(5), 349–356.

Charil, A., Laplante, D. P., Vaillancourt, C., & King, S. (2010). Prenatal stress and brain development. *Brain Research Reviews*, *65*(1), 56–79.

Chazan, S., & Cohen, E. (2010). Adaptive and defensive strategies in post-traumatic play of young children exposed to violent attacks. *Journal of Child Psychotherapy*, *36*(2), 133–151.

Chu, A. T., Bond, M. H., Rogowski, B., Leba, N. V., Ghosh Ippen, C., Cirolia, A., & Lieberman, A. F. (2025). Posttraumatic stress in infancy: The roles of cumulative trauma and caregiving context. *Infant Mental Health Journal*, *46*(5), 536–548.

Chung, E. H., Chou, J., & Brown, K. A. (2020). Neurodevelopmental outcomes of preterm infants: A recent literature review. *Translational Pediatrics*, *9*(Suppl 1), S3.

Cieslak, R., Shoji, K., Douglas, A., Melville, E., Luszczynska, A., & Benight, C. C. (2014). A meta-analysis of the relationship between job burnout and secondary traumatic stress among workers with indirect exposure to trauma. *Psychological Services, 11*(1), 75–86.

Clark, D. A., & Beck, A. T. (2010). Cognitive theory and therapy of anxiety and depression: Convergence with neurobiological findings. *Trends in Cognitive Sciences, 14*(9), 418–424.

Cohen, E., Chazan, S., Lerner, M., & Maimon, E. (2010). Posttraumatic play in young children exposed to terrorism: An empirical study. *Infant Mental Health Journal, 31*, 159–181.

de Schipper, E. J., Riksen-Walraven, J. M., Geurts, S. A., & de Weerth, C. (2009). Cortisol levels of caregivers in child care centers as related to the quality of their caregiving. *Early Childhood Research Quarterly, 24*(1), 55–63.

Del Giudice, M., Ellis, B. J., & Shirtcliff, E. A. (2011). The adaptive calibration model of stress responsivity. *Neuroscience & Biobehavioral Reviews, 35*(7), 1562–1592.

Del Giudice, M., & Belsky, J. (2010). Evolving attachment theory: Beyond Bowlby and back to Darwin. *Child Development Perspectives, 4*, 112–113.

Dempsey, I., & Keen, D. (2008). A review of processes and outcomes in family-centered services for children with a disability. *Topics in Early Childhood Special Education, 28*(1), 42–52.

Department for Education (2025). *Early years foundation stage statutory framework*. Department for Education.

Dixon, M. L., & Dweck, C. S. (2022). The amygdala and the prefrontal cortex: The co-construction of intelligent decision-making. *Psychological Review, 129*(6), 1414–1441.

Dorahy, M. J., Corry, M., Shannon, M., Webb, K., McDermott, B., Ryan, M., & Dyer, K. F. (2013). Complex trauma and intimate relationships: The impact of shame, guilt and dissociation. *Journal of Affective Disorders, 147*(1–3), 72–79.

Douglass, A., & Gittell, J. H. (2012). Transforming professionalism: Relational bureaucracy and parent-teacher partnerships in child care settings. *Journal of Early Childhood Research, 10*(3), 267–281.

Douglass, A., Chickerella, R., & Maroney, M. (2021). Becoming trauma-informed: A case study of early educator professional development and organizational change. *Journal of Early Childhood Teacher Education, 42*(2), 182–202.

Duffy, R. D., Allan, B. A., Autin, K. L., & Bott, E. M. (2013). Calling and life satisfaction: It's not about having it, it's about living it. *Journal of Counseling Psychology, 60*, 605–615.

Dunn, E. C., Nishimi, K., Powers, A., & Bradley, B. (2017). Is developmental timing of trauma exposure associated with depressive and post-traumatic stress disorder symptoms in adulthood? *Journal of Psychiatric Research, 84*, 119–127.

Dwyer, P., Gurba, A. N., Kapp, S. K., Kilgallon, E., Hersh, L. H., Chang, D. S., Rivera, S. M., & Gillespie-Lynch, K. (2024). Community views of neurodiversity, models of disability and autism intervention: Mixed methods reveal shared goals and key tensions. *Autism, 29*(9), 2297–2314.

Dyregrov, A., & Regel, S. (2012). Early interventions following exposure to traumatic events: implications for practice from recent research. *Journal of Loss and Trauma, 17*(3), 271–291.

Education Scotland (2020). *Realising the ambition: National practice guidance for early years in Scotland*. Education Scotland.

Ehlers, A., Hackmann, A., & Michael, T. (2004). Intrusive re-experiencing in post-traumatic stress disorder: Phenomenology, theory, and therapy. *Memory, 12*(4), 403–415.

Eisenberg, N., Spinrad, T. L., & Eggum, N. D. (2010). Emotion-related self-regulation and its relation to children's maladjustment. *Annual Review of Clinical Psychology, 6*(1), 495–525.

Ellis, B. J. (2018). Toward an adaptation-based approach to resilience. In J. G. Noll & I. Shalev (Eds.), *The biology of early life stress: Understanding child maltreatment and trauma* (pp. 31–43). Springer.

Ellis, B. J., Sheridan, M. A., Belsky, J., & McLaughlin, K. A. (2022). Why and how does early adversity influence development? Toward an integrated model of dimensions of environmental experience. *Development and Psychopathology, 34*(2), 447–471.

Feldman, R. (2020). What is resilience: An affiliative neuroscience approach. *World Psychiatry, 19*(2), 132–150.

Finkelhor, D. (2018). Screening for adverse childhood experiences (ACEs): Cautions and suggestions. *Child Abuse & Neglect, 85*, 174–179.

Fonagy, P., & Target, M. (2005). Bridging the transmission gap: An end to an important mystery of attachment research? *Attachment & Human Development, 7*(3), 333–343.

Forry, N. D., Moodie, S., Simkin, S., & Rothenberg, L. (2011). Family-provider relationships: A multidisciplinary review of high quality practices and associations with family, child, and provider outcomes. Issue Brief OPRE.

Frankenhuis, W., Young, E. S., & Ellis, B. J. (2020). The hidden talents approach: Theoretical and methodological challenges. *Trends in Cognitive Sciences, 24*(7), 569–581.

Frewen, P. A., Brown, M. F., & Lanius, R. A. (2017). Trauma-related altered states of consciousness (TRASC) in an online community sample: Further support for the 4-D model of trauma-related dissociation. *Psychology of Consciousness: Theory, Research, and Practice, 4*(1), 92–114.

Friedman-Krauss, A. H., Raver, C. C., Morris, P. A., & Jones, S. M. (2014). The role of classroom-level child behavior problems in predicting preschool teacher stress and classroom emotional climate. *Early Education and Development, 25*, 530–552.

Fusar-Poli, P., Placentino, A., Carletti, F., Landi, P., Allen, P., Surguladze, S., & Politi, P. (2009). Functional atlas of emotional faces processing: A voxel-based meta-analysis of 105 functional magnetic resonance imaging studies. *Journal of Psychiatry and Neuroscience, 34*(6), 418–432.

Gaensbauer, T. J. (2002). Representations of trauma in infancy: Clinical and theoretical implications for the understanding of early memory. *Infant Mental Health Journal, 23*(3), 259–277.

Gao, W., Biswal, B., Chen, S., Wu, X., & Yuan, J. (2021). Functional coupling of the orbitofrontal cortex and the basolateral amygdala mediates the association between spontaneous reappraisal and emotional response. *Neuroimage, 232*, 117918.

Gilbert, R., Abel, M. R., Vernberg, E. M., & Jacobs, A. K. (2021). The use of psychological first aid in children exposed to mass trauma. *Current Psychiatry Reports, 23*(9), 53.

Golkar, A., Lonsdorf, T. B., Olsson, A., Lindstrom, K. M., Berrebi, J., Fransson, P., & Öhman, A. (2012). Distinct contributions of the dorsolateral prefrontal and orbitofrontal cortex during emotion regulation. *PloS One, 7*(11), e48107.

Greenberger, D., & Padesky, C. A. (2015). *Mind over mood: Change how you feel by changing the way you think*. Guilford Publications.

Gunnar, M. (2017). Social buffering of stress in development: A career perspective. *Perspectives on Psychological Science, 12*(3), 355–373.

Gunnar, M., Frenn, K., Wewerka, S. S., & Van Ryzin, M. J. (2009). Moderate versus severe early life stress: Associations with stress reactivity and regulation in 10–12-year-old children. *Psychoneuroendocrinology, 34*(1), 62–75.

Hackmann, A., Ehlers, A., Speckens, A., & Clark, D. M. (2004). Characteristics and content of intrusive memories in PTSD and their changes with treatment. *Journal of Traumatic Stress, 17*(3), 231–240.

Hambrick, E. P., Brawner, T. W., Perry, B. D., Brandt, K., Hofmeister, C., & Collins, J. O. (2019). Beyond the ACE score: Examining relationships between timing of developmental adversity, relational health and developmental outcomes in children. *Archives of Psychiatric Nursing, 33*(3), 238–247.

Helton, J. J., Gochez-Kerr, T., & Gruber, E. (2017). Sexual abuse of children with learning disabilities. *Child Maltreatment, 23*(2), 157–165.

Henderson, A. A., Matthews, R. A., & Ford, M. T. (2023). The temporal dynamics between work stressors and health behaviors. *Journal of Occupational Health Psychology, 28*(1), 1–19.

Hensley, L., & Varela, R. E. (2008). PTSD symptoms and somatic complaints following Hurricane Katrina: The roles of trait anxiety and anxiety sensitivity. *Journal of Clinical Child and Adolescent Psychology, 37*(3), 542–552.

Herculano-Houzel, S. (2009). The human brain in numbers: A linearly scaled-up primate brain. *Frontiers in Human Neuroscience, 3*, 857.

Hobfoll, S. E., Watson, P., Bell, C. C., Bryant, R. A., Brymer, M. J., Friedman, M. J., & Ursano, R. J. (2007). Five essential elements of immediate and mid-term mass trauma intervention: Empirical evidence. *Psychiatry: Interpersonal and Biological Processes, 70*(4), 283–315.

Huffhines, L., Herman, R., Silver, R. B., Low, C. M., Newland, R., & Parade, S. H. (2023). Reflective supervision and consultation and its impact within early childhood-serving programs: A systematic review. *Infant Mental Health Journal, 44*, 803–836.

Humphreys, K. L., King, L. S., Guyon-Harris, K. L., & Zeanah, C. H. (2022). Caregiver regulation: A modifiable target promoting resilience to early adverse experiences. *Psychological Trauma: Theory, Research, Practice, and Policy, 14*(S1), S63–S71.

Jimenez, M. E., Wade, R. Jr, Lin, Y., Morrow, L. M., & Reichman, N. E. (2016). Adverse experiences in early childhood and kindergarten outcomes. *Pediatrics, 137*(2), e20151839.

Jones, C., Hadley, F., Waniganayake, M., & Johnstone, M. (2019). Find your tribe! Early childhood educators defining and identifying key factors that support their workplace wellbeing. *Australasian Journal of Early Childhood, 44*(4), 326–338.

Jones, L., Bellis, M. A., Wood, S., Hughes, K., McCoy, E., Eckley, L., & Officer, A. (2012). Prevalence and risk of violence against children with disabilities: A systematic review and meta-analysis of observational studies. *The Lancet, 380*(9845), 899–907.

Kaye, K., & Wells, A. J. (1980). Mothers' jiggling and the burst-pause pattern in neonatal feeding. *Infant Behavior and Development, 3*, 29–46.

Kearney, B. E., & Lanius, R. A. (2022). The brain-body disconnect: A somatic sensory basis for trauma-related disorders. *Frontiers in Neuroscience, 16*, 1015749.

Keding, T. J., Heyn, S. A., Russell, J. D., Zhu, X., Cisler, J., McLaughlin, K. A., & Herringa, R. J. (2021). Differential patterns of delayed emotion circuit maturation in abused girls with and without internalizing psychopathology. *American Journal of Psychiatry, 178*(11), 1026–1036.

Kerns, C. M., Newschaffer, C. J., & Berkowitz, S. J. (2015). Traumatic childhood events and autism spectrum disorder. *Journal of Autism and Developmental Disorders, 45*, 3475–3486.

Keyser, J. (2006). *From parents to partners: Building a family-centered early childhood program*. Redleaf Press.

Kip, A., Diele, J., Holling, H., & Morina, N. (2022). The relationship of trauma-related guilt with PTSD symptoms in adult trauma survivors: A meta-analysis. *Psychological Medicine, 52*(12), 2201–2211.

Koss, K. J., Kronaizl, S., Brown, R., & Brooks-Gunn, J. (2025). Childhood environmental unpredictability and adolescent mental health and behavioral problems. *Child Development, 96*, 1424–1442.

Kross, E., Ayduk, O., & Mischel, W. (2014). Self-talk as a regulatory mechanism: How you do it matters. *Journal of Personality and Social Psychology, 106*, 304.

Kurki, K., Järvenoja, H., Järvelä, S., & Mykkänen, A. (2016). How teachers co-regulate children's emotions and behaviour in socio-emotionally challenging situations in day-care settings. *International Journal of Educational Research, 76*, 76–88.

Kwon, K., Jeon, S., Jeon, L., & Castle, S. (2019). Teachers' depressive symptoms, classroom quality, and children's developmental outcomes in Early Head Start. *Learning and Individual Differences, 74*, 101748.

Lanius, R. A., Vermetten, E., Loewenstein, R. J., Brand, B., Schmahl, C., Bremner, J. D., & Spiegel, D. (2010). Emotion modulation in PTSD: Clinical and neurobiological evidence for a dissociative subtype. *American Journal of Psychiatry, 167*(6), 640–647.

Laplante, D. P., Barr, R. G., Brunet, A., Du Fort, G. G., Meaney, M. L., Saucier, J. F., Zelazo, P. R. & King, S. (2004). Stress during pregnancy affects general intellectual and language functioning in human toddlers. *Pediatric Research, 56*(3), 400–410.

Lazarus, R. S. (2006). Emotions and interpersonal relationships: Toward a person-centered conceptualization of emotions and coping. *Journal of Personality, 74*(1), 9–46.

LeDoux, J. E. (1996). *The emotional brain: The mysterious underpinnings of emotional life*. Simon and Schuster.

LeDoux, J. E., & Pine, D. S. (2016). Using neuroscience to help understand fear and anxiety: A two-system framework. *American Journal of Psychiatry, 173*(11), 1083–1093.

Lee, R. T., & Brotheridge, C. M. (2011). Words from the heart speak to the heart: A study of deep acting, faking, and hiding among child care workers. *Career Development International, 16*(4), 401–420.

Lester, B. M., Conradt, E., LaGasse, L. L., Tronick, E. Z., Padbury, J. F., & Marsit, C. J. (2018). Epigenetic programming by maternal behavior in the human infant. *Pediatrics, 142*(4), 2017–1890.

Lewis, H. R., Lipscomb, S. T., Hatfield, B. E., Jäderholm, C. M., & Tominey, S. L. (2024). Early childhood teachers' relationships with families when children experience adversity. *Journal of Research in Childhood Education, 38*(4), 665–690.

Lieberman, A. F., & Van Horn, P. (2009). Giving voice to the unsayable: Repairing the effects of trauma in infancy and early childhood. *Child and Adolescent Psychiatric Clinics, 18*(3), 707–720.

Lloyd, S. (2020). *Building sensorimotor systems in children with developmental trauma: A model for practice*. Jessica Kingsley Publishers.

Lloyd, S. (2023). An innovative approach to working with children who have experienced developmental trauma: An introduction to the Building Underdeveloped Sensorimotor Systems (BUSS®) model. *Adoption & Fostering, 47*(2), 157–173.

Loomis, A. M. (2018). The role of preschool as a point of intervention and prevention for trauma-exposed children: Recommendations for practice, policy, and research. *Topics in Early Childhood Special Education, 38*(3), 134–145.

Ludick, M., & Figley, C. R. (2017). Toward a mechanism for secondary trauma induction and reduction: Reimagining a theory of secondary traumatic stress. *Traumatology, 23*(1), 112.

Ma, X., Shen, J., Krenn, H. Y., Hu, S., & Yuan, J. (2016). A meta-analysis of the relationship between learning outcomes and parental involvement during early childhood education and early elementary education. *Educational Psychology Review*, *28*, 771–801.

Machado, S. A., & Anderson, P. N. (2022). The perspectives of preschool teachers regarding their ability to respond to various crises in the childcare center. *Journal of Early Childhood Research*, *21*(1), 18–30.

MacLean, P. D. (1990). *The triune brain in evolution: Role in paleocerebral functions*: Springer.

Marini, S., Davis, K. A., Soare, T. W., Zhu, Y., Suderman, M. J., Simpkin, A. J., Smith, A. D. A. C., Wolf, E. J., Relton, C. L., & Dunn, E. C. (2020). Adversity exposure during sensitive periods predicts accelerated epigenetic aging in children. *Psychoneuroendocrinology*, *113*, 104484.

Maslach, C., & Leiter, M. P. (2016). Understanding the burnout experience: Recent research and its implications for psychiatry. *World Psychiatry*, *15*(2), 103–111.

Matson, R., Barnes-Brown, V., & Stonall, R. (2024). The impact of childhood trauma on sensory processing and connected motor planning and skills: A scoping review. *Journal of Child & Adolescent Trauma*, *17*(2), 447–456.

McBryde, M., Fitzallen, G. C., Liley, H. G., Taylor, H. G., & Bora, S. (2020). Academic outcomes of school-aged children born preterm: A systematic review and meta-analysis. *JAMA Network Open*, *3*(4), e202027-e202027.

McDonnell, C. G., Boan, A. D., Bradley, C. C., Seay, K. D., Charles, J. M., & Carpenter, L. A. (2019). Child maltreatment in autism spectrum disorder and intellectual disability: Results from a population-based sample. *Journal of Child Psychology and Psychiatry*, *60*(5), 576–584.

McLeroy, K. R., Bibeau, D., Steckler, A., & Glanz, K. (1988). An ecological perspective on health promotion programs. *Health Education Quarterly*, *15*(4), 351–377.

McMullen, M. B., Lee, S. C., McCormick, K. I., & Choi, J. (2020). Early childhood professional well-being as a predictor of the risk of turnover in child care: A matter of quality. *Journal of Research in Childhood Education*, *34*(3), 331–345.

McQuade, J. D., Breslend, N. L., & Groff, D. (2018). Experiences of physical and relational victimization in children with ADHD: The role of social problems and aggression. *Aggressive Behavior*, *44*(4), 416–425.

Mehta, T. R., Monegro, A., & Nene, Y. (2019). Neurobiology of ADHD: A Review. *Current Developmental Disorders Reports*, *6*, 235–240.

Meins, E., Fernyhough, C., Wainwright, R., Clark-Carter, D., Das Gupta, M., Fradley, E., & Tuckey, M. (2003). Pathways to understanding mind: Construct validity and predictive validity of maternal mind-mindedness. *Child Development*, *74*(4), 1194–1211.

Minnis, H., Marwick, H., Arthur, J., & McLaughlin, A. (2006). Reactive attachment disorder – A theoretical model beyond attachment. *European Child & Adolescent Psychiatry*, *15*, 336–342.

Missiuna, C., & Campbell, W. N. (2014). Psychological aspects of developmental coordination disorder: Can we establish causality? *Current Developmental Disorders Reports*, *1*, 125–131.

Mittal, C., Griskevicius, V., Simpson, J. A., Sung, S., & Young, E. S. (2015). Cognitive adaptations to stressful environments: When childhood adversity enhances adult executive function. *Journal of Personality and Social Psychology*, *109*(4), 604.

Moner, N., Soubelet, A., Barbieri, L., & Askenazy, F. (2022). Assessment of PTSD and posttraumatic symptomatology in very young children: A systematic review. *Journal of Child and Adolescent Psychiatric Nursing*, *35*(1), 7–23.

Morawetz, C., Riedel, M. C., Salo, T., Berboth, S., Eickhoff, S. B., Laird, A. R., & Kohn, N. (2020). Multiple large-scale neural networks underlying emotion regulation. *Neuroscience & Biobehavioral Reviews*, *116*, 382–395.

National Association for the Education of Young Children. (2020). *Early Childhood Program Standards*. National Association for the Education of Young Children.

National Child Traumatic Stress Network. (2006). *Psychological first aid: A fieldworkers guide* (2nd ed.). NCTSN.

National Institute for Health and Care Excellence (NICE). (2018). *Posttraumatic stress disorder*. NICE guideline.

Nejati, V., Majdi, R., Salehinejad, M. A., & Nitsche, M. A. (2021). The role of dorsolateral and ventromedial prefrontal cortex in the processing of emotional dimensions. *Scientific Reports*, *11*(1), 1971.

Nolvi, S., Merz, E. C., Kataja, E. L., & Parsons, C. E. (2023). Prenatal stress and the developing brain: Postnatal environments promoting resilience. *Biological Psychiatry*, *93*(10), 942–952.

Norbury, C. F., & Sparks, A. (2013). Difference or disorder? Cultural issues in understanding neurodevelopmental disorders. *Developmental Psychology*, *49*(1), 45–58.

O'Mahony, S. M., Clarke, G., Dinan, T. G., & Cryan, J. F. (2017). Irritable bowel syndrome and stress-related psychiatric co-morbidities: Focus on early life stress. In B. Greenwood-Van Meerveld (Eds.), *Gastrointestinal pharmacology: Handbook of experimental pharmacology*, vol. 239. Springer.

Oberg, G., Carroll, A., & Macmahon, S. (2023). Compassion fatigue and secondary traumatic stress in teachers: How they contribute to burnout and how they are related to trauma-awareness. *Frontiers in Education*, *8*, 129.

Oleś, P. K., Brinthaupt, T. M., Dier, R., & Polak, D. (2020). Types of inner dialogues and functions of self-talk: Comparisons and implications. *Frontiers in Psychology*, *11*, 227.

Ormiston, H. E., Nygaard, M. A., & Apgar, S. (2022). A systematic review of secondary traumatic stress and compassion fatigue in teachers. *School Mental Health*, *14*(4), 802–817.

Patel, R., Spreng, R. N., Shin, L. M., & Girard, T. A. (2012). Neurocircuitry models of posttraumatic stress disorder and beyond: A meta-analysis of functional neuroimaging studies. *Neuroscience & Biobehavioral Reviews*, *36*(9), 2130–2142.

Pauen, S. (2016). Understanding early development of self-regulation and co-regulation: EDOS and PROSECO. *Journal of Self-Regulation and Regulation*, *2*, 3–16.

Perry, B. D. (2009). Examining child maltreatment through a neurodevelopmental lens: Clinical applications of the neurosequential model of therapeutics. *Journal of Loss and Trauma*, *14*(4), 240–255.

Pessoa, L. (2017). A network model of the emotional brain. *Trends in Cognitive Sciences*, *21*(5), 357–371.

Phillips, M. L., Ladouceur, C. D., & Drevets, W. C. (2008). A neural model of voluntary and automatic emotion regulation: Implications for understanding the pathophysiology and neurodevelopment of bipolar disorder. *Molecular Psychiatry*, *13*(9), 833–857.

Puig, J., Englund, M. M., Simpson, J. A., & Collins, W. A. (2013). Predicting adult physical illness from infant attachment: A prospective longitudinal study. *Health Psychology*, *32*(4), 409–417.

Rovee-Collier, C., & Cuevas, K. (2008). The development of infant memory. In M. L. Courage & N. Cowan (Eds.), *The development of memory in infancy and childhood* (pp. 23–54). Psychology Press.

Ryan, K., Lane, S. J., & Powers, D. (2017). A multidisciplinary model for treating complex trauma in early childhood. *International Journal of Play Therapy*, *26*(2), 111.

SAMHSA. (2014). *SAMHSA's concept of trauma and guidance for a trauma-informed approach*. Substance Abuse and Mental Health Services Administration.

Sandman, C. A., Davis, E. P., Buss, C., & Glynn, L. M. (2011). Prenatal programming of human neurological function. *International Journal of Peptides*, *2011*(1), 837596.

Scheeringa, M. S., & Zeanah, C. H. (2001). A relational perspective on PTSD in early childhood. *Journal of Traumatic Stress*, *14*(4), 799–815.

Seal, S. V., & Turner, J. D. (2021). The "Jekyll and Hyde" of gluconeogenesis: Early life adversity, later life stress, and metabolic disturbances. *International Journal of Molecular Sciences*, *22*(7), 3344.

Seligman, M. E. P. (1990). *Learned optimism: How to change your mind and your life*. Knopf.

Selye, H. (1978). *The stress of life*. McGraw Hill.

Seth, A. K., & Tsakiris, M. (2018). Being a beast machine: The somatic basis of selfhood. *Trends in Cognitive Sciences*, *22*(11), 969–981.

Shalev, A., Cho, D., & Marmar, C. R. (2024). Neurobiology and treatment of posttraumatic stress disorder. *American Journal of Psychiatry*, *181*(8), 705–719.

Silkenbeumer, J. R., Schiller, E. M., & Kärtner, J. (2018). Co-and self-regulation of emotions in the preschool setting. *Early Childhood Research Quarterly*, *44*, 72–81.

Silvers, J. A., Weber, J., Wager, T. D., & Ochsner, K. N. (2015). Bad and worse: Neural systems underlying reappraisal of high- and low-intensity negative emotions. *Social Cognitive and Affective Neuroscience*, *10*(2), 172–179.

Simons, C., Harden, B. J., Lee, K. A., & Tirrell-Corbin, C. (2022). Infant-toddler teachers' early adversity, current wellbeing, and engaged support of early learning. *Early Childhood Research Quarterly*, *61*, 158–169.

Smith, R., & Lane, R. D. (2015). The neural basis of one's own conscious and unconscious emotional states. *Neuroscience & Biobehavioral Reviews*, *57*, 1–29.

Sokolowski, K., & Corbin, J. G. (2012). Wired for behaviors: From development to function of innate limbic system circuitry. *Frontiers in Molecular Neuroscience*, *5*, 55.

Sonnentag, S., & Bayer, U. (2005). Switching off mentally: Predictors and consequences of psychological detachment from work during off-job time. *Journal of Occupational Health Psychology*, *10*, 393–414.

Southall, A. (2024). The trauma challenge: How teachers experience students with complex trauma. *British Journal of Special Education*, *51*(1), 3–14.

Sutton Trust. (2023). *Parental engagement*. Sutton Trust.

Szepsenwol, O. (2022). Identifying developmental adaptations to early-life stress. *Infant and Child Development*, *31*(1), e2290.

Tebben, E., Lang, S. N., Sproat, E., Tyree Owens, J., & Helms, S. (2021). Identifying primary and secondary stressors, buffers, and supports that impact ECE teacher wellbeing: Implications for teacher education. *Journal of Early Childhood Teacher Education*, *42*(2), 143–161.

Terranova, A., Morris, A. S., Myers, S., Kithakye, M., & Morris, M. D. S. (2015). Preschool children's adjustment following a hurricane: Risk and resilience in the face of adversity. *Early Education and Development*, *26*(4), 534–548.

Thome, J., Terpou, B. A., McKinnon, M. C., & Lanius, R. A. (2020). The neural correlates of trauma-related autobiographical memory in posttraumatic stress disorder: A meta-analysis. *Depression and Anxiety*, *37*(4), 321–345.

Trivette, C. M., Dunst, C. J., & Hamby, D. W. (2010). Influences of family-systems intervention practices on parent-child interactions and child development. *Topics in Early Childhood Special Education*, *30*(1), 3-19.

Tronick, E., & Hunter, R. G. (2024). Rethinking early childhood trauma as a dynamic developmental process in making meaning, emerging from chronic, repeated experiences and reiterated mental processes. In J. D. Osofsky, H. E. Fitzgerald, M. Keren, & K. Puura (Eds), *WAIMH handbook of infant and early childhood mental health: Biopsychosocial factors*, Vol. 1 (pp. 461–479). Springer International Publishing.

Tung, I., Hipwell, A. E., Grosse, P., Battaglia, L., Cannova, E., English, G.,. . .& Foust, J. E. (2024). Prenatal stress and externalizing behaviors in childhood and adolescence: A systematic review and meta-analysis. *Psychological Bulletin*, *150*(2), 107–131.

Underwood, R., Tolmeijer, E., Wibroe, J., Peters, E., & Mason, L. (2021). Networks underpinning emotion: A systematic review and synthesis of functional and effective connectivity. *Neuroimage*, *243*, 118486.

Ungar, M. (2015). Practitioner review: Diagnosing childhood resilience – a systemic approach to the diagnosis of adaptation in adverse social and physical ecologies. *Journal of Child Psychology and Psychiatry*, *56*(1), 4-17.

van der Kolk, B., Burbridge, J. A., & Suzuki, J. (1997). The psychobiology of traumatic memory. *Annals of the New York Academy of Sciences*, *821*(1), 99–113.

Vernberg, E. M., Steinberg, A M., Jacobs, A. K., Brymer, M. J., Watson, P. J., Osofsky, J. D., & Ruzek, J. I. (2008). Innovations in disaster mental health: Psychological first aid. *Professional Psychology: Research and Practice*, *39*(4), 381.

Wang, L., Norman, I., Edleston, V., Oyo, C., & Leamy, M. (2024). The effectiveness and implementation of psychological first aid as a therapeutic intervention after trauma: An integrative review. *Trauma, Violence, & Abuse*, *25*(4), 2638–2656.

Weiner, B. (1985). An attributional theory of achievement motivation and emotion. *Psychological Review*, *92*(4), 548–573.

Whitaker, R. C., Dearth-Wesley, T., & Gooze, R. A. (2015). Workplace stress and the quality of teacher-children relationships in Head Start. *Early Childhood Research Quarterly*, *30*, 57–69.

Williams, R. C. (2023). From ACEs to early relational health: Implications for clinical practice. *Paediatrics & Child Health*, *28*(6), 377–384.

Wodka, E. L., Mahone, E. M., Blankner, J. G., Gidley Larson, J. C., Fotedar, S., Denckla, M. B., & Mostofsky, S. H. (2007). Evidence that response inhibition is a primary deficit in ADHD. *Journal of Clinical and Experimental Neuropsychology*, *29*(4), 345–356.

Woolgar, F., Garfield, H., Dalgleish, T., & Meiser-Stedman, R. (2022). Systematic review and meta-analysis: Prevalence of posttraumatic stress disorder in trauma-exposed preschool-aged children. *Journal of the American Academy of Child & Adolescent Psychiatry*, *61*(3), 366–377.

World Health Organization. (2019). *International statistical classification of diseases and related health problems* (11th edition). WHO.

Wu, Q. (2021). A biopsychosocial perspective on maternal parenting in the first two years of infant life. *Behavioural Brain Research*, *411*, 113375.

Xie, Y., Hu, Z., Ma, W., Sang, B., & Wang, M. (2019). Different neural correlates of automatic emotion regulation at implicit and explicit perceptual level: A functional magnetic resonance imaging study. *i-Perception*, *10*(1), 2041669519831028.

Yang, H., Park, S., & Chau, L. (2025). A snapshot of time allocation and influencing factors in US early childhood education. *Early Childhood Education Journal*. https://doi.org/10.1007/s10643-025-01938-3

Zwicker, J. G., & Lee, E. J. (2021). Early intervention for children with/at risk of developmental coordination disorder: A scoping review. *Developmental Medicine and Child Neurology*, *63*, 659–667.

Index

For Product Safety Concerns and Information please contact our EU
representative GPSR@taylorandfrancis.com
Taylor & Francis Verlag GmbH, Kaufingerstraße 24, 80331 München, Germany

www.ingramcontent.com/pod-product-compliance
Lightning Source LLC
LaVergne TN
LVHW081322110826
845149LV00007B/1571

* 9 7 8 1 0 3 2 9 1 5 4 3 2 *